REAI
A JOURNAL FOR PHILOSOPHICAL
DISCOURSE

THE PHILOSOPHY OF REALISM

Volume I | Number I

2020

To learn more about REALITY, please visit

https://realityjournal.org.

This page intentionally left blank.

Table of Contents

Editorial Introduction

Reality as Katharsis (κᾰθαρσις)[1]

Attaining the Real

Daniel C. Wagner, PhD
Professor and Chair of Philosophy
Aquinas College, Grand Rapids MI
Editor, REALITY

Brian Kemple, PhD
Continuum Philosophical Insight
Executive Editor, REALITY

This first issue of REALITY—*The Philosophy of Realism*—like most publications and especially those of a collaborative effort, signifies innumerable hours of effort. The goal of our journal is simple: to reinvigorate an intelligent discussion about realism as a philosophical approach. By a realist approach, we mean not simply as pertains to theories of knowledge, but rather a kind of thinking that perfuses itself throughout all philosophical inquiries: all questions of truth, of meaning and purpose, of good, of human action, the political, the physical and the metaphysical, of thought and thing, and anything else about which one might ask, "What does this *mean*?" To clarify this pursuit of reality, and expound on its importance, our first issue asks the question: what *is* realism? It is an important question, not simply for our purposes here, but for philosophy as a whole, and thus an important question for all human beings. Without maintenance of a sound answer—which must be sustained dialogically—philosophy wilts into one or another sophistical theory that begins by denying some aspect of the real; and a small error in the beginning becomes great in the end.

---

[1] Correspondence to editors@realityjournal.org.

To safeguard against such slippery slopes, we take a cue from the first philosopher of the Western tradition, Socrates, and seek to define our terms: "what is reality?"

§

Reality—the English term, that is—has its etymological roots in the Latin noun *res* and its later medieval adjectival form, *reale* (n.). The noun signifies "thing," "event," "affair," or even "cause," while the adjective modifies a noun or verbal noun to signify that its referent has the intrinsic possibility of existing, as opposed to, say, something contrived in the imagination, or expressed in a proposition, that cannot exist independently of our cognitive actions, e.g., a "heffalump" or a "square-circle."[2]

Res has more ancient corresponding Greek progenitors in τὸ ὄν (*to on*), meaning "the being/existence," and οὐσία (*ousia*), meaning, also, "being" in the sense of "what belongs to something properly" such that, if it is removed, the thing in question will not *really* be what it is—e.g., if it is not an arthropod, it is not a honey bee, or if it is not mammalian it is not a dolphin, making the features of

---

[2] Notably, the term *res* as used by Aquinas indicates the imposition of a name from the quiddity understood; thus it primarily signifies the intelligibility of a thing and only by a kind of consignification does it signify the existence. See c.1252/56: *In Sent.*, lib.1, d.25, q.1, a.4, c.: "Respondeo dicendum, quod secundum Avicennam, ut supra dictum est, dist. 2, qu. 1, art. 3, hoc nomen ens et res differunt secundum quod est duo considerare in re, scilicet quidditatem et rationem ejus, et esse ipsius; et a quidditate sumitur hoc nomen res. Et quia quidditas potest habere esse, et in singulari quod est extra animam et in anima, secundum quod est apprehensa ab intellectu; ideo nomen rei ad utrumque se habet: et ad id quod est in anima, prout res dicitur a reor reris, et ad id quod est extra animam, prout res dicitur quasi aliquid ratum et firmum in natura. Sed nomen entis sumitur ab esse rei..." – "It must be said that, according to Avicenna, as mentioned above (d.2, q.1, .a3), that these nouns 'being' [*ens*] and 'thing' [*res*] differ insofar as there are two objects of consideration in a thing [*in re*], namely the quiddity or intelligible rationale of it, and the existence of it; and it is from the quiddity that the noun 'thing' [*res*] is taken. And because the quiddity is able to have existence, both in the singular existent which is outside the soul and in the soul, insofar as it is apprehended by the intellect, therefore the noun 'thing' [*res*] is related to each: both to that which is in the soul, insofar as it is said to be the thing of thought, and to that which is outside the soul, insofar as a thing is said to be as established and firmed in nature. But the noun 'being' [*ens*] is taken from the existence of the thing..."

arthropod and *mammalian* part of the *reality* of the honey bee and dolphin.[3] *Reality*, then, to put it simply, pertains to and signifies *what is*, and to *things actually existing in the world*. *Realism*, what many philosophers would now call an *epistemological* theory, in the broadest of terms, means that (i) there is *reality*—that things actually exist in the world—*and* (ii) that we can comprehend and express true (or conversely false) statements/propositions about this reality.

Realism, in this broad sense, is a perennial philosophy having its source in antiquity and including, but not limited to, such a broad range of thinkers as Socrates (469/70—399BC), Plato (427—347BC), Aristotle (384—322BC), St. Augustine (354—430AD), St. Thomas Aquinas (1224/5—1274) and the many thinkers of his school, such as John Poinsot (1589—1644), as well as Charles Sanders Pierce (1839—1914), Edmund Husserl (1859—1938), Martin Heidegger (1889—1976), Edith Stein (1889—1942), Karol Wojtyła (1920—2005), and many others.[4] Common to these monumental figures is the doctrine that thought and language are determined by existing things in the world through real relations and that thoughts and words are capable of expressing true meaning about these things. Aristotle and St. Thomas Aquinas, the most comprehensive and consistent champions of the realist philosophical world view, offer concise statements of the doctrine. In defining truth and falsity, Aristotle notes the following:[5]

> For to say that 'what is (τὸ ὂν) does not exist (μὴ εἶναι)' or that 'what is not (τὸ μὴ ὂν) does exist' (εἶναι) is to speak falsehood (ψεῦδος), but to say that 'what is (τὸ ὂν) exists (εἶναι)' and that 'what is not (τὸ μὴ ὂν) does not exist (μὴ εἶναι)'

---

[3] ὂν (*on*) and οὐσία (*ousia*) are both participial forms of the Greek verb 'to be' (εἰμί/*eimi*), meaning literally, 'being' and 'beingness,' respectively. For a helpful account of the history of the meaning of these terms and there translations in Latin and English, see Joseph Owens 1951: *The Doctrine of Being in the Aristotelian Metaphysics*, 139; and, see also, R.E. Houser 2010: "The Language of Being and the Nature of God in the Aristotelian Tradition," in *Proceedings of the ACPA*, vol.84, 117. On the best translation of οὐσία as 'being' and not the common 'substance,' from Boethius' translation of the term in Latin (*'substantia'*), see Chapter 2, pp. 104-109, of Daniel C. Wagner 2018: *φύσις καί τὸ ἀνθρώπινον ἀγαθὸν: The Aristotelian Foundations of the Human Good*, available through ProQuest.

[4] This list is meant to be neither comprehensive nor indisputable, and thoughtfully articulate disputations are most welcome as submissions to REALITY.

[5] Aristotle i.348-30BC: *Metaphysics* IV.7 (1011b24-28): "τὸ μὲν γὰρ λέγειν τὸ ὂν μὴ εἶναι ἢ τὸ μὴ ὂν εἶναι ψεῦδος, τὸ δὲ τὸ ὂν εἶναι καὶ τὸ μὴ ὂν μὴ εἶναι ἀληθές, ὥστε καὶ ὁ λέγων εἶναι ἢ μὴ ἀληθεύσει ἢ ψεύσεται." Translations of all Greek texts here are by Daniel C. Wagner.

> is to say the truth (ἀληθές), so that something said to exist or not to exist will either be said truly or falsely.

According to Aristotle, meaningful thoughts and statements (i.e., ones that can be true or false) are not an imposition, construction, or fabrication of the mind—as though a proposition is true *because* we think it or want it to be so. Rather, on this realist approach, reality or being determines the mind fitted for its comprehension and provides the measure by which the truth or falsity of a thought or proposition is to be judged. Thus, and for example:[6]

> ...it is not because we think truly that you are white that you are white, but rather it is because you are white that we are speaking this assertion truly.

Developing this realist approach and explaining how truth and being are related and yet distinct, St. Thomas Aquinas expresses that truth is the *conformity* or "*adequation* (*adaequatio*) of the intellect and the thing or reality."[7]

An uncritical and ahistorical approach will likely suggest that *realism* is one of multiple equally tenable alternative philosophies—that it is just one of many -*isms* from which one must choose "one's own philosophy."[8] This claim about the reality of philosophy and its relation to realism is false. That is, all proclaimed philosophies or philosophical systems deserve to be considered at least in terms of their principles, but many of them deserve also to be discounted on the basis of those same principles. For example, deconstructionism, which although it often portrays "reality" as consisting in extramentally existent relations, denies

---

[6] i.348-30BC: *Metaphysics*, IX.10 (1051b1-10): οὐ γὰρ διὰ τὸ ἡμᾶς οἴεσθαι ἀληθῶς σε λευκὸν εἶναι εἶ σὺ λευκός, ἀλλὰ διὰ τὸ σὲ εἶναι λευκὸν ἡμεῖς οἱ φάντες τοῦτο ἀληθεύομεν.

[7] Aquinas i.1256-59: *Questiones Disputates de Veritate*, q.1, a.1, c.: "Prima ergo comparatio entis ad intellectum est ut ens intellectui concordet: quae quidem concordia adaequatio intellectus et rei dicitur; et in hoc formaliter ratio veri perficitur. Hoc est ergo quod addit verum super ens, scilicet conformitatem, sive adaequationem rei et intellectus; ad quam conformitatem, ut dictum est, sequitur cognitio rei. Sic ergo entitas rei praecedit rationem veritatis, sed cognitio est quidam veritatis effectus." – "Therefore, the primary relation of being to the intellect is such that being concords to the intellect; this concordance is called a certain *adequation/equality* (*adaequatio*) of the intellect and the thing (*rei*); and in this [*adequation*] the formal principle of truth is completed. This, therefore, is what truth (*verum*) adds to being, namely, a conformity or adequation of the thing and the intellect."

[8] Of course, such a notion is, on the realist conception of philosophy, absurd and self-contradictory as it entails that what I might say is true about reality is at the same time not true about reality according to someone else's "personal philosophy."

that these relations connect any really existent things; there is only the pattern of relations, and nothing really related as such.[9] Not being a true realism, it cannot be considered a true philosophy any more than Roscelian nominalism or Cartesian idealism.

We can see the necessary exclusion of these non-realist theories from the argument that a proper understanding of *philosophy* and *realism* shows them to be coextensive, both as historical fact and in terms of their essential meaning. First, in its source in Ancient Greece, as indicated above, Socrates, Plato, and Aristotle were all realists.[10] Realism, thus—whatever position one might take as a "personal philosophy"—must be given a preeminent position in the history of philosophy as *philosophy*. Second, some brief reflection on the ancient source and meaning of the word *philosophy* shows that it is essentially realist in its meaning. The Greek term φῐλοσοφία (*philosophia*) is a compound form of φίλος/*philos* meaning "love" (from the verb φιλέω/*phileo*), and σοφία (*sophia*), meaning "wisdom." The question is, of course: what is the meaning of this *wisdom*, which Socrates, Plato, and Aristotle were driven to seek by love? As Aristotle makes clear at the outset of his *Metaphysics*, *sophia* was long associated with expert technical knowledge in production, i.e., it was the highest level of knowledge in τέχνη (*techne*)—*craft*, *trade*, or *art*. The master craftsmen, Aristotle tells us, was respected and called wise precisely because he understood the *things and state of affairs* in the production and because he could *causally*

---

[9] See Kemple 2019: "Signs and Reality",78n6 below.

[10] The fact that Plato, for some portion of his philosophical career, proposed *an* idealist theory of knowledge in making *separated* Ideas/Forms (τὰ εἴδη/*ta eide*) what is real (οὐσία) (c.370BC: *Parmenides*, 130b-d; 133c) does not militate against the thesis that he was a realist as his teacher Socrates and student Aristotle. His realism will be displayed below, alongside that of Socrates. While it must be qualified that his sometime position that what is real, and perhaps, only real, is the separated Idea is not ultimately compatible with sense-perceptive realism, it is also to be noted that Plato himself appears to have recognized the fundamental problems with this theory and to have rejected it accordingly (see *Parmenides* and *Sophist*). In any case, and following Socrates, Plato adopted and employed the Ancient Greek oratorical, mathematical, and medical tradition of classifying and defining by division of *forms* or *species* (τὰ εἴδη/*ta eide*), which is manifestly realist. See, A.E. Taylor 1911: "The words εἶδος, ἰδέα in Pre-Platonic Literature". As Aristotle shows succinctly at i.360-330BC: *Categories* 5 (3b10-18), Plato's realist approach to defining the particular things in the world is simply incompatible with the claim that ideas/forms exist as separated individuals. Following Socrates, Plato clearly believed that rational-discourse (λόγος/logos) is ordered toward expression of the truth (ἀλήθεια/aletheia) about reality through definition (see, e.g., *Euthyphro*, *Meno*, *Phaedo*, *Phaedrus*, *Republic*, *Cratylus*, *Sophist*, *Parmenides*).

explain them. The physician knows not only that an herb is medicinal as an empirical fact, but why and how it is medicinal given its properties and the disposition of the body being healed. He knows that aspirin alleviates the headache, and that it does this chemically at the cellular level by stopping the production of the enzymes responsible for inflammation, etc. The master carpenter knows the things that exist in the production of the house at this particular stage here and now and he knows why they are so with respect to the end or goal being sought, i.e., the house for the sake of shelter and protection. This distinguishes him from the apprentices and laborers who lack such comprehension, but produce through his intelligent direction. He knows the fact that the foundation has been set in the dimensions it has been set in; that it has been plated level; and that this state of reality will causally allow for the construction of the floor box, framed walls, roof, etc., which will then provide the shelter and protection. Those who are masters of a τέχνη (*techne*), then, clearly operate in a realist framework: they are wise because they know the realities of their artistic productions and they can explain their causes.

Similarly, in leisure and inspired by wonder and curiosity as opposed to utility, the philosopher is the one who seeks wisdom, which is theoretical knowledge sought for its own sake, of the factual states of affairs in the world and their causes.[11] For example, wisdom is knowing not only the fact that the light of the sun is absent and no shadows are being cast at midday (though the sky appears clear), but also the causal explanation of this phenomenon by appeal to interposition of the moon between the earth and the sun.[12] In fact, Aristotle—who, incidentally, was also the first historian of Philosophy—tells us that Socrates sought precisely this sort of wisdom. Socrates was famous for asking the question τὶ ἐστι (*ti esti*) or "what is it?" Given a particular subject of inquiry, Socrates sought a rational-account or expression, i.e., a λόγος/*logos*, so that he could reason from it causally to important conclusions about the subject.[13] This method of inquiry is thematic in Plato's dialogues, where Socrates is often the star interlocutor. For example, Socrates requests a definition of piety (in the *Euthyphro*) so that he can reason to the conclusion that he is not impious (in the

---

[11] See i.348-30BC: *Metaphysics*, I.1.

[12] See, Aristotle i.348-30BC: *Metaphysics* I.1 (981a28-30): οἱ μὲν γὰρ ἔμπειροι τὸ ὅτι μὲν ἴσασι, διότι δ' οὐκ ἴσασιν· οἱ δὲ τὸ διότι καὶ τὴν αἰτίαν γνωρίζουσιν. Or, "Those with experience have grasped that something is the case, but not the account of why it is so. But those [with science or art] know also the account of why it is so and the cause." The translation is my own.

[13]i.348-30BC: *Metaphysics*, XIII.4 (1078b24-25): συλλογίζεσθαι γὰρ ἐζήτει, ἀρχὴ δὲ τῶν συλλογισμῶν τὸ τί ἐστιν. Or, Socrates "was seeking to syllogize/argue and the principle (ἀρχὴ) of syllogisms/arguments is the definition (τὸ τί ἐστιν)

Apology); or, he requests a definition of virtue in order to show the sense in which it is teachable (as a form of knowledge) and the sense in which it is not teachable (as a voluntary practice; in the *Meno*). There is, perhaps, no better example of this in the case of Socrates than that found in the *Apology* where, having discovered about himself and human beings in general that our defining and perfective characteristic lies in knowing and rational inquiry (attracting the ire of many Athenians), he can draw the conclusion that "the unexamined life," i.e., a life devoid of giving "rational-accounts of human virtue/excellence...," is not worth living for the human being."[14] It is no wonder, then, that Aristotle would characterize Socrates as a realist, asserting that he was the first to seek universal definitions and to draw conclusions from them regarding the human good.[15]

Socrates, who we must recognize as the first Philosopher, was a realist, holding that *things exist in the world*—there is reality—and we can know these things and express truths about them. Thus we see philosophy, as the love of wisdom, is from its deepest roots historically and essentially coextensive with realism.

Having expressed the basic meaning of *reality* and the realist philosophy that is married to it, it is fitting now to say a word regarding motivation. **Why reality?** Which is to say: what is the importance and significance of realist philosophy?

First, the realist holds that the expression of the truth about reality is good for the human being, as it constitutes the perfection of the highest faculty of the human being: the intellect, which, as we have already seen St. Thomas indicate, is ordered toward and harmoniously fitted for reality and its disclosure. Apprehending the reality of ourselves and the world we live in, apprehending that things are in various manners, we have wonder and then the desire to know the distinction of all things real and their causes. This innate yearning is precisely why Aristotle famously begins his *Metaphysics* with the line, "All human beings desire to know by nature."[16] In a way, thus, if we ask the question "why reality, realism, and philosophy?", as looking for some extrinsic justification of their connection, we run afoul of a category error: it is tantamount to asking why plants grow, photosynthesize, flower, and reproduce with the same expectation of extrinsic justification. That is: we philosophize as the most free and highest expression of our being, because it is our inescapable end, good, perfection, and fulfillment. To be human—to be at our *most* human—is to philosophize, just as

---

[14] Plato c.399BC: *Apology*, 38a1-6: ὁ δὲ ἀνεξέταστος βίος οὐ βιωτὸς ἀνθρώπῳ. All translations of Plato by Daniel C. Wagner, unless indicated otherwise.

[15] i.348-30BC: *Metaphysics*, XIII.4 (1078b16-29).

[16] i.348-30BC: *Metaphysics*, I.1 (980a20): Πάντες ἄνθρωποι τοῦ εἰδέναι ὀρέγονται φύσει.

plants find their fulfillment in flowering. There is a second and essentially related reason driving our need for reality: *katharsis*.

The English word "catharsis" has come to mean "a release, or relief from powerful repressed emotions." The term's original Greek meaning (as is usually the case) is a good deal more profound, enlightening, and pertains to processes of *human_reason* rather than of *emotion*. Etymologically, κἄθαρσις (*katharsis*) looks to be a compound of the preposition κατά, meaning here "toward," "into," or "according to," and a form of the Greek verb, ἀείρω (*aeiro*), which can mean both "a taking away/removing" and a "lifting up, raising, or elevating." Literally, therefore, the term κἄθαρσις means "toward-taking away" and "toward-raising up or elevating." Both of these meanings, i.e., "removing" and "elevating," are essential to *katharsis*. In the Pythogoreans (famous now for mathematical contributions, but also known in antiquity for strong philosophical and religious convictions), κἄθαρσις (*katharsis*) is a kind of *purification* of the soul through education (μουσἴκός/*musikos*), where impurity is *removed* from the soul so that it can obtain what is fitting for it in a state of health (ὑγίειἄ/*hugeia*) and harmony (ἁρμονία/*harmonia*). An ἁρμονία/*harmonia* was literally a carpenter's joint, e.g., a dovetail; thus the soul being in a *harmonia* meant, for the Pythagoreans, that it obtained what was fitting for it, or what it belongs with as its end, as tenons and mortises are ordered to fit together in formation of the joint and the box. Here, the notion of *katharsis*, then, is already connected to *health* and flourishing of the human being.

Similarly, in the medical tradition championed by Hippocrates, *katharsis* is a *purgation* or a *purification*, whereby the physician "takes away" some alien harm from the body (disease, or some dietary harm or imbalance), an impediment to healthy function, so that the body in turn can be *elevated* and returned to the state of health or proper biological functioning. To use a modern example, which we think Hippocrates would appreciate, overconsumption of caffeine can result in blurred vision—an unhealthy state of the eye. This state is *disharmonious* and unhealthy because the eye has a proper object or end, to which it is fitted: generally the reception of color; specifically shape[s]. Too much caffeine results in the eye not achieving this end/object well, or bad vision. The physician, then, removes this excess from the patient, proscribing caffeine, which process of *katharsis* will *elevate* the eye back to a state of health allowing the person to obtain what is fitting in the case of vision.

Following and developing the Pythagorean and Hippocratic traditions, Plato appropriates the term κἄθαρσις/*katharsis* and applies it in his expression of the meaning and purpose of philosophy and rational-discourse (λόγος/*logos*). In the *Phaedo*, Plato's Socrates, speaking to an audience of Pythagoreans, identifies the practice of philosophy with *katharsis*. Philosophy as *katharsis*, he explains, is a process of "purification" or "moral cleansing" in removal of carnal desire and evil associated with the body so that the soul can obtain its good—i.e., knowledge (*Phaedo*, 67a-c).[17] In the *Sophist*, Plato then appeals to *katharsis* in order to contrast Socrates' vocation as a philosopher with the dubious activities of sophists.

The sophists were, in fact, the first anti-realists, and anti-philosophers, rejecting the order of reason/speech—λόγος/*logos*—to the true expression of reality or being. These were figures such as Protagoras (490—420BC), who denied the principle of non-contradiction and, thus, truth and meaning,[18] and Gorgias (483—376BC), who reduced spoken discourse (λόγος/*logos*) to power for the sake of self-aggrandizement through the manipulation of others.[19] This radical skepticism was fundamentally connected to subjectivism and a moral relativism that would allow for the justification of virtually any human behavior and, most importantly, would prevent human beings (if subscribed to) from obtaining their good in the perfection of the intellect. Here, the morally dubious character of anti-realist sophistry, which caused Socrates, Plato, and Aristotle to have much contempt for these figures, comes to the fore: where there is no truth in speech about reality, all human discourse in language becomes eristic and coercive manipulation.[20] The skeptical rejection of reality must also lead us (if we are thinking at all) to a dark and cynical view of human relations in speech.

Contra this anti-realist approach, Plato explains that, by way of "critical examination" and "refutation" (ἔλεγχος/*elenchus*), Socrates the philosopher *removes* false opinions from the minds and souls of his interlocutors so that they can *elevate* themselves through learning the truth about what is fitting,

---

[17] It turns out there is a need for a κᾰθαρσις of Plato's κᾰθαρσις in the *Phaedo*, as he deems the body and matter evil, but that is the topic of another essay!

[18] Diogenes Laertius c.210-40AD: *Lives of Philosophers*, 9.53 (DK): "Contradiction is impossible." And, 9.531 (DK). "...there are two mutually opposed [but equal] arguments on any subject." Translations by Daniel C. Wagner.

[19] In his *Encomium to Helen*, and aside from implying a denial of the principle of non-contradiction by holding that all persuasive "discourse" (λόγος/*logos*) is false, Gorgias (c.380BC) repeatedly identifies discourse with "power" (δύνᾰμις/dunamis), he compares it to a "drug" (φάρμακον/*pharmakon*) (14), he calls it a "plaything" (21) for his own wants and desires.

[20] For a classic example of eristic discourse from one of Gorgias' admirers, see Plato's c.385BC: *Meno* (80a-e), where Socrates calls Meno's self-contradicting argument that learning is impossible an ἐριστικὸν λόγον (*eristikon logon*).

beautiful, and good (*Sophist*, 230b-d).[21] *Reality is therefore attained through katharsis*. In this technical sense, realist Philosophy provides (i) *the removal or refutation of harmful ideas that are impediments to the good of the human person so that* (ii) *the human person can actually achieve the human good*. Because of the possibility of falsity in the expression of reality, there is ever a need for the realist philosopher to correct error and aid all humans in the pursuit toward expression of the truth, the only good which may satisfy the deepest yearnings of our human nature.[22]

§

The need for *katharis* by way of realist philosophy stretches beyond the Protagorases and Gorgiases[23] of antiquity, through the medieval and modern periods and all the way to our own contemporary period. For beginning with Jean Roscelin (c.1050-112) and continuing through William of Ockham (c.1287—1349), the Latin age of philosophy contended with nominalist theories that made thought essentially unrelated to things. These early nominalisms would indirectly lay the ground of those that permeated modernity, which still undermine philosophy in the Western world today. Though it takes many forms—comprising not only that of Roscelin and Ockham, but the conceptualism of John of Salisbury (1115—1180) and all the best known philosophers of modernity, such as Descartes (1596—1650), Locke (1632—1704), Hume (1711—1776) and Kant (1724—1804), as well as many of the prominent philosophical thinkers and theories influential today—nominalism may be commonly defined as the denial that relations as such possess an ontological status independent of the mind, or, being effectively the same thing, if they do exist they cannot be known.

---

[21] C.f., F.E. Peters, *Greek Philosophical Terms: A Historical Lexicon*, 98-99. I have conferred with the Greek of Iamblichus in the case of the claims regarding the Pythagoreans, along with that of Plato in the *Phaedo* and *Sophist*.

[22] St. Thomas Aquinas also understood philosophy in terms of the realist expression of truth and *katharsis*, as we have set it out here. At 1259/65: *Summa Contra Gentiles* lib.1, c.1, n.4, thus, he notes that the twofold office of the wise man is "meditating to speak divine truth (*veritatem divinam*) [...] and to refute error that is contrary to the truth (*et errorem contra veritatem impugnare*)".

[23] We do want to qualify that not all figures in the history of philosophy who have taken what we would consider an anti-realist stance are sophists in terms of principles or motivations.

We see this nominalism grown especially by William of Ockham, who held there to exist nothing other than individuals.[24] That is, the heart of his objection to the notion of universals is objecting to their possibility of holding existence; for Ockham conceived existence on the model of substantial being alone, *in esse*; i.e., being as in a substance—either *in se* (in itself, as a relatively-independent substance, such as this or that human individual) or *in alio* (in another, in a substance as an accident, such as the color of this or that human being's hair). Anything universal in itself, or even anything general (if we may assume a distinction between universality and generality), could not be either a substance or an accident; for then it would be subsisting within an individual and therefore constrained to particularity and thus not predicable of others and not universal.[25]

In short, this entails that conceptual meaning apprehended by and in the mind cannot signify what is real and commonly possessed in particular beings in the world. On this view, for example, when we predicate 'animal' of a particular ox and a particular human, all that these particular things have in common (in terms of meaning) is the name, 'animal' (thus, 'nominalism'), and it is not the case that we call them both 'animal' because they really each possess the identical ontological features pertaining to animality—organic, living, bodily, etc. It is little surprise, given the prevalence of nominalism among the thinkers of the Enlightenment, that social contracts became the norm for enforcing moral order: for, absent belief in real relations as governing cognition-independent reality, only convention can nominate an action as good or bad, right or wrong. The influence of this nominalist thinking on our morality can be seen still today, where morality and the political exist not in a continuum—as they did for Aristotle—but as separately divided into private and public spheres.

But while nominalism still shows itself today explicitly through undermining our moral and political realism, it begins always with errors concerning the knowability of the real itself. The nominalism of modernity, for instance, culminated in one of the more severe expressions of anti-realism and skeptical idealism (albeit, under the guise of empiricism) in the history of philosophy:

---

[24] Cf. Armand Maurer 1962: *Medieval Philosophy: An Introduction*, 277-81.

[25] The nonsense here, of course, is that if a sign is an individual thing–a sign being for Ockham the means whereby "universality" occurs, namely in that one individual thing, the sign, can signify many (cf. Maurer 1962: *Medieval Philosophy*, 280-81)–there is no explanation for the existential status of its connection to those things its signifies; that is, if a sign is not a relation, or does not entail a relation, how can it bring about a connection between the mind and its object? (Cf. Deely 2010: *Medieval Philosophy Redefined*, 326-27).

David Hume. Aware of the full consequences of nominalism[26] and Cartesian Dualism with respect to our ability to know things in the world, Hume notes that:[27]

> The mind has never anything present to it but the [immanent] perceptions, and cannot possibly reach any experience of their connexion with objects. The supposition of such a connexion is, therefore, without any foundation in reasoning.

Reducing human knowledge to the matter of fact customary conjunction of ideas in the mind (which he conflated with perceptions[28]), Hume denied the possibility of wisdom (*sophia*) about the world altogether. In the same vein, Fredrick Nietzsche (1844—1900)—a new instantiation of Gorgias—redefined truth as "the will to power", which is to say one will's domination of that of another.[29] Truth for Nietzsche, then, is not, as Aristotle and St. Thomas expressed it, an expression of the way things really are or are not; rather, it is merely an instrumental expression of power which gets one what one wants—control and domination of other. Richard Rorty (1931—2007) holds a similar view, re-naming truth "anti-representationalism," which "...does not view knowledge as a matter of getting reality right, but rather as a matter of acquiring habits of action for coping with reality."[30] Dialogue, on this view, is not about the expression of what is truly good, it is eristic verbal combat aimed merely at a "consensus."

Coincident sophistry can be found in the resurgent rise of scientism, not merely as the ephemeral positivism and verificationism popular in the early 20th century, but as an emergent cultural ethos among the increasingly-secularized West, exemplified in thinkers such as Sam Harris, who has proposed that advances in neuroscience—chief among other idioscopic scientific disciplines—will enable us to regulate morality.[31]

The implicit and unconscious nominalism behind the popularity of our current (and recent) sophists—found in adherents of contemporary nihilism and

---

[26] For Hume's nominalism, see 1748: *An Enquiry Concerning Human Understanding*, sec. XII, part 1, 244.
[27] 1748: *An Enquiry Concerning Human Understanding*, sec. XII, p. 114.
[28] 1748: *An Enquiry Concerning Human Understanding*, sec. II.
[29] 1886: *Jenseits von Gut und Böse: Vorspiel einer Philosophie der Zukunft* in the English translation by Helen Zimmern, *Beyond Good and Evil: Prelude to a Philosophy of the Future* c.1, sec.4.
[30] Richard Rorty 1990: *Objectivity, Relativism and Truth*, 1.
[31] 2010: *The Moral Landscape: How Science Can Determine Human Values*.

scientism alike, both beliefs alike often coinciding in the same individual—demands a rigorous, candid, insightful, and *kathartically*-exercised realist inquiry into the truth of what is. Within the pages of this volume, you will find just such an approach to realism.

§

Reality proposes a unique structure for all its issues. Every article is accompanied by the review of a peer, not given in the form of hastily-written notes sent anonymously to an editor, but in a thoughtful composition: either a **comment**, a short discussion of the papers merits and demerits in scholarship and argumentation, or a **response**, which goes to greater lengths providing not only consideration of the original article, but the reviewer's own thinking as well.

In "The Logical Terms of Sense Realism: A Thomistic-Aristotelian & Phenomenological Defense", Daniel C. Wagner presents critical exegesis of Aristotle's treatment of definition and subsequent defense of univocal predication. By drawing on the traditions of Thomism and Husserlian phenomenology, Wagner is able to show both the philosophical indefensibility of nominalism and the possibility of discovering the identity between individuals and what is given in universal definitions.

Commenting upon Wagner's article is James D. Capehart, in "The Philosophical Implications of Sense Realism". Capehart's comment succinctly presents the key merits of Wagner's position and suggests further developments: namely, integrating the explicit doctrine of universals presented by Thomas Aquinas and demonstrating the relevance of true univocal predication for moral questions.

Brian Kemple provides an advocation for "semiotic realism" in his "Signs and Reality", which provides resolution to a lasting problem in the Thomistic tradition: namely, *how* it is that the cognitive means of knowing have a similitude to the objects known. Beyond resolving the immediate textual dispute, this semiotic realism—building upon the philosophy of John Deely, Charles Peirce, John Poinsot, and Thomas Aquinas—is upheld also as the means to unraveling the tangled knots of "meaning" in our present day.

Responding to Kemple is Matthew Minerd, who provides a series of complementary remarks in "The Analogy of *Res*-ality". These remarks focus on the importance of the as-yet underdeveloped application of semiotics to *signa practica* and provide a critical a clarified understanding of the operations of the intellect.

Following is Kirk Kanzelberger's "Reality and the Meaning of Evil: On the Moral Causality of Signs", an investigation of the nature of moral evil which builds upon the consequences of semiotics and the "reality" of beings of reason. Aided by a piece of dramatic fiction, a reflection on the nature of fiction itself, and profound insights into the semiotic traditions of Deely, Peirce, Poinsot, and Aquinas, Kanzelberger demonstrates that what is meant by evil in the world of real human experience cannot be understood *simply* as privation.

Commenting upon Kanzelberger's work is Michael Dodds, OP, in "Made of Flame and Air", providing both original insight and commentary. Fr. Dodds' contribution deftly weaves C.S. Lewis and Miguel de Cervantes into the narrative wrought by Kanzelberger, bringing further illumination to the complexities of evil's reality.

Finally, Francisco E. Plaza provides us an article on "Political Science and Realism" which challenges both the brusque pragmaticism of value-free materialism and the utopian-idealist subjectivism which dominate contemporary political thought. Instead, Plaza proposes, political science must seek the actual common good with a realist metaphysical foundation. This proposal is enlivened with the thinking of not only Aristotle, but Strauss, Voegelin, and Maritain.

Responding to Plaza is Brian Jones, whose "Classical Realism in a Democratic Context" furthers the challenge of modern politics, astutely pointing out how contemporary political science ignores the explanatory power of ideas in the reality of political life, and further that the *context* of modern politics as pervasive if unconsciously religious.

§

These four articles and their four peer responses are far from an exhaustive presentation of the philosophy of realism: not only is there variation in the thinking of the authors and topics, but realism by its very nature—as discussed above—pertains to the whole of rightly-conducted philosophical inquiry. To *encapsulate* realism is not the intent of this issue.

Rather, this is a *primer* for realism: not one which endeavors simply to prove that realism is true, but moreover that realist philosophy holds answers to questions beyond the "*yes or no*" question of whether we know what is real. We do: and within these pages, the weighty philosophical impact of that truth will be felt.

References Historically Layered

THOMAS AQUINAS (1225—1274).

c.1252/6. *Scriptum super libros Sententiarum*

i.1256-59. *Quaestiones disputatae de veritate*.

1259/65. *Summa contra Gentiles*.

ARISTOTLE (384-322BC).

i.360-330BC. Κατηγορίαι, Greek from *Aristotelis categoriae et liber de interpretatione*, edited by L. Minio–Paluello (Oxford: Clarendon Press, 1949; reprinted in 1966).

i.348-30BC. Μετά τα Φυσικά, all translations by Daniel C. Wagner from the Greek in *Aristotlelis metaphysica*, 2 vols, edited by W. D. Ross (Oxford: Clarendon Press, 1924; 1953 corrected edition, reprinted in 1970).

DEELY, John (26 April 1942—2017 January 7).

2010. *Medieval Philosophy Redefined: The Development of Cenoscopic Science, AD354 to 1644 (From the Birth of Augustine to the Death of Poinsot)* (Chicago: Scranton University Press).

DIOGENES Laertius (c.180—240AD).

c.210-40AD. Lives of Philosophers

HARRIS, Sam (9 April 1967—).

2010. *The Moral Landscape: How Science Can Determine Human Values* (New York: Free Press).

HOUSER, Rollen Edward.

2010. "The Language of Being and the Nature of God in the Aristotelian Tradition," in *Proceedings of the ACPA*, vol.84: 113-32.

HUME, David (7 May 1711—1776 August 25).

1748. *An Enquiry Concerning Human Understanding* (originally published under the title *Philosophical Essays Concerning Human Understanding* and retitled in 1758), edited by Tom L. Beauchamp (New York: Oxford University Press, 2000).

MAURER, Armand (21 January 1915—2008 March 22).

1962. *Medieval Philosophy: An Introduction*, second edition (Toronto: Pontifical Institute of Medieval Studies, 1982).

NIETZSCHE, Friedrich (15 October 1844—1900 August 25).

1886. *Jenseits von Gut und Böse: Vorspiel einer Philosophie der Zukunft* in the English translation by Hene Zimmern, *Beyond Good and Evil: Prelude to a Philosophy of the Future* (T.N. Foulis: Edinburgh, 1907).

OWENS, Joseph, C.S.B. (17 April 1908—2005 October 30).

1951. *The Doctrine of Being in the Aristotelian Metaphysics* (Toronto: PIMS, 1978).

PETERS, Francis Edward (23 June 1927—).

1967. *Greek Philosophical Terms: A Historical Lexicon* (New York: New York University Press).

PLATO (c.429/424—348/47BC).

All Plato's Greek is taken from *Platonis opera*, vol. 1, ed. by J. Burnet (Oxford: Clarendon Press, 1900, Reprinted. 1967) and translations are by Daniel C. Wagner.

c.399BC. Ἀπολογία Σωκράτους – *Apology.*

c.385BC. Μένων – *Meno.*

c.380BC. Γοργίας – *Gorgias.*

c.370BC. Παρμενίδης – *Parmenides.*

RORTY, Richard (4 October 1931—2007 June 8).

1990. *Objectivity, Relativism and Truth* (Cambridge University Press, 1990).

TAYLOR, Alfred Edward (22 December 1869—1945 October 31).

1911. "The words εἶδος, ἰδέα in Pre-Platonic Literature," in *Varia Socratica* (Oxford: St. Andrews University Publications, No. IX, 1911).

WAGNER, Daniel C.

2018. *φύσις καί τὸ ἀνθρώπινον ἀγαθὸν: The Aristotelian Foundations of the Human Good*. Doctoral dissertation, University of St. Thomas, Houston TX. Available through ProQuest.

The Logical Terms of Sense Realism

A Thomistic-Aristotelian & Phenomenological Defense[1]

Daniel C. Wagner
Professor and Chair of Philosophy
Aquinas College, Grand Rapids, MI
Editor, REALITY

At the heart of realist philosophy is the doctrine of univocal predication of definitions or the universal terms genus, species, and difference. This doctrine, first set down by Aristotle in the *Categories*, was famously rejected in the medieval period by William of Ockham. Ockham's nominalism consisted in the claim that all that is common when a term is predicated of particular individuals is the term or name (*nomen*) and not essential meaning or nature. His position was accepted by virtually all the major modern philosophers, and still stands as one of the most formidable obstacles to realism.

After giving a detailed textual presentation of Aristotle's treatment of definition—the logical terms of sense-realism—in the *Topics* and *Categories*, this article offers a critical defense of the doctrine of univocal predication in two stages. First, by analysis of the phenomenon of predication as it is exercised in human language, it shown that the nominalist position is untenable by *reductio ad impossibile*: nominalism results in contradiction as human knowers do not

---

[1] Correspondence to wagner@realityjournal.org

Table of Contents

predicate names and conceptual meaning unless they suppose the truth of the doctrine of univocal predication. Second, looking to key texts in Aristotle, and inspired by Avicenna and St. Thomas Aquinas, a plausible account of the identity between individuals and universal definitions is articulated, which avoids the major criticism of univocal predication offered by nominalists, i.e., that the doctrine reduces to contradiction in equating individuals and universals. Form provides a principle of identity between individuals and universal, as the same form can be conceived in two modes of existence: (i) in the individual and (ii) as a separated universal. The critique of nominalism offered in defense of sense-realism is taken up under the umbrella of the phenomenological method. Beginning from an attitude of neutrality regarding the question of whether or not definitions signify what is real in the particulars of sense-experience, the profound unreasonableness of nominalism is exhibited while the sense-realism of Aristotle and St. Thomas Aquinas is shown to be the most reasonable account of the phenomena.

I. Introduction

As the introduction to this issue of *Reality* has explained in some detail, philosophical realism, in the broadest of terms, "means that (i) there is *reality*—that things actually exist in the world—*and* (ii) that we can comprehend and express true (or conversely false) statements/propositions about this reality." So, for example, the realist holds that a buzzing being with a stinger, collecting nectar, really exists over there on the flower and that I express knowledge of this being when I apply the name 'honey bee' and its corresponding definition to this buzzing being, distinguishing it from the flower, the pond, the frog, the lily, etc. In answering the question "what is realism" in a manner sensitive to the historical fact that the essential tenets of realism have been, and especially now are, often rejected, it will be helpful to think of realism as a *problem* in light of this general meaning. Setting out *the correct problem* is of the utmost import.

Broadly speaking, one *might* say that the problem lies in explaining how it is that we can know there is reality and how it is that this reality comes to exist in the mind in such a way that the mind can know and express it as it is. So, to stick with our example, the problem would lie in explaining how it is that I come to possess the notion that the buzzing being *is* over there on the flower and then apply the name 'honey bee' to it understanding that what it is in itself is captured by the definition corresponding to the name. Given the formulation of the problem in this manner, one *might* then immediately attempt to give a **genetic account** of knowledge, that is explaining the genesis of knowledge of things in the world beginning with sensation through the sense organs and culminating in abstract understanding of things sensed in the world—the move from the buzzing being to the definition of the honey bee and its application in judgement. Given the widely accepted Modern, Cartesian-idealist assertion that what the mind knows is not things in the world but ideas, concepts, impressions, or, as David Hume says, "copies," of those things which exist only immanently in the mind, the urgency of giving a genetic account of human knowledge seems even greater.[2] If my knowledge that the buzzing being is a honey bee is true because my idea of the honey bee is an accurate "copy" of the honey bee itself, then it seems that I must first give an account of how I came to possess this idea in such a manner as to explain its truthful accuracy in relation to the thing I apply it to in the act of judgment. On this "impression-to-thing-itself" model of knowledge, if one cannot account for accurate concept formation, then, one cannot be sure that what one thinks one knows (that the buzzing being on the flower is a honey bee) is true.

But then, perhaps, the genetic account is not quite the fundamental problem, and we have jumped the gun, as it were. While a comprehensive account of the genesis of the abstract meanings, ideas, or concepts that make knowing possible is important and necessary for a complete explanation and defense of sense realism, moving immediately into this account would be a hasty methodological error. To begin, this approach falsely suggests that, if one could not give a comprehensive account of all the possible details of the genesis of knowledge in physical, psychological, and mental terms, then our natural mode of assuming we know things would be naïve, illegitimate, and false. This is problematic, however, as it is motivated by the uncritical assumption that the mind knows only immanent ideas (which are "copies") and not things in the world. In my natural attitude and mode of judging things in the world to be honey bees, lilies, ponds, and frogs, I am not even hyper-reflectively focusing on the concepts I use to form these judgments. It is a methodological error to think that the genetic account comes first in the realist approach to knowledge because, objectively speaking, human beings are already regularly engaged in thinking and speaking acts characteristic of a realist attitude using concepts *as though* they signify what things in the world *really* are. The priority, then, lies in the *problem* of giving an account of the terms of human knowing and expression as they present

---

[2] Descartes commits himself to this epistemology through his mind body dualism in 1641: *Meditations on First Philosophy*. See, especially, *Meditations* I, II, and VI. David Hume describes the mind and its concepts in relation to things in the world in this manner in 1748: *An Enquiry Concerning Human Understanding*, §12.

themselves in thought and language. Here, I do not mean "logical terms" in the modern sense of pure meaning abstracted from being or existence. This would, again, be to import an unfounded assumption into my analysis of the phenomena of thought and language—namely, that all logical notions can be conceived in the first place as pure meaning without a relation to being or existence in some sense. As the careful analysis to follow will bring to light, this is false. Aristotle will show us that the essential parts of human language and their syntax cannot be conceived except as through a relation to being and reality.

The methodological priority of an account of the terms of realism over the genetic account becomes even clearer through recognizing that only after one reflectively thinks about the use of terms in thought and language which constitute supposed acts of knowing things in the world can the question and problem of the genesis of such knowledge even be formulated. If, while I sit and read in this garden by this pond, I have not *already* made the intellectual judgement 'that buzzing being is a honey bee,' I cannot yet even ask the question of whether or not my application of this predicate 'honey bee' to this subject 'buzzing being' constitutes a true expression of the way this thing (the buzzing being) is in itself. Accordingly, the primary goal of this article is the presentation and defense of the fundamental terms of reality and human knowing acts that grasp it. As it turns out, a thorough, systematic, and critical presentation of the phenomenon of human language and the terms and order of human judgement has already been conducted in antiquity by Aristotle. Thus, this article will begin in section 2 by presenting Aristotle's treatment of logic and grammar in the *Topics* and *Categories*. Here, the primary goal will be to understand Aristotle's division of being/substance (οὐσία/ousia) into two senses: primary, signifying (i) individual subjects existing in the world, and secondary, signifying (ii) the universal meanings by which we know primary beings, i.e., the defining terms of genus, species, and difference. Having an adequate grasp of the basic terms of realism in this manner, its most formidable historical opposition will be presented in section 3 through a historical account of the problem of universals and its culmination in the nominalism of William of Ockham, which was accepted by virtually every modern philosopher. Finally, in section 4, a defense of the logical doctrine of sense realism contra nominalism will be offered in two parts. First, following the approach of Avicenna and St. Thomas Aquinas, an Aristotelian account of the identity between primary and secondary being/substance through the principle of form (εἶδος/*species*) will show the plausibility of sense realism in the face of the nominalism. By appeal to form, the Aristotelian and the Thomist realist can, in fact, explain an identity and *adaequatio* between the knowing mind and its object. Second, it will be shown that the denial of sense realism is not reasonable, given the objective phenomenon of human language. Here, a *reductio ad impossibile* style argument will show that the nominalist rejection of universal meaning and realism (i.e., the denial of secondary being/substance) results in manifest contradiction and is, therefore, untenable. As Aristotle, then, performed a *reductio ad vegetabilie* on the sophist who would deny the principle of non-contradiction at *Metaphysics* IV.4, so here a similar *reductio ad vegetabile* will be performed on the nominalist position.

I do not share David Hume's naiveté that any one who reflects on knowledge will see that our ideas are mere copies of things in the world.[3] To the contrary, I think, following the post-modern philosopher Edmund Husserl (1859-1938), that Hume himself needed to spend a bit more time in careful philosophical reflection. While this article presents the account of the terms of realism offered by Aristotle in antiquity, it will also operate under the umbrella of the phenomenological method, as formulated by Husserl. In the realist spirit, and in order 'to get back to the things themselves' in contradistinction to modern idealism, Husserl proposed using an ἐποχή (*epoche*), or a *suspense of judgement* regarding the relation of the mind to what it knows. Rather than taking a Cartesian approach, which naïvely assumes that the mind does not know things but only ideas of things, or what might be called a naïve realist approach, which uncritically takes for granted that the mind knows things in the world as they are, the ἐποχή places one in an attitude of neutrality so that candid analysis of the phenomenon of human knowing can be achieved.[4] By utilizing this

---

[3] See, again, 1748: *An Enquiry Concerning Human Understanding*, §12.

[4] For Husserl's account of the phenomenological method and the natural and phenomenological attitudes to which I have appealed throughout this introduction, see 1907: *The Idea of Phenomenology* and 1913: *Ideas Pertaining to a Pure Phenomenology and to a Phenomenological Philosophy*. For the most helpful general presentation of Husserlian phenomenology, see Robert Sokolowski's 2000: *Introduction to Phenomenology*. For a general account of Husserl's method and epistemological accomplishments in contrast to the Cartesian approach, and for an account of the compatibility of Aristotelian and Thomistic sense-perceptive realism with phenomenology, see also, Daniel C. Wagner 2019: "On the Foundational Compatibility of Phenomenology & Thomism," in *Studia Gilsoniana* (forthcoming).

methodology, Husserl achieved a necessary apprehension of the fact that human conscious knowing is essentially *intentional*—that it is always a relation of knower and known (*noesis-noema*)—thus showing the absurdity of idealist positions that divorce the mind from what is known. If the essential from and structure of human knowing is not thinking in itself without an object, as Descartes and his modern followers held, but *thinking of something*, the idealist descriptive account of knowing as thought alone is false.

Here, in this article, a similar approach will be taken regarding the basic terms of realism as they are set out by Aristotle. After reflective awareness of the phenomenon of judgement about things in the world through definitions, one may reasonably ask about the nature and meaning of a supposed knowing act, and may even be open to the possibility of a skepticism about whether or not he knows things in the world like honey bees in the way he naturally tends to think he knows them. Of course, I ought also to be open to the converse possibility, that critical enquiry into the matter might verify my natural realist orientation—that *that is a honey bee*, after all. On the other hand, it would not be reasonable for me to begin an inquiry into this phenomenon by naïvely assuming from the outset that my mind knows only immanent ideas and that these ideas or definitions of things like honey bees are not accurate representations of the things to which I suppose they correspond. By utilizing the ἐποχή, then, this study achieves the phenomenological attitude, initially taking a neutral stance regarding the application of conceptual meaning to things in the world. Indeed, the point already made above that proper methodology requires a critical treatment of the terms of realism prior to the genetic account is in line with this phenomenological method, which has us begin by examining the organic constitution of realism in the objective and publicly given phenomenon of human language, grammar, and logic.

Through an initial suspense of judgement, we hold that perhaps the realist stance described at the outset of this paper is true or perhaps it is not. After such an ἐποχή, however, it will be shown that, in fact, contradiction arises when the realist conception of the terms of defining (genus, species, and difference) is denied. A comprehensive genetic account of human knowledge, though certainly important, is not even necessary for establishing that realism is the most reasonable view of reality and human understanding—that it is absurd and self-contradictory to deny the basic tenets of realism.

2. Primary Terms of Classical Sense-Perceptive Realism: Aristotle's *Topics and Categories*[5]

Categories belongs to a group of works in the Aristotelian corpus called the Organon. These works were taken to express the foundational *instruments* (ὄργανον/*organon* = *instrument*) by which knowledge is to be achieved.[6] If the whole of these texts together is taken as the foundational "organ" or "instrument" of knowledge, the *Categories* must be taken as the very footing of this foundational structure. The *Categories'* primary subject matter, as Aristotle clearly indicates in chapter four, pertains to "expressions not one of which is complex," i.e., the simple concepts which make all human thought through judgment and reasoning possible.[7] These concepts are the *categories* (κατηγορίαι/*kategoriai*), which are the simple notions communicated by linguistic terms that may be grammatically predicated of a subject through a connecting verb, forming complex judgments. Literally, and as will be explained in more detail below, they classify the concepts of the mind by which we can "accuse" beings in the world of *being in some respect*.[8] In what follows in this section, a detailed and rigorous account of the first five chapters of Aristotle's *Categories* will be given. The primary goal is an understanding of Aristotle's doctrine of primary and secondary being/substance, offered in chapter 5, as this

---

[5] Significant portions of the treatment of *Topics* and *Categories*, here, along with the argument in defense of Aristotle's realist conception of definition are taken from chapter 2 of my dissertation, 2018: *φύσις καὶ τὸ ἀνθρώπινον ἀγαθόν: The Aristotelian Foundations of the Human Good*, 83-117, available through ProQuest. Hereafter, the work will simply be referred to as *The Aristotelian Foundations of the Human Good*.

[6] This follows the organization of the Aristotelian corpus by Andronicus of Rhodes in the 1st century BC. See, E.S. Forster's 1960 introductory essay to the Loeb edition of the *Topics*, 266.

[7] Aristotle i.360-330BC: *Categories*, 4 (1b25): Τῶν κατὰ μηδεμίαν συμπλοκὴν λεγομένων... This passage will be treated in more detail below. Aristotle's Greek is taken from Aristoteles et Corpus Aristotelicum Phil., ed. by W.D. Ross (Oxford: Clarendon Press, 1950, repr. 1966). All translations are my own, unless indicated otherwise.

[8] Though it is beyond the scope of the current study, it must be acknowledged that Aristotle develops and contributes to a tradition on categories going back through his teacher, Plato, to Socrates and the pre-Socratic traditions on oratory, mathematics, and medicine. For a recent treatment of definition, division, and classification in Socrates, Plato, and the pre-Socrates, and for comparison and contrast of Aristotle's approach to his predecessors, see chapters 1 and 2 of *The Aristotelian Foundations of the Human Good*.

doctrine constitutes the essence of the realist approach to reality and our knowledge of it.[9]

2.1. Definitional propositions in the *Topics*

A brief presentation of the basic terms composing propositions expressing definitions, as Aristotle presents them in his earlier work *Topics*, will provide a helpful propaedeutic to our treatment of the *Categories*.[10] Here, treating the topic of defining, Aristotle classifies the manners in which an attribute may be *said of something*. For this reason, these modes of predicating are often called the "predicables." Aristotle's predicables are definition (ὅρος/*horos*), property (ἴδιον/*idion*), genus (γένος/*genos*), difference (διαφορά/*diaphora*), and accident (συμβεβηκὸς/*sumbebekos*).[11] Aristotle defines definition as "the account

---

[9] I am much indebted to Michael W. Tkacz, who first made this fact known to me in his treatment of the problem of universals in Medieval philosophy.

[10] Following Jonathan J. Sanford 2004: "Categories and Metaphysics: Aristotle's Science of Being", 6, and contra the view of Michael Frede 1981: "Categories in Aristotle", it is not necessary to give a full treatment of *Topics* in order to grasp the *Categories*. The appeal here is limited to the extent that it is helpful for understanding the *Categories*. In point of fact, the *Topics* is a less mature work of Aristotle, often reflecting Platonic accounts of division (thus, the primary concern is "dialectic"). One should give priority to *Categories* in treating Aristotle's approach to definition (along with *Posterior Analytics*, and *De partibus animalium*). On this latter claim, see E.S. Forester's introduction to his 1960 translation of the *Topics*, in the Loeb edition, 265-269. For an analysis showing that the *Topics* represents an earlier, less developed stage of Aristotelian logic in comparison to the *Categories* and the *Analytics*, see C.M. Gillespie 1925: "The Aristotelian Categories", 77-79. Regarding the claim that the *Topics* reflects Platonic division, cf., again, Gillespie's 1925: "The Aristotelian Categories," 76-77. One fairly obvious indication of this fact is that when Aristotle gives a complete list of the categories in c.353BC: *Topics*, I.9 (103b20-24), he lists the first category as τί ἐστι, i.e., "definition" and not οὐσία, i.e., being/substance. This suggests that his interest was largely in the quiddative meaning of things, like his teacher Plato, as it does not manifest the radical break of the *Categories* by making concrete existing individuals of experience the basis of reality and knowledge. For more on the topic of definition and division and the relation of the *Topics* to the *Categories*, see, Wagner 2018: *The Aristotelian Foundations of the Human Good*, chapter 2, sec. A.

[11] See c.353BC: *Topics*, I.4 (101b17023): "Now, every premise and problem manifests either property, genus, or accident; for one must also arrange difference—being

(λόγος/*logos*) signifying the essence (τὸ τί ἦν εἶναι/*to ti en einai*) (e.g., a human being is an animal with the capacities of reason and language."[12] "Property" is defined as "that which does not manifest the essence of a thing, but belongs to the thing alone and is convertible with the thing,"[13] which is to say that, wherever you find the thing, you will find the property (e.g., 'having interior angles equal to two right angles' is a property of triangle). "Genus" is defined as "what is predicated in reference to what a thing is (ἐν τῷ τί ἐστι/*en to ti esti*) of several things also differing in species" (e.g., shape is the genus to which triangle, circle, etc., belong).[14] "Difference" is an essential attribute added to the genus and constituting the species (e.g., 'with three equal sides' differentiates the equilateral from the isosceles and the scalene).[15] Finally, an accident is neither definition, property, genus, nor difference, but it is an attribute which can belong or not belong to a thing (e.g., the triangle is blue or red or black, etc.).[16]

---

generic—together with genus. However, since one sense of property signifies essence, and another does not signify essence, let property be divided into both the priorly mentioned parts, and let that sense called the essence signify the definition, and the remaining sense let us call property according to commonly rendered language." Or, πᾶσα δὲ πρότασις καὶ πᾶν πρόβλημα ἢ ἴδιον ἢ γένος ἢ συμβεβηκὸς δηλοῖ· καὶ γὰρ τὴν διαφορὰν ὡς οὖσαν γενικὴν ὁμοῦ τῷ γένει τακτέον. ἐπεὶ δὲ τοῦ ἰδίου τὸ μὲν τὸ τί ἦν εἶναι σημαίνει, τὸ δ' οὐ σημαίνει, διῃρήσθω τὸ ἴδιον εἰς ἄμφω τὰ προειρημένα μέρη, καὶ καλείσθω τὸ μὲν τὸ τί ἦν εἶναι σημαῖνον ὅρος, τὸ δὲ λοιπὸν κατὰ τὴν κοινὴν περὶ αὐτῶν ἀποδοθεῖσαν ὀνομασίαν προσαγορευέσθω ἴδιον.

[12] See c.353BC: *Topics*, I.5 (101b38-102a): ἔστι δ' ὅρος μὲν λόγος ὁ τὸ τί ἦν εἶναι σημαίνων.

[13] c.353BC: *Topics*, I.5(102a18-19): Ἴδιον δ' ἐστὶν ὃ μὴ δηλοῖ μὲν τὸ τί ἦν εἶναι, μόνῳ δ' ὑπάρχει καὶ ἀντικατηγορεῖται τοῦ πράγματος. Aristotle's example here is that a human has the property of being grammatical.

[14] c.353BC: *Topics*, I.5 (102a31-32): Γένος δ' ἐστὶ τὸ κατὰ πλειόνων καὶ διαφερόντων τῷ εἴδει ἐν τῷ τί ἐστι κατηγορούμενον.

[15] c.353BC: *Topics*, I.9 (103b15-16): ...ἐπειδὴ ὁ ὁρισμὸς ἐκ γένους καὶ διαφορῶν ἐστιν· Or, "...since the definition is [formed] from the genera and differentia." See also, *Topics* VI.1 (139a28-29) δεῖ γὰρ τὸν ὁριζόμενον εἰς τὸ γένος θέντα τὰς διαφορὰς προσάπτειν· Or, "For the one defining must have set it [i.e., the defined] into a genus to then ascribe differences."

[16] c.353BC: *Topics*, I.5 (102b4-7): Συμβεβηκὸς δέ ἐστιν ὃ μηδὲν μὲν τούτων ἐστί, μήτε ὅρος μήτε ἴδιον μήτε γένος, ὑπάρχει δὲ τῷ πράγματι, καὶ ὃ ἐνδέχεται ὑπάρχειν ὁτῳοῦν ἑνὶ καὶ τῷ αὐτῷ καὶ μὴ ὑπάρχειν· Or, "An accident is that which is not one of these

Most importantly, in stating the essence of a thing, the proper differences must be connected to the things' genus. Thus, in order to define what something is through genus and specific difference, one must make use of various manners of characterization. This is precisely where the categories come to the fore in the *Topics*, as they logically classify the various manners of characterization. Not yet distinguishing between what something is (definition) and its existence as an atomic, individual whole, separate from other things in the world—as we will see him do presently in *Categories* 4 and 5—Aristotle here lists 10 categories giving the first as τί ἐστι (*ti esti*), i.e., the 'what it is' or 'definition.'[17] The other nine categories are stated in identical form to those we will treat presently in more detail in the *Categories* itself: quantity, quality, relation, place, time, position, possession, action, and passion.[18] Here, then, by identifying these categories, we have clearly transcended first order predication of concepts (as when one says, 'the frog is green') to second order predication, where concepts themselves are classified by concepts (as when I say that 'green is a quality'). We are, then, properly in the realm of logic.

Importantly, Aristotle explains the relation between these categories and the four predicables. When a category is applied so as to signify what something is and what kind of thing it is, as in its genus or through its differentia and species, it is taken as a predicable precisely in the sense that it defines the thing. Otherwise, the predicated categorial term is merely an accident.[19] The point, then, is that while the quality 'animal' is predicable of a cat and a dog as a genus, 'being in the backyard' (place) or 'being shaved' (affection/quality) are predicated merely as accidents. The former generic attribute tells us *what* a cat and a dog are in common and essentially (living organisms in possession of nutritive and sensitive capacities), while the latter attributes are merely accidental—they could not be and then be denied of these subjects and these subjects would still be the same beings. So, knowledge pursued in rational discourse is a matter of determining how various categorial predicates are connected to the subject of inquiry, either as definitive (genus, species,

---

things, neither the definition, nor a property, nor genus, but still belongs to a thing, and it is also that which can belong to any one and self-same thing whatsoever and not belong [to it]."

[17] c.353BC: *Topics*, I.9 (103b22).

[18] c.353BC: *Topics*, I.9 (103b22-23): ... ποσόν, ποιόν, πρός τι, ποῦ, ποτέ, κεῖσθαι, ἔχειν, ποιεῖν, πάσχειν.

[19] Cf. Sanford 2004: "Categories and Metaphysics: Aristotle's Science of Being", 6-12.

difference), or as accidental (accident). Aristotle's realism is already incipient: he believes that by appealing to the terms classified by the categories, we can know what things are essentially. To see this approach to the language and terms of realism further developed, let us turn now to Aristotle's mature treatment of the topic in the *Categories*.

2.2. Predication and reality

Making it clear that the *Categories* is a work about knowing things in the world by definition at the very outset, Aristotle begins chapter one by distinguishing things said that are equivocal and things said that are univocal. "Things are said to be equivocal," he says, "when only the name is common, but the account of the being [i.e., the definition] in accord with the name is different."[20] The term 'animal,' for example, is predicated equivocally when it is said of the particular man and also of the picture, i.e., of a man or some other animal. The reason for this, Aristotle explains is that the definition (τί ἐστιν) of each thing termed 'animal' will be different (one is actually an animal, while the other is a picture).[21] On the other hand, "Something is said univocally," he says, "when both the name is common along with the account of the being itself in accordance with the name, as in the case of both the human and the ox being animals."[22] Aristotle further explains:

---

[20] i.360-330BC: *Categories*, 1 (1a1-3): Ὁμώνυμα λέγεται ὧν ὄνομα μόνον κοινόν, ὁ δὲ κατὰ τοὔνομα λόγος τῆς οὐσίας ἕτερος, οἷον ζῷον ὅ τε ἄνθρωπος καὶ τὸ γεγραμμένον·

[21] i.360-330BC: *Categories*, 1 (1a4-6): ἐὰν γὰρ ἀποδιδῷ τις τί ἐστιν αὐτῶν ἑκατέρῳ τὸ ζῴῳ εἶναι, ἴδιον ἑκατέρου λόγον ἀποδώσει. Or, "For, if one were to set down the definition of these with respect to each being called an 'animal,' one will set down a different account of each."

[22] i.360-330BC: *Categories*, 1 (1a6-8): συνώνυμα δὲ λέγεται ὧν τό τε ὄνομα κοινὸν καὶ ὁ κατὰ τοὔνομα λόγος τῆς οὐσίας ὁ αὐτός, οἷον ζῷον ὅ τε ἄνθρωπος καὶ ὁ βοῦς· Following Harold P. Cooke, E.M. Edghill and Fr. Owens, I have rendered ὁμώνῦμος and συνώνῦμος 'equivocal' and 'univocal,' not giving the literal equivalents of 'homonymous' and 'synonymous.' As Owens points out, the definitions given at *Categories*, 1 are not of *terms*, to which 'homonymous' and 'synonymous' refer alone in English, but to the *things* denoted by the terms. This is clear immediately in the definition of things that are ὁμώνῦμος. The name or term is, in fact, common to the things, which differ in what they are in their being. See Owens 1951: *The Doctrine of Being in the Aristotelian*

> For each of these is called by the name 'animal,' and the account of the being of each is also the same; for, if it were demanded of one to set down what the account of the definition (τὸν λόγον τί ἐστιν) of each of these themselves is—with respect to each being an 'animal'—one would set down the same account (τὸν αὐτὸν λόγον).[23]

Univocal predication occurs, then, when a term and the content of the definition attached to it are applied identically to a set of individual existing beings.[24] Univocal predication constitutes the foundation of realism: if univocal predication of the term 'honey bee' to particular buzzing beings is not possible, the realist conception of reality and knowledge is false. If all predication is equivocal, so that all that would be common to a multiplicity of buzzing beings in the garden is the name 'honey bee' and not an essential meaning, then my natural mode of thinking that I know such a multiplicity through an identical essential meaning is false.

Chapter two of the *Categories* begins by drawing a further distinction in the manner that things are said, which was already implied by the treatment of equivocal and univocal predication. When things are said equivocally or univocally there is a complex expression or, rather, expressions. Knowing the term 'animal' to be univocal, for example, follows on the statements, 'The human is an animal' and 'The ox is an animal,' along with the understanding that 'animal' means precisely the same thing in both propositions. Having these kinds of expressions as data, a further distinction may be drawn, since they can be analyzed into simple components.

1) First, there is a subject, which is that which "under-lies" (the literal meaning of ὑποκείμενον) and receives some predicable *categorization* of its being. 'Subject' can refer to an existing individual in the world and the grammatical

---

Metaphysics, 112. For the alternative translation, see J.J. Ackrill's translation of *Categories* in the *Complete Works (Aristotle)*, 2.

[23] i.360-330BC: *Categories*, 1 (1a8-12): τούτων γὰρ ἑκάτερον κοινῷ ὀνόματι προσαγορεύεται ζῷον, καὶ ὁ λόγος δὲ τῆς οὐσίας ὁ αὐτός· ἐὰν γὰρ ἀποδιδῷ τις τὸν ἑκατέρου λόγον τί ἐστιν αὐτῶν ἑκατέρῳ τὸ ζῴῳ εἶναι, τὸν αὐτὸν λόγον ἀποδώσει.

[24] Aristotle concludes chapter 1 by distinguishing a third manner in which things may be said, which is beyond our scope. Things may also be said as 'derivatives' or 'paronyms' (παρώνῦμος). In this case, a thing derives its name from some other name, but is different in its object than the source, as for example, says Aristotle, when 'grammarian' (the one who does grammar) is derived from 'grammar,' or the man is called 'courageous' by derivation from the term 'courage.'

subject of a sentence. Sometimes a grammatical subject refers to an individual being in the world, e.g., 'Willis' in the statement, 'Willis is a K-9.' 'Subject' may also refer, however, to a grammatical subject, which refers to a generic or specific feature, not an individual in the world, e.g., 'animal' in the statement 'animal is a living organism, etc.' **2)** Second, there is the simple predicate said of the subject in order to *categorize* it in some manner, e.g., 'golden' in the statement 'Willis is a golden.' And, **3)** third, there is some kind of connecting verb (*is/belongs*) linking the predicate to the subject, e.g., 'Willis *is* a dog' or 'It belongs to Willis to have non-retractable claws.' So, Aristotle begins by noting that, "Of things said, some are said in accord with complexity, while other things are without complexity."[25] He then explains by way of examples. Complex sayings include a subject and a predicate, e.g., 'the man runs' or 'the man wins.' The simple sayings include the subjects, i.e., 'man' or 'ox,' along with the predicates applied to them in complex sayings, i.e., 'runs' or 'wins.'[26] Definitions applied to beings, then, will be complex sayings which connect a subject to a predicate signifying what the subject is essentially. The categories will be the modes of predicating an attribute of a subject.

> Without in any way suggesting Wagner's essay to be incomplete in what it was attempting and I think successfully did, any follow up essay would do well to tie in this previous account to a more developed treatment of St. Thomas' own explicit doctrine on the problem of universals as presented in De Ente et Essentia, III. Wagner had already indicated that the more genetic account of the problem of universals should come after his logically rooted treatment, so Thomas' more detailed explanation for how form exists in singulars and in the mind would map on quite profitably either in an extended version of this essay or as a follow up.
>
> *Capehart, "Philosophical Implications" [p.72].*

---

[25] i.360-330BC: *Categories*, 2 (1a16-17): Τῶν λεγομένων τὰ μὲν κατὰ συμπλοκὴν λέγεται, τὰ δὲ ἄνευ συμπλοκῆς.
[26] i.360-330BC: *Categories*, 2 (1a17-19).

See also Kreeger, "Aquinas on Suppositum, Essence & Universals" [online at RealityJournal.org].

In the remainder of chapter two, Aristotle sets down **four** syntactic modes in which things can be said in relation to the subject of predication. These modes are highly relevant to the realist approach to definition, as they capture the grammatical manner in which predicates may be applied to existing things in the world depending upon whether they signify the meaning of an individual essentially and its corresponding class, or some part or accidental feature. **1)** First, Aristotle notes that,[27]

> Some things are said of beings with respect to some subject, which are not in a subject, as is the case with 'human' being said of the subject of some [particular] human, though it is not said to be in the subject.

Here, then, the mode of predication is 'predicated of, but not present in' a subject.

2) Second, "some things are in a subject, but are not said of a subject," for example, a single point of grammatical knowledge is in a subject, i.e., the soul of the grammarian, but not predicable of a subject.[28] Immediately prior to giving the example, Aristotle explains what he means by 'present in,' shedding light on the meaning of these modes of predication, generally: [29]

> Saying 'in a subject,' [I refer] not to that which belongs to something as a part, but to that which in it [i.e., the subject] is incapable of separate existence.

---

[27] i.360-330BC: *Categories*, 2 (1a20-22): Τῶν ὄντων τὰ μὲν καθ' ὑποκειμένου τινὸς λέγεται, ἐν ὑποκειμένῳ δὲ οὐδενί ἐστιν, οἷον ἄνθρωπος καθ' ὑποκειμένου μὲν λέγεται τοῦ τινὸς ἀνθρώπου, ἐν ὑποκειμένῳ δὲ οὐδενί ἐστιν·

[28] i.360-330BC: *Categories*, 2 (1a23-24): τὰ δὲ ἐν ὑποκειμένῳ μέν ἐστι, καθ' ὑποκειμένου δὲ οὐδενὸς λέγεται. Aristotle also uses the attribute 'white' as an example. See 1a25-29: οἷον ἡ τὶς γραμματικὴ ἐν ὑποκειμένῳ μέν ἐστι τῇ ψυχῇ, καθ' ὑποκειμένου δὲ οὐδενὸς λέγεται, καὶ τὸ τὶ λευκὸν ἐν ὑποκειμένῳ μέν ἐστι τῷ σώματι, – ἅπαν γὰρ χρῶμα ἐν σώματι, – καθ' ὑποκειμένου δὲ οὐδενὸς λέγεται· Or, "As, for example, a certain point of grammar is in a subject of the soul, but it is not predicated of a subject, and white is in the subject of a body—for it is from color in a body—but it is not said of a subject."

[29] i.360-330BC: *Categories*, 2 (1a24-25): ἐν ὑποκειμένῳ δὲ λέγω ὃ ἔν τινι μὴ ὡς μέρος ὑπάρχον ἀδύνατον χωρὶς εἶναι τοῦ ἐν ᾧ ἐστίν

Thus, by 'present in' Aristotle means something which is accidental to the subject—a feature that exists only in the subject and not separately. In the first mode of predication, i.e., 'predicated of, but not present in,' 'human' is predicable of the subject 'Socrates,' because it signifies what he is as a human being. It is not 'present in' any subject precisely because it not an accidental feature of any subject that has it—it is again, precisely, what it is. On the other hand, and returning back to the second mode of predication, accidental features 'present in' a subject cannot be 'predicated of' a subject because they are not the subject—i.e., they do not belong to it as its being and what it is, but only inhere in it in such a manner as to be incapable of existence without it. Thus, we would not say 'Socrates is grammar,' as this would reduce Socrates to one of his accidental parts. He happens to be in possession of grammar here and now, but he was Socrates prior to possessing this attribute and he would remain Socrates also after losing it.

3) Third, Aristotle notes that, "Some things are both said of a subject and are in subject, as science is in a subject, i.e., the soul, and it is also said of a subject, e.g., grammar."[30] **4)** Fourth and finally, Aristotle states that,[31]

> Some things are neither in a subject, nor said of a subject, such as an individual human or an individual horse—for none of these types of things is in a subject or said of a subject.

This mode of predication, then, pertains to the expression of individual separately existing beings. Aristotle immediately notes that, "Without qualification, things indivisible and one with respect to number are not said of a subject..."[32] Since an individual man or horse *is* not another individual thing, but

---

[30] i.360-330BC: *Categories*, 2 (1a29-1b3): τὰ δὲ καθ' ὑποκειμένου τε λέγεται καὶ ἐν ὑποκειμένῳ ἐστίν, οἷον ἡ ἐπιστήμη ἐν ὑποκειμένῳ μέν ἐστι τῇ ψυχῇ, καθ' ὑποκειμένου δὲ λέγεται τῆς γραμματικῆς·

[31] i.360-330BC: *Categories*, 2 (1b3-6): τὰ δὲ οὔτε ἐν ὑποκειμένῳ ἐστὶν οὔτε καθ' ὑποκειμένου λέγεται, οἷον ὁ τὶς ἄνθρωπος ἢ ὁ τὶς ἵππος, – οὐδὲν γὰρ τῶν τοιούτων οὔτε ἐν ὑποκειμένῳ ἐστὶν οὔτε καθ' ὑποκειμένου λέγεται· By the combination of the indefinite pronoun "τὶς" (*tis*) and the definite article "ὁ" (*ho*) in "ὁ τὶς ἄνθρωπος ἢ ὁ τὶς ἵππος" Aristotle is emphatically designating an individual and not a common feature predicable of an individual.

[32] i.360-330BC: *Categories*, 2 (1b6-9) ἁπλῶς δὲ τὰ ἄτομα καὶ ἓν ἀριθμῷ κατ' οὐδενὸς ὑποκειμένου λέγεται, ἐν ὑποκειμένῳ δὲ ἔνια οὐδὲν κωλύει εἶναι· ἡ γὰρ τὶς γραμματικὴ

has its own separate existence in reality, it is not predicable of any such other thing in speech. Most importantly, this rule of grammar and logic flows immediately from the nature of being and reality. Thus, for Aristotle, the logic of terms which allows for the expression of being results and is inextricable from the nature of being. The *Categories* is simultaneously *logical* and *ontological* in its content.[33] Without the experiential notion of an 'individual being,' the grammatical concept of a subject and the rules that apply to it could not be

---

τῶν ἐν ὑποκειμένῳ ἐστίν. Or, "Without qualification, things indivisible (ἄτομα) and one (ἓν) with respect to number are not said of a subject, although nothing prevents some [sorts of things] from being in subject. For, a certain point of grammar belongs to such things as are in a subject."

[33] This interpretation mirrors that of Owens, Sanford, and also Grene. See Owens 1951: *The Doctrine of Being in the Aristotelian Metaphysics*, Ch. 3; Sanford 2004: "Categories and Metaphysics: Aristotle's Science of Being" and, Marjorie Grene 1963: *A Portrait of Aristotle*, 73. It is at odds with that of David Sachs, G.E.L. Owen, Michael Frede, C.M. Gillespie, Walter E. Wehrle. Sachs opts for reading *Categories* as merely a work in logic (David Sachs 1948: "Does Aristotle have a Doctrine of Secondary Substance?" 221-225). G.E.L. Owen sees *Categories* as fundamentally metaphysical in its content in 1986: "Logic and Metaphysics in Some Earlier Works of Aristotle", 180-199; cf. Michael Frede holds a similar view. C.M. Gillespie, and Walter E. Wehrle, hold that *Categories* is logical in its contents in 1925: "The Aristotelian Categories" and 2000: *The Myth of Aristotle's Development and Betrayal of Metaphysics*, respectively (again, cf., Sanford). There is also the erroneous and modernistic view that Aristotle "invented" the categories, grounded in epistemological relativism and subjectivism. See, e.g., Fredrick J.E. Woodbridge 1965: *Aristotle's Vision of Nature*, 7. Ackrill articulates the correct position extremely well, in his introductory remarks to the *Categories*. The primary goal of Aristotle is to provide a logical structure for the sciences of φυσις (nature) and τὰ ὄντα (existing things) in general. Thus, *Categories* is not just about names and their relations, but it is about the things that names signify. *Categories* is not merely a linguistic and logical work: "Aristotle relies greatly on linguistic facts and test, but his aim is to discover truths about non-linguistic items." We can add to this point the fact that for Aristotle, a treatment of language which is to express what is true of beings in the sciences is in principle inseparable from being. This is because being determines the structure and meaning of language whenever it expresses what is true. i.348-30BC: *Metaphysics*, IX.10 (1051b1-10): οὐ γὰρ διὰ τὸ ἡμᾶς οἴεσθαι ἀληθῶς σε λευκὸν εἶναι εἶ σὺ λευκός, ἀλλὰ διὰ τὸ σὲ εἶναι λευκὸν ἡμεῖς οἱ φάντες τοῦτο ἀληθεύομεν. Or, "For it is not because we think truly that you are white that you are white, but rather it is because you are white that we are speaking this assertion truly." Cf. Owens 1951: *Doctrine of Being*, 138.

formed.[34] The nature of being is determinative of the nature of language expressing being.

Looking forward, note that the first and fourth modes of predication, i.e., (i) 'predicated of but not present in a subject' and (iv) 'neither in a subject, nor said of a subject,' will be immensely important in the Aristotelian account of definition, as will be seen in the treatment of chapter 5, where Aristotle appeal to them to in order to define the first category, "being" or οὐσία (*ousia*).

After a brief discussion of the rules of relation between genus, species, and subject in *Categories* 3, which is beyond our scope, Aristotle sets out the list of the categories by which definitions through these predicables would be obtained in chapter 4. The verb κατηγορέω (*kategoreo*) and its derivatives literally mean 'to speak against' (κατὰ + ἀγορεύω) or 'to accuse.' In its origins, it is a legal term. Indeed, Socrates refers to his own "accusers" in the very opening lines of his trial as κατηγοροῖ (*kategoroi*).[35] Thus, Aristotle's goal is to set out the various modes of categorizing or of 'accusing' things of experience. He explains that he is treating simple notions or concepts and then he sets out a list of 10 such categories without delay:[36]

---

[34] John Herman Randall, Jr. has suggested that Aristotle held that "the structure of Greek language and the structure of the world are ultimately the same..." Charitably, Randall does point out that Aristotle's view would be no more naïve than the modern view that mathematics and the structure of the world are the same. See 1960: *Aristotle*, 7. However, we can see that the *Categories* constitutes a careful analysis of language as it follows on and is expressive of being. Aristotle is, in fact, on extremely solid ground following extremely critical analysis. If there is a human language at all, capable of conveying meaningful (i.e., true or false) statements/propositions, it will be factually the same in its basic structures as Aristotle has expressed. The fact that, perhaps, some human beings are unable to communicate being in language at the level of the Greeks, Latins, Germans, English, etc., is, of course, no evidence at all that language is not as Aristotle says it is at its base. It merely shows that there may be some cultures lacking the more complete expression of being.

[35] Plato, *Apology* (17a1-2): Ὅτι μὲν ὑμεῖς, ὦ ἄνδρες Ἀθηναῖοι, πεπόνθατε ὑπὸ τῶν ἐμῶν κατηγόρων, οὐκ οἶδα· Or, "What you, oh Athenian men, have experienced at the hands of my accusers, I have no idea."

[36] i.360-330BC: *Categories*, 4 (1b25-27): Τῶν κατὰ μηδεμίαν συμπλοκὴν λεγομένων ἕκαστον ἤτοι οὐσίαν σημαίνει ἢ ποσὸν ἢ ποιὸν ἢ πρός τι ἢ ποὺ ἢ ποτὲ ἢ κεῖσθαι ἢ ἔχειν ἢ ποιεῖν ἢ πάσχειν.

> Concerning expressions not one of which is complex, we signify each of the following: being (οὐσία/*ousia*), quantity (πόσον/*poson*), quality (ποιὸν/*poion*), relation (πρός τι/*pros ti*), place (ποὺ/*pou*), time (ποτὲ/*pote*), position (κεῖσθαι/*keisthai*), possession (ἔχειν/*ekein*), action (ποιεῖν/*poien*), and passion (πάσχειν/*paskein*).

As is seen in the Greek, quantity, quality, place, and time are actually interrogatives or question phrases. Quantity is literally, 'how much?' quality, 'of what sort?' place, 'where?' and time, 'when?' Position, possession, action, and passion are all the infinitive forms of verbs. Position is literally, 'to lie;' possession, 'to possess;' action, 'to act;' and passion, 'to be acted upon.' Relation, which takes Aristotle some work to define in the end, is literally the prepositional phrase, 'toward something.' 'Being' or οὐσία (*ousia*), the first category, is an abstractive noun formed from the feminine present participle of the Greek verb to be, εἰμί (*eimi*).[37] Its core etymological meaning is 'that which is one's own,' or 'one's property/belonging.' Be aware that, while "substance" has become the standard translation of the term, as a result of Boethius' Latin rendering (*substantia*) in his translation of the *Categories*, I will consistently use "being" here.[38]

To return to the text at hand, Aristotle proceeds to give examples for each category, and in the remainder of the work he takes up the task of defining each in itself. Aristotle provides "human" and "horse" as a "vague sketch" of what is meant by being. He does not restrict the meaning of the terms to an individual

---

[37] For a helpful treatment of the term οὐσία and the history of its various translations in Latin and English, see Fr. Joseph Owens 1951: *The Doctrine of Being*, 139. See Also, R.E. Houser 2010: "The Language of Being and the Nature of God in the Aristotelian Tradition," in *Proceedings of the ACPA*, vol.84, 117.

[38] See, for example, Boethius c.509-11: *Aristoteles Latinus: Aristoteles: Categoriae*, c.5: "Substantia [οὐσία] autem est, quae proprie et principaliter et maxime dicitur, quae neque de subiecto praedicatur neque in subiecto est, ut aliqui homo vel aliqui equus." Or, "Now, substance is, which is said properly, primarily, and in the highest degree, that which is neither predicated of a subject, nor is it in a subject, as for example a particular human or a particular horse." For my argument as to why, though it is not a perfect translation, "being" is still the best translation of οὐσία over and above the alternatives, including the standard "substance," see Wagner 2018: *The Aristotelian Foundations of the Human Good*, Chapter 2, 104-109.

human and an individual horse.[39] This is because, as will be seen presently, he will divide the meaning of being as the first category to capture both individuals and the proper universals by which they are defined, in chapter 5. Accordingly, "human" and "horse" could here refer either to individuals or to universal meanings or definitions signifying what the individuals are as members of kinds—thus, the indication that it is a "vague and general sketch." Aristotle gives a similar sketch of examples for the other nine categories. Examples of quantity are '2 or 3 cubits;' of quality, 'white' or 'grammatical;' of relation, 'double,' 'half,' or 'larger;' of place, 'in the Lyceum' or 'in the marketplace;' of time, 'yesterday,' or 'last year;' of position, 'lying' or 'sitting;' of possession, 'having shoes on' or 'being armed;' of action, 'to cut' or 'to burn;' of passion, 'to be cut' or 'to be burned.'[40]

When these predicates are brought into combination with each other in complex thought or propositions, an affirmation is made which, in turn, may be true or false. In and of itself "human" is not true or false, nor is "white," "three," or "wins." These are simple notions of things that come to be through concept formation. Once a particular categorical term is composed with another, e.g., 'the human is white,' or the 'human wins,' i.e., where a subject is connected through a verb to a predicate, an affirmative judgment which can be characterized as *true* or *false* comes into being.[41] In general, each of the nine categories after being may be called accidents or attributes. These are sayings

---

[39] i.360-330BC: *Categories*, 4 (1b27-28): ἔστι δὲ οὐσία μὲν ὡς τύπῳ εἰπεῖν οἷον ἄνθρωπος, ἵππος· Or, "To speak in the manner of a vague or general sketch, being is, for example, human or horse."

[40] i.360-330BC: *Categories*, 4 (1b28-2a4): ποσὸν δὲ οἷον δίπηχυ, τρίπηχυ· ποιὸν δὲ οἷον λευκόν, γραμματικόν· πρός τι δὲ οἷον διπλάσιον, ἥμισυ, μεῖζον· ποὺ δὲ οἷον ἐν Λυκείῳ, ἐν ἀγορᾷ· ποτὲ δὲ οἷον χθές, πέρυσιν· κεῖσθαι δὲ οἷον ἀνάκειται, κάθηται· ἔχειν δὲ οἷον ὑποδέδεται, ὥπλισται· ποιεῖν δὲ οἷον τέμνειν, καίειν· πάσχειν δὲ οἷον τέμνεσθαι, καίεσθαι.

[41] i.360-330BC: *Categories*, 4 (2a4-10): ἕκαστον δὲ τῶν εἰρημένων αὐτὸ μὲν καθ' αὑτὸ ἐν οὐδεμιᾷ καταφάσει λέγεται, τῇ δὲ πρὸς ἄλληλα τούτων συμπλοκῇ κατάφασις γίγνεται· ἅπασα γὰρ δοκεῖ κατάφασις ἤτοι ἀληθὴς ἢ ψευδὴς εἶναι, τῶν δὲ κατὰ μηδεμίαν συμπλοκὴν λεγομένων οὐδὲν οὔτε ἀληθὲς οὔτε ψεῦδός ἐστιν, οἷον ἄνθρωπος, λευκόν, τρέχει, νικᾷ. Or, "Each of these predicates itself by itself is not said in the manner of affirmation, but by the combination of these in relation to one another affirmation comes to be; for every affirmation seems to be either true or false, but of things said in which there is no composition, neither is there truth nor falsity, such as is the case with 'human,' 'white,' 'three,' or 'wins.'

sayable of beings taking the role of the subject in the sentence. On the other hand, it is also true that these categories will be said of individuals at times, when the proper methodology has been used, in such a manner as to signify what they are as in their essence and definition. This point becomes clear in *Categories* 5, to which we must now turn in our exposition.

2.3. Primary and secondary being

Aristotle begins chapter five by explicitly drawing a distinction between being in a primary and a secondary sense, only implicit to this point. First, being in its primary sense refers to individual existing things in the world. The fourth mode of predication from chapter two provides the grammatical and logical sense of primary being:[42]

> Being (Οὐσία) is said most properly, primarily, and to the highest degree, of that which is neither said of a subject nor is it in any subject, as for example 'this individual human' or 'this individual horse.'

Οὐσία, thus, is a universal notion—the first of the categories to which the rest belong as predicaments—which signifies in its primary meaning the individual existing being. It is not said of a subject, because this would entail the contradiction that one individual in the world is identical with another, e.g., in the statement 'Willis the dog is the oak tree.' Further, such a predication would also entail the absurdity that "the oak tree, "an individual, is a universal. It is not 'present' in a subject, because that would entail that it be accidental, e.g., holding that 'Willis is an accidental feature of his dog house,' which is false, since the latter need not exist for Willis to exist as the individual he is. Primary being, then, refers to the reality of individual existing things in the world of experience as distinct from accidents.

---

[42] i.360-330BC: *Categories*, 5 (2a11-14): Οὐσία δέ ἐστιν ἡ κυριώτατά τε καὶ πρώτως καὶ μάλιστα λεγομένη, ἣ μήτε καθ' ὑποκειμένου τινὸς λέγεται μήτε ἐν ὑποκειμένῳ τινί ἐστιν, οἷον ὁ τὶς ἄνθρωπος ἢ ὁ τὶς ἵππος.

Aristotle then sets down, however, the second sense of being. The universal terms species and genus, which are used to define primary beings by expressing what they are, are also called beings in a secondary manner:[43]

> Those things are called secondary beings (δεύτεραι οὐσίαι), however, under which as species (εἴδεσιν) the primary beings are said to belong—these and also the genera (τὰ γένη) of these species (τῶν εἰδῶν); for example, this individual human belongs under the species 'human,' and the species is [under] the genus 'animal;' therefore, these are also called secondary beings, namely, both 'human' and 'animal.'

Aristotle then appeals back to chapter 2, expressing that both the name and the account or definition constituting the secondary being are 'said of a subject'—because they signify what the individual subject is. For this same reason, they cannot be present in a subject as accidents. Thus, and in line with the first mode of syntactical predication, 'human' and its definition, which is a secondary being, is *predicated of* the individual human, because "the individual human is 'human.'"[44]

---

[43] i.360-330BC: *Categories*, 5 (2a14-19): δεύτεραι δὲ οὐσίαι λέγονται, ἐν οἷς εἴδεσιν αἱ πρώτως οὐσίαι λεγόμεναι ὑπάρχουσιν, ταῦτά τε καὶ τὰ τῶν εἰδῶν τούτων γένη· οἷον ὁ τὶς ἄνθρωπος ἐν εἴδει μὲν ὑπάρχει τῷ ἀνθρώπῳ, γένος δὲ τοῦ εἴδους ἐστὶ τὸ ζῷον· δεύτεραι οὖν αὗται λέγονται οὐσίαι, οἷον ὅ τε ἄνθρωπος καὶ τὸ ζῷον.

[44] i.360-330BC: *Categories*, 5 (2a19-27): – φανερὸν δὲ ἐκ τῶν εἰρημένων ὅτι τῶν καθ' ὑποκειμένου λεγομένων ἀναγκαῖον καὶ τοὔνομα καὶ τὸν λόγον κατηγορεῖσθαι τοῦ ὑποκειμένου· οἷον ἄνθρωπος καθ' ὑποκειμένου λέγεται τοῦ τινὸς ἀνθρώπου, καὶ κατηγορεῖταί γε τοὔνομα, – τὸν γὰρ ἄνθρωπον κατὰ τοῦ τινὸς ἀνθρώπου κατηγορήσεις· – καὶ δὲ τοῦ ἀνθρώπου κατὰ τοῦ τινὸς ἀνθρώπου κατηγορηθήσεται, – ὁ γὰρ τὶς ἄνθρωπος καὶ ἄνθρωπός ἐστιν· – ὥστε καὶ τοὔνομα καὶ ὁ λόγος κατὰ τοῦ ὑποκειμένου κατηγορηθήσεται. Or, "It is manifest from what has been said that, regarding what is said of a subject, both the name and the account (τὸν λόγον) are predicated (κατηγορεῖσθαι) of the subject; this is the case when 'human' is said of an individual human, and the name is certainly predicated (for you will predicate 'human' of the individual human); and the account (ὁ λόγος) of 'human' will be predicated of the individual human—for the individual human *is human*. Therefore, both the name and the account will be predicated of the subject." In contrast, and properly speaking, the definition or account of what is *present in* a subject, like the accidental quality, 'white,' cannot be predicated of the subject—even though loosely speaking the term may sometimes be predicated of the subject, as when Socrates is called white. See i.360-

Having drawn the initial distinction between primary and secondary being in this manner, Aristotle proceeds to spell out the distinct characteristics of each, along with their commonalities and differences, in the remainder of chapter 5. The presentation that follows proceeds analytically, for the sake of clarity and concision, presenting first Aristotle's full treatment of primary beings, and then secondary beings. However, it needs to be noted that this is not Aristotle's procedure. Rather, he circles back and forth presenting distinctive and common features of primary and secondary beings. The reason for this lies in the reciprocal ontological and epistemological dependence of these notions upon one another, which should be kept in mind.[45]

Aristotle gives primary being absolute ontological priority over secondary being and the other nine categories. "All other things" he says, "are either said of

---

330BC: *Categories*, 5 (2a27-34). As an accidental feature, 'white' cannot be equated with the whole of Socrates, which is why it cannot properly be predicated of Socrates in its meaning. Here, what is meant is that Socrates is white, in his skin, not that Socrates is 'whiteness,' since he is not this accidental attribute.

[45] Here, in the *Categories*, the ontological dependence of secondary οὐσίαι on primary οὐσίαι is emphasized, and the role of secondary οὐσίαι as that by which we know the primary οὐσίαι as what they are is shown. At the same time, it is already clear that the essential forms which secondary οὐσίαι signify and *are*, in a way, have an ontological role to play, as Aristotle will say that primary οὐσίαι do not differ by degree. This claim is only intelligible because the primary οὐσίαι are defined by the secondary οὐσίαι, which signify or mean *what they are*. In *Metaphysics* VII, where Aristotle sets out to explain what makes primary οὐσίαι to be primary οὐσίαι, he in fact appeals to the principle of form, which makes the primary οὐσίαι to be what they are essentially and is ultimately the cause of their being the individuals that they are. The definition, of course, is an account of the form, so that now second οὐσία expresses the ontological principle making primary οὐσίαι to be the unitary things that they are. See, Michael V. Wedin 2002: *Aristotle's Theory of Substance: The Categories and Metaphysics Zeta*. The circular dependence of these terms is benign and can be explained in terms of the order of knowledge. Sense-perception and consequent concept formation gives us a vague and better-known idea of individuals and of what they are. I do not need a rigorous definition of a pig to know that it is an individual of a certain type. This is clear from sense experience, which discloses the pig as a single organism, separated from other beings in the world, and experiment, since when the pig is cut into pieces it ceases to be a pig so that I know that it is, *qua* pig, an indivisible unit. When I ask, however, what makes the pig to be an individual pig, I must then appeal to the form making it to be what it is as a unity, which will require a more rigorous definition of the animal.

primary beings as subjects," i.e., as species or genus, "or are in subjects themselves," i.e., as accidental features expressed through the other nine categories.[46] He defends this claim, here, in a manner that clearly maps onto the view of the generation of concepts (universals) that he gives in other texts (e.g., *Posterior Analytics* II.19, and *Metaphysics* I.1). Since universals are formed in the intellect by a collection of what is common to a set of individual primary beings given first to sensation, it follows that the non-existence of an essential feature in the primary beings will result in its non-existence as a secondary being, i.e., as genus or species. Simply said, were there no primary beings possessing the features meant by 'human' and 'animality,' for example, there would be no such secondary beings. Similarly, an accident cannot be said of a generic subject, except that it actually exists in the primary beings which the generic term signifies. Without individual colored bodies, for example, 'body' in general cannot be called 'colored'—the accident will not exist in connection to the generic subject because it would not actually be present in any individual body.[47] Because of this, Aristotle can repeat his initial claim and conclude emphatically that primary beings are the ground of all being, i.e., secondary being and the accidents:[48]

> Thus, all other things are either said of primary beings as subjects or are in subjects themselves. Therefore, except that there have been primary beings it is not possible that any other type of beings be.

Here, then, the Aristotelian logic of the terms of realism clearly holds that the primary sense of being—what is, or reality—is individual things in the world of

---

[46] i.360-330BC: *Categories*, 5 (2a34-35): τὰ δ' ἄλλα πάντα ἤτοι καθ' ὑποκειμένων λέγεται τῶν πρώτων οὐσιῶν ἢ ἐν ὑποκειμέναις αὐταῖς ἐστίν.

[47] i.360-330BC: *Categories*, 5 (2a35-2b3): τοῦτο δὲ φανερὸν ἐκ τῶν καθ' ἕκαστα προχειριζομένων· οἷον τὸ ζῷον κατὰ τοῦ ἀνθρώπου κατηγορεῖται, οὐκοῦν καὶ κατὰ τοῦ τινὸς ἀνθρώπου, – εἰ γὰρ κατὰ μηδενὸς τῶν τινῶν ἀνθρώπων, οὐδὲ κατὰ ἀνθρώπου ὅλως· – πάλιν τὸ χρῶμα ἐν σώματι, οὐκοῦν καὶ ἐν τινὶ σώματι· εἰ γὰρ μὴ ἐν τινὶ τῶν καθ' ἕκαστα, οὐδὲ ἐν σώματι ὅλως· Or, "This is manifest by examining the particulars; for example, 'animal' is predicated of 'human,' and therefore also of the individual human—for, if it were not predicated of individual humans, it would not be predicated of the whole of 'human.' Again, color is in 'body,' and therefore also in an individual body; for, if it were not in a particular individual, neither would it be in 'body' as a whole.

[48] i.360-330BC: *Categories*, 5 (2b3-6): ὥστε τὰ ἄλλα πάντα ἤτοι καθ' ὑποκειμένων τῶν πρώτων οὐσιῶν λέγεται ἢ ἐν ὑποκειμέναις αὐταῖς ἐστίν. μὴ οὐσῶν οὖν τῶν πρώτων οὐσιῶν ἀδύνατον τῶν ἄλλων τι εἶναι·

experience. The concepts by which we know these beings are then real only to the extent that they signify what is essentially present and real in primary beings. Finally, there is the accidental type of being in the world (of which we can also form corresponding concepts through the other nine categories), which exists as dependent ontologically on primary beings.

Indicating further characteristics of primary being, Aristotle notes also that primary beings are always a 'this one' or individuals,[49] and for this reason they are the proper subjects, ontologically and predicatively.[50] Further, as individuals they have no contraries in themselves (e.g., there is no contrary state of being 'a human'),[51] and they do not admit of degrees in the individual, which is to say that something either is or is not a particular primary being—the same as any other member of its species—and not more or less so.[52] Finally, primary beings are capable, while remaining numerically one and the same, of receiving contrary predicates (e.g., the same primary being can receive the contrary predicates 'hot' and 'cold,' though not in the same respect at the same time).[53]

---

[49] i.360-330BC: *Categories*, 5: Πᾶσα δὲ οὐσία δοκεῖ τόδε τι σημαίνειν. ἐπὶ μὲν οὖν τῶν πρώτων οὐσιῶν ἀναμφισβήτητον καὶ ἀληθές ἐστιν ὅτι τόδε τι σημαίνει· ἄτομον γὰρ καὶ ἓν ἀριθμῷ τὸ δηλούμενόν ἐστιν. Or, "It seems that all being signifies a 'this one' [i.e., an individual]. In the case of primary beings, it is indisputable and true that it signifies an individual, for it is signifying what is indivisible and one numerically."

[50] i.360-330BC: *Categories*, 5 (2b37-3a1): ἔτι αἱ πρῶται οὐσίαι διὰ τὸ τοῖς ἄλλοις ἅπασιν ὑποκεῖσθαι κυριώτατα οὐσίαι λέγονται· Or, "Moreover, primary beings are most properly called beings because they are the subjects for all other things."

[51] i.360-330BC: *Categories*, 5 (3b25).

[52] i.360-330BC: *Categories*, 5 (3b33-4a9), especially 4a5-8: ἡ δέ γε οὐσία οὐδὲν λέγεται, – οὐδὲ γὰρ ἄνθρωπος μᾶλλον νῦν ἄνθρωπος ἢ πρότερον λέγεται, οὐδὲ τῶν ἄλλων οὐδέν, ὅσα ἐστὶν οὐσία· Or, " For being is not spoken of in this manner; for a human is not said to be more human now than before, nor is any other thing which is being." This claim is not defended in the *Categories*. In fact, its validity is founded on the concept of φύσις (*phusis*) or nature. Unless primary beings have a static natural form and essential intrinsic principle of motion and rest making them to be what they are regardless of where they stand in the process of generation and corruption, they will necessarily admit of differing degrees of the species to which they belong. Of course, without the notion of nature, it would also be unintelligible to talk of such individuals as members of a species at all—which is one reason nature must be posited as a first principle in the natural sciences. In the end, without the ontological ground of nature, the concept of species itself would be nearly meaningless.

[53] i.360-330BC: *Categories*, 5 (4a10).

This point, of course, allows for a logical expression of change and, thus, for the possibility of a science of natural beings (one of Aristotle's primary goals in composing the *Categories*, along with the other works of the *Organon*).

Aristotle's treatment of secondary being occurs with constant reference to primary being as its ontological ground. Aristotle first explains that, regarding the secondary beings of species and genus, species has ontological priority, i.e., it is 'more being,' as it signifies most properly what a primary being is:[54]

> Of secondary beings, species is more being than genus, for it is nearest to primary being; for, if one were to state the definition (τί ἐστι) of some primary being, he will state more informatively and properly the species, rather than stating the genus.

It is more informative, for example, to state that an individual is a human or a tree, than to say that it is an animal or a plant. This is because these species signify more properly what the things are in distinction from other things and, of course, they also imply and entail the generic attributes. Because of this ontological priority of species, Aristotle can further explain that just as primary beings are most properly called 'being' because all things are either present in them or said of them, so too species holds an analogous relationship to genera as the subject of their predication:[55]

---

[54] i.360-330BC: *Categories*, 5 (2b7-10): Τῶν δὲ δευτέρων οὐσιῶν μᾶλλον οὐσία τὸ εἶδος τοῦ γένους· ἔγγιον γὰρ τῆς πρώτης οὐσίας ἐστίν. ἐὰν γὰρ ἀποδιδῷ τις τὴν πρώτην οὐσίαν τί ἐστι, γνωριμώτερον καὶ οἰκειότερον ἀποδώσει τὸ εἶδος ἀποδιδοὺς ἢ τὸ γένος·

[55] i.360-330BC: *Categories*, 5 (2b15-22): ἔτι αἱ πρῶται οὐσίαι διὰ τὸ τοῖς ἄλλοις ἅπασιν ὑποκεῖσθαι καὶ πάντα τὰ ἄλλα κατὰ τούτων κατηγορεῖσθαι ἢ ἐν ταύταις εἶναι διὰ τοῦτο μάλιστα οὐσίαι λέγονται· ὡς δέ γε αἱ πρῶται οὐσίαι πρὸς τὰ ἄλλα ἔχουσιν, οὕτω καὶ τὸ εἶδος πρὸς τὸ γένος ἔχει· – ὑπόκειται γὰρ τὸ εἶδος τῷ γένει· τὰ μὲν γὰρ γένη κατὰ τῶν εἰδῶν κατηγορεῖται, τὰ δὲ εἴδη κατὰ τῶν γενῶν οὐκ ἀντιστρέφει· – ὥστε καὶ ἐκ τούτων τὸ εἶδος τοῦ γένους μᾶλλον οὐσία. Aristotle repeats this conclusion again, at 2b29-34: Εἰκότως δὲ μετὰ τὰς πρώτας οὐσίας μόνα τῶν ἄλλων τὰ εἴδη καὶ τὰ γένη δεύτεραι οὐσίαι λέγονται· μόνα γὰρ δηλοῖ τὴν πρώτην οὐσίαν τῶν κατηγορουμένων· τὸν γὰρ τινὰ ἄνθρωπον ἐὰν ἀποδιδῷ τις τί ἐστιν, τὸ μὲν εἶδος ἢ τὸ γένος ἀποδιδοὺς οἰκείως ἀποδώσει, – καὶ γνωριμώτερον ποιήσει ἄνθρωπον ἢ ζῷον ἀποδιδούς· Or, "For good reason, thus, after primary beings, of all others, species and genera are alone called secondary being; for it is manifest that these alone are predicated of primary being; for if one were to state the definition (τί ἐστιν) of some individual human, he will more

> Further, because primary beings are the subjects for all other things, and all other things are either predicated of them or are in them, they are called being especially. Nevertheless, as primary beings possess this relation to all other things, so also species holds a relation to genus; for the species is the subject for the genus; this is because the genera are predicated of the species, but the species are not conversely predicable of the genera. Therefore, from this point also, it follows that the species is more being than the genus."[56]

With respect to species themselves, as was also the case with primary beings, no one species is more properly being than another.[57] In other words, a secondary being as signifying *what* a primary being is, does not admit of difference of degree. The account of the Socrates as 'human,' we might say, is thus equal to an account of Otis as 'horse.' This, again, is apparent from the relation of primary beings themselves, which secondary beings (species) signify, for "In a similar manner," says Aristotle, "no one of the primary beings is more a being than another; for this individual man is not more a being than this individual ox."[58] Since all the other features are accidents, they are irrelevant to the definition so that only species and genus are to be called secondary beings.

Having expressed the ontological priority of primary being to secondary, and of species to genus in this manner, Aristotle then focuses on the meaning of secondary being in relation to the logical or syntactical notions of being 'present in' and 'said of.' First, a commonality between primary and secondary being is to be noted in regard to predication: "It is common to all beings not to be in a subject."[59] Primary beings cannot be 'in a subject' for they are the individual subjects—both ontologically and logically—providing the ontological and predicative foundation for all things. Secondary beings, again, cannot be 'in a

---

properly render a statement of the species or the genus—and more informatively, he will produce a the statement of 'human,' rather than 'animal.'"

[56] For an interesting discussion showing that primary and secondary being/substance are both the valid subject of demonstrative predication for Aristotle, see, Mary Catherine Sommers 1987: "Substance and Predication in Aristotle: A Medieval View", 61.

[57] i.360-330BC: *Categories*, 5 (2b22-24): αὐτῶν δὲ τῶν εἰδῶν ὅσα μή ἐστι γένη, οὐδὲν μᾶλλον ἕτερον ἑτέρου οὐσία ἐστίν· Or, "Of species themselves, which are not genera, no one is more a being than another."

[58] i.360-330BC: *Categories*, 5 (2b26-28): ὡσαύτως δὲ καὶ τῶν πρώτων οὐσιῶν οὐδὲν μᾶλλον ἕτερον ἑτέρου οὐσία ἐστίν· οὐδὲν γὰρ μᾶλλον ὁ τὶς ἄνθρωπος οὐσία ἢ ὁ τὶς βοῦς.

[59] i.360-330BC: *Categories*, 5 (3a7-8): Κοινὸν δὲ κατὰ πάσης οὐσίας τὸ μὴ ἐν ὑποκειμένῳ εἶναι.

subject' because they signify what the subject is essentially, and not accidental features.[60]

Most importantly for Aristotelian realism, not being 'in a subject,' secondary beings are predicated of subjects univocally:[61]

> It properly belongs to [secondary] beings and differentia to be said univocally of the things themselves of which they are said.

This means that secondary beings define what primary beings are—they are, to use Aristotle's expression from chapter 1, ὁ λόγος τῆς οὐσίας καί τί ἐστι (*ho logos tes ousias kai ti esti*) or "the account of the being/essence and the definition." Defining, then, must be a matter of sorting out which attributes of a subject of enquiry belong to it essentially, and which belong to it only accidentally. Genus, species, and difference, thus, will make use of the nine categories under primary being to define it, but they will do this by signifying what properly belongs—being. So, Aristotle says,[62]

> They [i.e., secondary beings] do not simply signify any quality, such as 'white;' for white signifies nothing but another quality, but species and genus define (ἀφορίζει) the quality or 'what kind' in accord with being (περὶ οὐσίαν)—they signify the quality or 'what kind' (ποιὰν) with respect to being/essence.

Finally, contrasting it with primary being as signifying what is individual, Aristotle further explains that secondary being is not individual itself as it is predicated of the many primary individual beings. In other words, and while it might seem that secondary beings are individuals, they are, in fact, universal meanings, common to many:[63]

---

[60] i.360-330BC: *Categories*, 5 (3a10-21). At *Categories*, 5 (3a22-32), Aristotle notes also that this point applies to difference.

[61] i.360-330BC: *Categories*, 5 (3a33-34): Ὑπάρχει δὲ ταῖς οὐσίαις καὶ ταῖς διαφοραῖς τὸ πάντα συνωνύμως ἀπ' αὐτῶν λέγεσθαι·

[62] i.360-330BC: *Categories*, 5 (3b18-21): οὐχ ἁπλῶς δὲ ποιόν τι σημαίνει, ὥσπερ τὸ λευκόν· οὐδὲν γὰρ ἄλλο σημαίνει τὸ λευκὸν ἀλλ' ἢ ποιόν, τὸ δὲ εἶδος καὶ τὸ γένος περὶ οὐσίαν τὸ ποιὸν ἀφορίζει, – ποιὰν γάρ τινα οὐσίαν σημαίνει.

[63] i.360-330BC: *Categories*, 5 (3b10-18): Πᾶσα δὲ οὐσία δοκεῖ τόδε τι σημαίνειν. ἐπὶ μὲν οὖν τῶν πρώτων οὐσιῶν ἀναμφισβήτητον καὶ ἀληθές ἐστιν ὅτι τόδε τι σημαίνει· ἄτομον γὰρ καὶ ἓν ἀριθμῷ τὸ δηλούμενόν ἐστιν. ἐπὶ δὲ τῶν δευτέρων οὐσιῶν φαίνεται μὲν ὁμοίως τῷ σχήματι τῆς προσηγορίας τόδε τι σημαίνειν, ὅταν εἴπῃ ἄνθρωπον ἢ ζῷον· οὐ

> It seems that all being signifies a 'this one' [i.e., an individual]. In the case of primary beings it is indisputable and true that it signifies an individual, for it is signifying what is indivisible and one numerically. In the case of secondary beings, it seems similarly that they signify the individual (τόδε τι) with respect to the form of the term, when [for example] 'human' or 'animal' is said; however, this is not strictly true, but they signify quality [or 'what kind'] (ποιόν τι)—for as a subject [of predication] a secondary being is not one as a primary being, but 'human' and 'animal' are said of many.

The reason, thus, that a secondary being can be confused with a primary being as an individual is that, as Aristotle has already explained, it may be the grammatical subject of a predicate. The genus, 'animal,' for example may have 'organic,' 'living, etc., predicated of it, and this may give the impression that it itself is an individual. The reason that this is false, Aristotle explains, is that the secondary being itself signifies a qualitative difference that is *predicable of many*—it cannot be an individual *and* serve this function qua universal at the same time.[64] Secondary beings, then, are universals apprehended in the mind, and predicated of individuals in acts of judgment and understanding.

In the *Categories*, Aristotle has provided the technical, i.e., logical and grammatical, foundation for a realist conception of definition. He has explained the nature of equivocal and univocal predication and expressed the logical relations of genus, species, and difference through which various subjects can be defined. The logical terms of realism and their essential connection to reality have now been set out in their *locus classicus*. There is reality. There are actually existing things in the world, which we are aware of and can point out in language and through sense-perceptive experience. Aristotle refers to these constituents of reality, in technical terms, as primary beings. He defines primary beings logically and grammatically, given the role that they play in human language, as

---

μὴν ἀληθές γε, ἀλλὰ μᾶλλον ποιόν τι σημαίνει, – οὐ γὰρ ἕν ἐστι τὸ ὑποκείμενον ὥσπερ ἡ πρώτη οὐσία, ἀλλὰ κατὰ πολλῶν ὁ ἄνθρωπος λέγεται καὶ τὸ ζῷον· –

[64] This concisely stated argument constitutes Aristotle rejection of a Platonic theory of Forms. Secondary beings by which we know primary beings cannot, in principle, be separately existing individuals—as Plato at times claimed they were—lest they would not be predicable of the many primary beings. This is the foundation of Aristotle's famous 3rd man argument. The consequence of making genus and species individuals is that they no longer explain how we define members of the class; rather, they become more members of the class being defined, which results in an infinite regress. For further discussion, see Wagner 2018: *The Aristotelian Foundations of the Human Good*, especially 102-103.

'what is neither predicated of nor present in a subject,' which means ontologically speaking, what is *one* and *individuated*. The conceptions of the mind which, when predicated of primary beings, constitute knowledge through propositional judgements, i.e., genus, species, and difference, though they do not exist without qualification in themselves, are *real*—they are *being*—precisely to the extent that they universally signify the essential features of primary beings and, thus, can be predicated of them univocally. Without delving into a genetic account of *how* human beings come into mental possession of the secondary beings that make univocal prediction possible in human knowing acts, a concise and decisive argument can be given, showing *that* it is entirely unreasonable to deny univocal predication and sense-realism. Such an argument is a necessary task for the realist, given the fact that, historically speaking, univocal predication as conceived by Aristotle has been seriously called into question.

3. A Brief History of the Problem of Universals & Nominalism

The position commonly called "nominalism," which rejects univocal predication, has its focal source in the Medieval period in the thought of the logician, William of Ockham, although the question of the ontological status and reality of universals goes back at least as far as Porphyry (233-305AD). In his famous *Isogoge* (Εἰσαγωγή), which is an introduction to Aristotle's *Categories*, Porphyry's purpose is to help the student of Aristotle's logic grasp the meanings of genus (γένος/*genos*), species (εἶδος/*eidos*), difference (διαφορά/*diaphora*), property (ἴδιον/*idion*), and accident (συμβεβηχός/*sumbebekos*). This knowledge is useful, he explains, in three ways: (1) For giving definitions; (2) for division (διαίρεσις); and (3) demonstration (ἀπόδειξις), as definitions provide the principle premises of syllogistic demonstrations. Before explaining the terms, however, Porphyry famously expresses that he will avoid certain "profound" questions, of which he lists three: (1) "Whether genera and species exist in themselves or reside in mere concepts alone." (2) "Whether, if they exist, they are corporeal or incorporeal." And, (3) "Whether they exist apart or in sense objects and in dependence on them."[65]

---

[65] See, Edward W. Warren's 1975 translation of the i.268-70: *Isogoge*, 1.

Of course, depending on how one answers these questions, one will go in an Aristotelian, Platonic, or nominalist and anti-realist direction. In abstract logical contemplation of these questions, i.e., without thinking about the organic connection between being and the logical terms that signify it, several prominent medieval thinkers began to deny the existence of secondary being or to reduce it to mere concept. Peter of Abelard (1079-1142) followed his first teacher Jean Roscelin (1050-1125), who reduced the universal (secondary being) to a mere vocal utterance (*flatus vocis*, or 'breath of the voice'). Rejecting the medieval realism of his teacher William of Champeaux (1070-1121), who held that there is something in the particular things themselves corresponding to predicated universal, Abelard famously held that universals are mere concepts, existing only in the mind. He argued from a simple disjunctive premise: either the universal (human) is partly in the particular (Socrates and Plato), or is wholly in the particular. If it is only partly present, the particulars cannot be said to be 'human,' and univocal predication is impossible. If it is wholly present, then it can only be present in one particular, and it cannot also be the universal. Thus, univocal predication is impossible.[66]

William of Ockham picked up and developed Abelard's approach, and his view was accepted by virtually every modern thinker after Descartes.[67] On Ockham's

---

[66] See Julius R. Weinberg 1964: *A Short History of Medieval Philosophy*, 72-91.

[67] See John Deely's article 2013: "Modern Epistemology and Solipsism". Nominalism becomes severely pronounced and apparently necessary after Descartes' ontological separation of the mind from its object[s], or perhaps better said, the things that correspond to its objects, through his reduction to the *cogito* and his subsequent substance or mind-body dualism. Descrates' nominalism is captured in the following passage: "...[N]umber, when it is considered simply in the abstract or in general, and not in any created things, is merely a mode of thinking; and the same applies to all the other universals, as we call them...These universals arise solely from the fact that we make use of one and the same idea for thinking of all individual items which resemble each other: we apply one and the same term [nomen] to all the things which are represented by the idea in question, and this is the universal term. Descartes 1644: *Principles of Philosophy*, I.58-59, I.212, AT VIIIA.27)" This passage is taken from "Descartes Theory of Ideas," in the *Stanford Encyclopedia of Philosophy*, where there is also a helpful treatment of his nominalism. Following Julius R. Weinberg, Deely has traced the modern problem of solipsism, which is first explicitly manifest in Descartes *cogito ergo sum*, to Ockham's nominalist view on the category of relation. On the Ockhamist view, relations have no being independent of immanent mental awareness. They are limited to the order of *ens*

view, there are no common natures or universals at all, i.e., there are no secondary beings in the sense of conceptions that signify a common identity between a multiplicity of individuals. Ockham gives logical reasons for his denial of secondary being, similar to the argumentation of Abelard. Essentially, he deems that universals signifying a common identical essence cannot exist because the doctrine entails a contradiction: what is universal will also be individual. Thus, and with respect to the definition of the human being, at *Summa Logicae* I, ch. 64, Ockham notes, "'man' is not established except for signifying these men; it does not signify something common to them."[68] The definition exists only *conceptually*, and does not have an ontological foundation in the individuals themselves since each is in fact other than each. Thus, predication of a definition over a plurality of individuals will always be equivocal. Definitions might be applied to individuals in virtue of some perceived resemblance, but are not ontologically grounded in what the individuals are.

---

rationis and do not extend to the order of *ens reale*. If this is the case, then a problem of the bridge (*problema pontis*) immediately presents itself, wherein we will not be able to explain how the cognitive contents of our own subjectivity (*ens rationis*) are related to mind independent being (*ens reale*) in such a manner as to account for proper knowledge of such beings. We will be left with concepts as objects of thought which have no real relation to the things of experience to which we commonly take them to correspond. Univocal predication will be impossible. See, Julius R. Weinberg 1965: *Abstraction, Relation, and Induction: three essays in the history of thought*. Also, for a similar discussion, see Deely's 2001: *Four Ages of Understanding: The first postmodern survey of philosophy from ancient times to the turn of the 20th century*, 542-44. Finally, see Brian Kemple's article in this issue of *Reality*, 2019: "Signs and Reality."

[68] See c.1323: *Summa Logicae* I, ch. 64, in *Opera Philosophica*, vol. 1, 195: "'homo' non imponitur nisi ad significandum istos homines; non enim significat proprie aliquid commune eis." The translation here is taken from Steven Striby's dissertation 2007: *Against the Principles of Nominalism*. I am most grateful to Steven for his helpful guidance on the nominalism of Ockham. As he explains in his dissertation, a distinction was drawn among Scholastic logicians like Peter of Spain, William of Sherwood, and Walter Burley, between the *significatum,* i.e., the meaning, of a general term and its *supposita,* i.e., the individuals to which the term refers. The *significatum* corresponds to the universal form or essence, which we have seen Aristotle refer to as second being. The *supposita* were the particular beings which fall under the second beings. Ockham identified *significatum* and *supposita.* In this case, predication of a single term over many individuals is always equivocal. See also c.1323: *Summa Logicae* I, chs. 5-10, and again in chapters 33. Also, for a helpful summary of Ockham's nominalism, see Julius R. Weinberg 1964: *A Short History of Medieval Philosophy*, 235-66.

Secondary beings, then, on Ockham's view, are not real or being in the sense that Aristotle held them to be, as they do not signify what is really common and identical among a set of particulars.

4. An Aristotelian-Phenomenological Defense of Secondary Being & Univocal Predication

In defending Aristotle's conception of univocal predication, it is first necessary to note that his approach in the *Categories* is analytic: the act of disclosing the categories by which we divide and define being is itself a form of division[69] presupposing the whole or general *phenomenon* of the objective experience of human language and the acts of defining that occur in language. In fact, Aristotle's approach can be treated as phenomenological. Aristotle is not arbitrarily contriving rules about the nature of human speech, communication, and the constitution of knowledge of reality by the application of definitions to primary beings. Rather, the *whole* of thought and language is public and already there for us to break down into its parts and syntactical order. It is a phenomenological datum. As we saw in the treatment of *Categories* 2, what is given is the linguistic sentence, statement, or proposition composed of subject, copula, and predicate. Aristotle does not fabricate these terms as a *post hoc* justification for some empirical epistemology that he has already constructed. Rather, he discovers them through the analysis of language.

This does not mean, of course, that there cannot be a development in human language and defining—indeed, Aristotle provides us with just such a development, as did Plato and Socrates, and many in the history of philosophy. Rather, the point is that human action in thought and speech already takes for granted that secondary beings are univocally predicated of primary beings. Because of this, any nominalist theory which works from abstract *a priori* asserted logical principles should already be highly suspect. Nominalism means that, when I predicate 'honey bee' of the buzzing being on the flower, and then later of another buzzing being in my window, I am not actually predicating as a result of the fact that I apprehend as ontologically present in both individuals the essential meaning of 'honey bee.' This, I am afraid, is quite a bizarre and absurd consequence, and it should lead us to enquire as to whether or not we

---

[69] Cf. c.353-47BC: *Physics* I.1, where Aristotle explains that this is the method for obtaining knowledge of the first principles of the study of nature.

might reject nominalism and find some principle for showing the identity between the universal (secondary being) and the individual (primary being) that allows us to avoid the contradiction. After all, I understand the meaning I apply to these bees and I also 'see' empirically that it belongs to each of them. Here, joining Aristotle in his enquiry into the categories with the post-modern phenomenological method of Husserl, we exercise an ἐποχή regarding the apparent existence of secondary being and its supposed univocal relation to primary being in acts of predication. In this attitude of neutrality, neither assuming that secondary being exists nor denying it existence, we will now discover that, in fact, human thought and language *make no sense* where secondary being is denied. In this attitude, by analyzing the phenomenon of defining in human language and thought, a *reductio ad impossibile*, or retorsive, argument can be preformed on the nominalist position, like that which Aristotle famously performed on the sophist that would deny the principle of non-contradiction at *Metaphysics*, IV.4.

4.I. A *reductio ad impossibile* argument against nominalism

In his defense of the axiomatic principle of non-contradiction, at *Metaphysics*, IV.4, Aristotle has shown us that one way to defend a first principle is to show the impossibility of its denial. Aristotle gives three formulations of the principle of non-contradiction, shifting from the perspective of being itself to our beliefs and propositions about being:

> (1) "It is impossible for the same attribute to belong and not to belong to the same being and in the same manner at one and the same time..."[70]
>
> (2) "For it is impossible to *understand* the same thing both to be and not to be..."[71]
>
> (3) "...opposite statements are not true at the same time..."[72]

---

[70] i.348-30BC: *Metaphysics*, IV.3 (1005b19-20): τὸ γὰρ αὐτὸ ἅμα ὑπάρχειν τε καὶ μὴ ὑπάρχειν ἀδύνατον τῷ αὐτῷ καὶ κατὰ τὸ αὐτό...

[71] i.348-30BC: *Metaphysics*, IV.3 (1005b23-24): ἀδύνατον γὰρ ὁντινοῦν ταὐτὸν ὑπολαμβάνειν εἶναι καὶ μὴ εἶναι...

[72] i.348-30BC: *Metaphysics*, IV.6 (1005b23): ...μὴ εἶναι ἀληθεῖς ἅμα τὰς ἀντικειμένας φάσεις...

Aristotle shows that, while the sophist might signify a denial of the principle, he could not practically function in thought, speech, or action, while consistently maintaining such a denial. This is because for the denial of the principle to be true, i.e., say, that "it is false that opposite assertion are not true at the same time," the principle must necessarily be true. The sophist then, engages in a performative contradiction, assuming the truth of what he denies. Further, and to be consistent, the sophist would have to stop thinking, speaking judgements, and acting: he could not think, e.g., 'this is bread' for it would also not be bread; he could not state, similarly, to himself or his friend that 'this is bread' because it would also not be bread; and then, he could not form an intentional desire to consume this judged to be bread, because it would also not be bread, preventing him from acting. Thus, to stay consistent, he would be reduced to the state of the vegetable—which, of course, is absurd and impossible for a human being who must think and speak presupposing the principle in order to act. In a similar manner, we can also perform a *reductio ad vegetabile* on the nominalist position that rejects univocal predication in denial of secondary being.[73] The predication of a singular definition over a plurality of individuals by human beings—from mundane activities like purchasing an apple at the store, all the way to the highest forms of scientific understanding regarding things like semen, ovum, elements, atoms, etc.,—is impossible and absurd to deny.

A puzzle does legitimately arise from reflection on this phenomenon as to the relation between definition (secondary being) and the individual subject of its predication (primary being). In attempting an answer to this puzzle, the nominalist may formulate the denial that the definition signifies what an individual primary being is in itself. Such a claim, however, is necessarily limited to the order of signification (*ut significata*). This is because, in the order of exercise (*ut exercita*), predication of the term is only intelligible *because* the one predicating *believes* that the attached definition signifies features that are ontologically immanent in the individual to which the definition is applied. In other words, whenever we predicate a meaning of an individual, we do so precisely because we *believe* that the meaning signifies what the individual is.

---

[73] The gist of the argument given here was first given in my paper 2012: "Definition and the *Reductio ad Vegetabilium*: Comments on Professor Tkacz's Treatment of Albertus Magnus and the Error Ptolemaei," at the Society for Thomistic Natural Philosophy Satellite session, during the National Meeting of the ACPA, Los Angeles. Professor Tkacz inspired the phrase "reductio ad vegetabile." Subsequently, it appeared in chapter 2 of 2018: *The Aristotelian Foundations of the Human Good*.

Without this belief, it will be in principle impossible to predicate the definition at all, because a contradiction will follow: one will both have to believe that the definition signifies what the individuals are, and not believe that the definition signifies what the individuals are. In this case, of course, predication is impossible and meaningless, as are all the human activities presupposing and following on such predication.

Let us return to the honey bee example to make our point. With some study (and or a good Oxford dictionary) I could come to know in a fairly rigorous manner that a honey bee is defined as "a stinging, winged insect that collects nectar and pollen, produces wax and honey, and lives in large communities/colonies." In this definition, the genus is insect meaning an *arthropod* with six legs and one or two pairs of wings. An arthropod is an invertebrate with segmented body, an exoskeleton, and jointed limbs. 'Stinging, 'winged,' 'collecting nectar and pollen,' 'producing wax and honey,' and 'living in large colonies,' are differentia which distinguish the honey bee from other members of the same genus, and are taken from the categories of action, quality, and possession/habit.[74] Having these attributes (secondary beings) is the cause of some individuals (primary beings) in nature being honey bees. When I run into such primary buzzing beings, I know them with a very high degree of accuracy, through these secondary beings. What is key is that, any time one has predicated a definition of a honey bee in the field, which is an expression (λόγος/*logos*) of his understanding it in itself and as distinct from other animals and species of its own genus, he does so precisely because he *believes* that the individual (primary being) displays those characteristics that are universally understood to apply to all such individuals through the relevant secondary beings (genus, species, and differentia).

This point is universalizable: predicating a definition of an individual is intelligible *because* the one predicating assumes that a relation of identity actually exists between the meaning of the term defining what the individual in the field is and

---

[74] I was inspired to choose this example by Plato's treatment of definition in the *Meno* (72b-c). It is an interesting example, as some of the essential attributes that belong to the whole, like stinging and collecting nectar and producing honey do not belong to each individual member. So, Drones lack these attributes, which belong to the workers. Of course, the queen simply reproduces. In any case, I am not worried about this fact, here, as the definition is sufficient for identifying the worker bees, which are the ones that I am worried about getting stung by in the garden!

the individual in itself. Without this belief, predication of the definition will not be possible. This is true, not only in the case of discerning honey bees in the garden, but it applies to activities as mundane as picking up trash (one must know what trash is and univocally predicate its meaning of individual pieces of trash in order to pick it up), and as complex as scientific research into things like light, the stars and the planets, animals, atoms and quarks, and so on. The only way to explain the phenomenon that natural scientists formulate their subject matter through formally defining characteristics, is to accept the Aristotelian account of secondary being and univocal predication. That scientists actually disclose the specifying characteristics of a particular subject allowing for demonstrative conclusions, is only possible because they determine those characteristics shared in common by the individuals who are members of the subject genus being studied. Without univocal predication, what scientists do when they define animals, elements, forces, etc., would be impossible. The nominalist might signify a denial of univocal predication of definitions. However, candid analysis of the phenomenon of the predication of definitions over individuals shows that such a denial is, in practice, absurd and impossible. Like the sophist that would deny the principle of non-contradiction, therefore, the nominalist is reduced in his position to the state of the vegetable.[75] If the nominalist needs to purchase an apple at the store, to be consistent, he will not be able to do so, since he will not be able to distinguish the apple from anything else. Examples such as this showing the impossibility of nominalism in human action are as infinite as the circumstances surrounding human existence. The state of neutrality with which we began this enquiry, then, must be abandoned: we can be as certain that secondary beings exist and allow for univocal

[75] Étienne Gilson makes a similar critique of the nominalist position in 1937: *The Unity of Philosophical Experience*, 4. Maritain employs the distinction between *ut significata ut exercita* in his critique of Husserl's phenomenology. See Jacques Maritain 1959: *Distinguer Pour Unir ou Les Degrés du Savoir*, 205. Finally, in the very opening lines of his 1867: "On a New List of Categories", Charles Sanders Peirce gives a brief argument similar to that given here for the validity of the concept/universal from the functionally fitted role that it must actually play in the unification of the sensuous manifold expressed in a proposition. Either the universal exists, or human knowledge cannot experience a unity from the sensuous manifold, which is actually expressed in the connection of a predicate to a subject through the copula. Since we do experience such a unity, thus, and express it linguistically, the universal or the concept must necessarily exist.

predication as we are (with Aristotle) that the principle of non-contradiction must be true, since absurdity follows from denying its reality.

4.2. An Aristotelian account of univocal predication

While it is clear that univocal predication must be accepted as valid given the impossibility of nominalism, it is also the case that the principles necessary for explaining how univocal predication is possible need to be set out in some detail. Mainly, we must give some account of how there can be an identity between primary (individual) and secondary (universal) being without the kind of contradiction following, which was identified by thinkers such as Ockham. Though he himself did not directly counter the nominalist position, Aristotle did provide us with such an account.

These principles are ready at hand by supplementing the treatment of *Categories* 5, with key texts from *Metaphysics* and the *Physics*. As has already been shown, secondary being is derivative from primary being, which is to say that its existential status is entirely dependent upon the individual primary beings it allows us to define. Holding that definitions fall under the category of being, albeit, in a secondary sense, the foundation for univocal predication of a definition is already laid. A definition is predicated univocally of each individual primary being because there is a relation of identity between the two terms: both are being (οὐσία/*ousia*). This Aristotelian account of definition already indicates a twofold relation of primary and secondary being. First, there must be some kind of relation of identity between the secondary being in the understanding and the primary beings of which it is predicated. Second, there must be a relation of primary beings to one another understood as having the same essence, the account of which is the definition. The appropriate question now becomes: what principle could provide the basis for an identity between primary and secondary being, which also allows us to classify individuals as being the same kinds of things?

Metaphysics, V.8, indicates the basis for this relation of identity between first and second being. "The essence (τὸ τί ἦν εἶναι), the account (λόγος) of which is a definition (ὁρισμός)," Aristotle tells us, is "called the being (οὐσία) of each thing."[76] Even though Aristotle is clear that matter is an element of the essential

[76] i.348-30BC: *Metaphysics*, V.8 (1017b21-22): ἔτι τὸ τί ἦν εἶναι, οὗ ὁ λόγος ὁρισμός, καὶ τοῦτο οὐσία λέγεται ἑκάστου.

subject of a physical being,[77] he nonetheless gives a special role to form as essence in the most proper sense at *Physics* II.3, saying that cause is said to be "the species/form and the model, which is to say the account of the essence."[78] In the final lines of *Metaphysics* V.8, he then relates that being "is also separable", we must understand, 'from the primary being,' "and of this nature is the shape or the species/form of each thing."[79] The definition of a primary being is attainable through apprehension of the species/form of each thing, which though in the individual is also separable in the understanding. Species/form as such, then, can be taken to provide the basis for second being, along with the basis of the unity of the individuals making up a defined class. Essence as species/form (εἶδος) extends from primary being to secondary being and is the intelligible unity of both: εἶδος extends to both οὐσία taken in its primary sense as the particular individual[s] of sense experience and taken in its secondary sense as essence in the understanding and definition (genus, species, and difference).[80] The identity between primary and secondary being is the

---

[77] See c.353-47BC: *Physics*, II.2 (193b37-194a8). Seeking to distinguish physics as an autonomous and proper science distinct from mathematics, he conveys that while mathematical objects are completely separable (χωριστὸν) in thought from matter and motion, natural subjects are separable (χωριστὸν), but to a lesser degree. This is because a complete definition of any natural subject must include its material cause.

[78] c.353-47BC: *Physics*, II.3: "...ἄλλον δὲ τὸ εἶδος καὶ τὸ παράδειγμα, τοῦτο δ' ἐστὶν ὁ λόγος ὁ τοῦ τί ἦν εἶναι..." In Aristotle, it is necessary to understand that εἶδος/*eidos* has a twofold sense, precisely because it can signify what makes ontologically makes and individual primary being to be what it is and the definition that captures this essence. In the former case, the best way to signify its meaning in English is with the term 'form.' In the latter case, and given his use of the term as we have seen it in categories, the best way to signify its meaning in English is with the term 'species.' Often, Aristotle would like us to think of both at the same time—precisely because he is a realist, believing that the mind knows the forms making things to be what they are ontological through species.

[79] i.348-30BC: *Metaphysics*, V.8 (1017b24-26): ...καὶ ὃ ἂν τόδε τι ὂν καὶ χωριστὸν ᾖ· τοιοῦτον δὲ ἑκάστου ἡ μορφὴ καὶ τὸ εἶδος. Or, "...and that which, being 'this here,' is also separable; and such is the shape and the form of each thing." Cf., also, *De Anima*, III.4 (429b10-23), where Aristotle argues that the intellect must be separate since its object, species/form, is separate. A materially individuated form, of course, cannot exist "in" the intellect.

[80] While Aristotle clearly grasps the distinction between the apprehension of essence in the understanding and its expressed definition, he appears to somewhat ambiguously apply the term "second substance" to both.

principle of form. This allows us to explain the phenomenon of defining, already given to us in common experience. Univocal predication is possible because **1)** the form captured by the definition in the intellect is identical to that existing in the individual—though we must say, following Avicenna and St. Thomas Aquinas, in a different mode of being[81]—and, **2)** because each particular primary being that is defined possesses a species/form identical to that of the other members of its class.

5. Conclusion

This article has presented a detailed account of the basic terms of sense-perceptive realism, as they were first set down by Aristotle in the *Categories*. Primary beings exist in the world as individuals possessing a myriad of attributes, and we can know these beings through the categories by sorting their attributes into those that are essential and those that are accidental. In the former case, we do this through the univocal predication of concepts that are generic, specific, or differentiating, which Aristotle calls secondary beings precisely because they signify what individual members of a class really are in themselves. In the latter case, we apply concepts falling under the nine categories after being, that belong to primary beings, but which do not make them to be what they are essentially. The realist doctrine of primary and secondary being was then defended against the nominalist critique through a *reductio ad impossibile* style argument coupled with an appeal to the phenomenological method. Understanding that the basic terms of realism are given to us as a phenomenological datum in human language, namely, the subject, copula, and predicate composing propositions expressing judgmental understanding, we first took a stance of neutrality regarding the question of whether or not

---

[81] Avicenna must be credited as the first philosopher to distinguish between two modes of existence of essence along these lines. See, Avicenna i.1020/27: *The Metaphysics of the Healing*, V, 1. Distinguishing between essence in the things themselves and in the intellect allows for a full resolution of the problem universals at the heart of the nominalist critique. It is the identical form and essence, though it exists in two different modes, which is how knowledge is possible. Following Avicenna, St. Thomas similarly utilizes the notion of modes of existence of essence in his dealing with universals in c.1252/56: *De ente et essentia*, III.

predicates taken as defining subjects of experience really captured universal and essential attributes.

> ...the ability to "buy an apple" or "take out the trash" entailed not only a universal meaning to be applicable to "apples" and "trash" but also to "buy" and "take out." While Nominalism can easily be shown to have laid waste to perennial natural philosophy and metaphysics, it has also contributed to the rejection of an objective ethics rooted in knowing what human beings are, what actions are in accord with that nature and bring about flourishing, and what actions do violence to that nature and thwart flourishing. Nominalism taken in its fullness would not only reject the intrinsic commonality of essences within things of like kind but also of a common essentiality to human actions of like kind. The specification of human actions as intrinsically evil in kind according to a knowable formal object of the act becomes unintelligible with such an epistemological, metaphysical, and physical worldview. Consequently, Wagner's defense of realism through our modes of thought and speech has significant implications for philosophical anthropology and ethics as a counter to Ethical Nominalism. In short, to make a case for an objective ethics depends upon knowing what human beings are and what is the human good—that is, having a definitional account of what human beings are and what constitutes the good for them as this type of being. Also, such an ethics entails that human actions have common natures which can be known and specified as good or evil in kind. Wagner's essay establishes a launching point, then, for what I think can be extremely valuable further philosophical discussion and development.
>
> *Capehart, "Philosophical Implications" [p.72].*

It was then shown, however, by appeal to examples of the practical exercise of univocal predication in human language that the nominalist denial of secondary being is not tenable. This is because it would not be possible for us to predicate a term like 'honey bee' of multiple individual beings in the world, when we do predicate the term, if we did not *believe* or *suppose* that the definition (secondary being) corresponding to the term actually signified immanently possessed ontological features (species/form) of the individuals. Therefore, just as Aristotle has shown us that the denial of the principle of non-contradiction is not tenable because it results in a contradiction, so also the nominalist denial of secondary beings is not tenable, as it would have the consequence that one could not predicate a secondary being of a primary being when one actually does so in exercise or practice.

Finally, key texts of Aristotle were appealed to in order to show that, in fact, it is possible to explain the identity between universal, secondary beings and the particular individuals of which they are predicated. A singular form, species, or essence is capable of two modes of existence, one in the primary being, making it to be what it is, and one separated or abstracted in the human intellect. Thus, there is an identity and an *adaequatio* between the intellect and the thing/being/reality known when one, sitting in the garden, says 'that is a honey bee.' The form making the honey bee to be what it is in itself is identical to the species/form in the intellect which, abstracted, becomes universally predicable of all individual honey bees sharing the form. The next major task in giving an account of and defending realist philosophy will be a more complete genetic account of the formation of secondary beings in the intellect starting with sense-perception of the primary beings. This, however, is a task for another article.

References Historically Layered

AQUINAS, Thomas (1225—1274).

c.1252/6. *De ente et essentia* in *Opera omnia iussu Leonis XIII P.M. edita, t.43* (Editori di San Tommasso, Roma, 1976): 315-81.

ARISTOTLE (384-322BC).

i.360-330BC. *Aristotelis categoriae et liber de interpretatione*, edited by L. Minio–Paluello (Oxford: Clarendon Press, 1949; reprinted in 1966).

c.348-47BC. *Aristotelis analytica priora et posteriora*, edited by W. D. Ross (New York: Oxford University Press, 1949).

i.348-30BC. *Aristotlelis metaphysica*, 2 vols, edited by W. D. Ross (Oxford: Clarendon Press, 1924; 1953 corrected edition, reprinted in 1970).

c.330BC. *Aristote: Les parties des animaux*, edited by P. Louis (Paris: Les Belles Lettres, 1956).

c.330BC. *Aristoteles et Corpus Aristotelicum Phil., De anima* "Aristotle. De anima", edited by W. D. Ross (Oxford: Clarendon Press 1961, reprinted in 1967)

Translations Consulted

c.360BC. Κατηγορίαι in the *Basic Works of Aristotle* prepared by Richard McKeon, in the English translation by E. M. Edghill, *Categories* (New York: Basic Books, 1941): 1-37 (complete).

Κατηγορίαι in the Loeb edition, English translation by Harold P. Cook, *The Categories* (Cambridge MA: Harvard University Press, 1938): 12-109.

Κατηγορίαι in the *Complete Works (Aristotle)* edited by Jonathan Barnes, in the English translation by J. J. Ackrill, *Categories* (Princeton, N.J.: Princeton University Press, 1991).

c.348-47BC. Ἀναλυτικὰ Ὕστερα in the *Basic Works of Aristotle* prepared by Richard McKeon, in the English translation by G. R. G. Mure,

Posterior Analytics (New York: Random House, 1941): 110-186 (complete).

Ἀναλυτικὰ Ὕστερα in the Loeb edition, English translation by Hugh Tredennick, *Posterior Analytics* (Cambridge MA: Harvard University Press, 1960): 24-261.

Ἀναλυτικὰ Ὕστερα in the translation by Hippocrates G. Apostle, *Posterior Analytics* (Grinell, IA: The Peripatetic Press, 1981).

c.353BC. Τοπικά, in the *Basic Works of Aristotle* prepared by Richard McKeon, English translation by W. A. Pickard-Cambridge, *Topics* (New York: Random House, 1941).

Τοπικά, in the Loeb edition, English translation by E. S. Forster, *Topics* (Cambridge MA: Harvard University Press, 1960): 272-739.

c.353-47BC. Φυσικὴ ἀκρόασις, in the *Basic Works of Aristotle*, prepared by Richard McKeon, in the English translation by R. P. Hardie and R. K. Gaye, *Physics* (New York: Random House, 1941): 218-394 (complete).

Φυσικὴ ἀκρόασις, in the Loeb edition, English translation by Philip H. Wicksteed and Francis M. Cornford (Cambridge, MA: Harvard University Press, Vol I. 1957, Vol. II. 1934).

Φυσικὴ ἀκρόασις, in the English translation by Joe Sachs, *Aristotle's Physics: A Guided Study* (New Brunswick, NJ: Rutgers University Press, 1998).

Φυσικὴ ἀκρόασις, in the translation by Glen Coughlin, *Physics* (South Bend, IN: St. Augustine's Press, 2005).

Φυσικὴ ἀκρόασις, in the translation by Hippocrates G. Apostle (Grinnell, Iowa: The Peripatetic Press, 1969).

c.330BC. Περὶ ζῴων μορίων, in the *Basic Works of Aristotle* prepared by Richard McKeon in the English translation by William Ogle, *De Partibus Animalium* (New York: Random House, 1941).

i.348-30BC. Μετά τα Φυσικά in the *Basic Works of Aristotle* prepared by Richard McKeon, in the English translation by W. D. Ross, *Metaphysics* (New York: Random House, 1941).

Μετά τα Φυσικά in the English translation by Hippocrates G. Apostle (Grinnell, IA: The Peripatetic Press, 1966).

BOETHIUS, Anicius Manlius Severinus (480—524AD)

c.509-11. *In Categorias Aristotelis* edited by L. Minio-Paluello (Desclée De Brouwer: Bruges-Paris 1961).

DEELY, John (26 April 1942—2017 January 7).

2001. *Four Ages of Understanding: the first postmodern survey of philosophy from ancient times to the turn of the 20th century* (Toronto: University of Toronto Press).

2013. "Modern Epistemology and Solipsism" in *The New Catholic Encyclopedia*.

DESCARTES, Rene (31 March 1596—1650 February 11).

1637. *Discours de la méthode pour bien conduire sa raison, et chercher la vérité dans les sciences* (Leyden: Ian Maire) in the English translation by Donald Cress with minor changes by Roger Ariew, *Discourse in Method* in *Philosophical Essays and Correspondence*, ed. Roger Ariew (Indianapolis, IN: Hackett Publishing Company, Inc., 2000): 46-82.

1641. *Meditationes de Prima Philosophiae* (Paris: Michel Soly). Reference is to the English translation by Donald Cress with minor changes by Roger Ariew, *Meditations on First Philosophy* in *Philosophical Essays and Correspondence*, ed. Roger Ariew (Indianapolis, IN: Hackett Publishing Company, Inc., 2000): 97-141.

1644. *Principia Philosophiae* (Amsterdam: L. Elzivier). Reference to the English translation by Donald Cress with minor changes by Roger Ariew, *Principles of Philosophy* in *Philosophical Essays and Correspondence*, ed. Roger Ariew (Indianapolis, IN: Hackett Publishing Company, Inc., 2000): 222-72.

FREDE, Michael

1981. "Categories in Aristotle" in D. O'Meara, ed., *Studies in Aristotle* (Washington, D.C.: CUA Press): 1-24.

GILLESPIE, C.M.

1925. "The Aristotelian Categories" in *The Classical Quarterly*, 19.2 (April): 75-84.

GILSON, Étienne (13 June 1884—1978 September 19).

1937. *The Unity of Philosophical Experience* (New York: Scribner's, 1948; reprinted, San Francisco, CA: St. Ignatius Press, 1999).

GRENE, Marjorie

1963. *A Portrait of Aristotle* (Chicago: The University of Chicago Press).

HOUSER, R.E.

2010. "The Language of Being and the Nature of God in the Aristotelian Tradition" in *Proceedings of the ACPA* 84: 113-32.

HUME, David (7 May 1711—1776 August 25).

1748. *An Enquiry Concerning Human Understanding* (originally published under the title *Philosophical Essays Concerning Human Understanding* and retitled in 1758), edited by Tom L. Beauchamp (New York: Oxford University Press, 2000).

HUSSERL, Edmund (8 April 1859—1938 April 27).

1907. *Der Idee des Phänomenologie* in the English translation by Lee Hardy, *The Idea of Phenomenology* (Dordrecht: Kluwer, 1999).

1913. *Ideen zur einer reinene Phänomenologie und phänomenologische Philosophie*, in the translation by F. Kersten, *Ideas Pertaining to a Pure Phenomenology and to a Phenomenological Philosophy*, in the *Collected Works*, vol.2 (The Hague: Martinus Nijhoff, 1983).

IBN SINA [Avicenna] (980—1037)

i.1020/27. *Al-Ilahiyyat Kitab al-Shifa* in the English translation by Michael E. Marmura, *The Metaphysics of the Book of the Healing* (Provo, UT: Brigham Young University Press, 2005).

KEMPLE, Brian (31 May 1986—).

2019. "Signs and Reality: an advocation for semiotic realism" in *Reality: a journal for philosophical discourse*, 1.1 (2020): 75-123.

MARITAIN, Jacques (18 November 1882—1973 April 28).

1959. *Distinguer Pour Unir: ou Les Degrés du Savoir* (Paris: Desclée de Brouwer, 1934) in the English translation overseen by Gerald B. Phelan (New York: Scribner's).

OWEN, G.E.L. (18 May 1922—1982 July 10).

1986. "Logic and Metaphysics in Some Earlier Works of Aristotle" in Martha Nussbaum, ed., *Logic, Science, and Dialectic: Collected Papers in Greek Philosophy* (Ithaca, NY: Cornell University Press): 180-220.

OWENS, Joseph C.S.B. (17 April 1908—2005 October 30).

1951. *The Doctrine of Being in the Aristotelian Metaphysics* (Toronto: PIMS, 1978).

PEIRCE, Charles Sanders (10 September 1839—1914 April 19).

1867. "On a New List of Categories" in *The Essential Peirce*, vol.1, 1867-1892 (Bloomington, IN: Indiana University Press, 1992): 1-10.

PLATO (c.429/424—348/347bc).

c.399BC. *Apologia* in *Platonis opera*, vol. 1, edited by J. Burnet (Oxford: Clarendon Press, 1900, reprinted in 1967).

c.385BC. *Meno* in *Platonis opera*, vol. 1, edited by J. Burnet (Oxford: Clarendon Press, 1900, reprinted in 1967).

PORPHYRY (234—305ad).

i.268-70. *Isagoge*, in the English translation by Edward W. Warren (Toronto: PIMS, 1975).

RANDALL, John Herman Jr. (14 February 1899—1980 December 1).

1960. *Aristotle* (New York: Columbia University Press).

SACHS, David (1921—1992 November 23).

1948. "Does Aristotle have a Doctrine of Secondary Substance?" in *Mind*, vol.57 (April): 221-25.

SANFORD, Johnathan J.

2004. "Categories and Metaphysics: Aristotle's Science of Being" in Michael Gorman and Jonathan J. Sanford, eds., *Categories: Historical and Systematic Essays* (Washington, D.C.: CUA Press): 3-20.

SOKOLOWSKI, Robert (3 May 1934—).

2000. *Introduction to Phenomenology* (New York: Cambridge University Press).

SOMMERS, Mary Catherine.

1987. "Aristotle on Substance and Predication: A Medieval View" in *Proceedings of the ACPA*, 61: 78-87.

STRIBY, Steve.

2007. *Against the Principles of Nominalism*. Dissertation, Center for Thomistic Studies, 2007, available in ProQuest.

WAGNER, Daniel C.

2012. "Definition and the *Reductio ad Vegetabilium*: Comments on Professor Tkacz's Treatment of Albertus Magnus and the Error Ptolemaei", presented at the Society for Thomistic Natural Philosophy Satellite session, National Meeting of the ACPA, Los Angeles.

2018. *φύσις καὶ τὸ ἀνθρώπινον ἀγαθόν: The Aristotelian Foundations of the Human Good*. Dissertation available through ProQuest, 2018.

2019. "On the Foundational Compatibility of Phenomenology & Thomism", forthcoming in *Studia Gilsoniana*, 2019.

WEDIN, Michael V.

2002. *Aristotle's Theory of Substance: The Categories and Metaphysics Zeta* (Oxford: Oxford University Press).

WEHRLE, Walter E.

2000. *The Myth of Aristotle's Development and Betrayal of Metaphysics* (Oxford: Rowman & Littlefield).

WEINBERG, Julius R (3 September 1908—1971 January 17).

1964. *A Short History of Medieval Philosophy* (Princeton, NJ: Princeton University Press).

1965. *Abstraction, Relation, and Induction: three essays in the history of thought* (Madison, WI: University of Wisconsin Press).

WILLIAM of Ockham (c.1287—1349).

c.1323. *Summa Logicae* in *Opera Philosophica*, vol.I, edited by Philotheus Boehner, Gedeon Gal, and Stephanus Brown (St. Bonaventure NY: The Franciscan Institute at St. Bonaventure University, 1974).

WOODBRIDGE, Fredrick J.E. (26 March 1867—1940 June 1).

1965. *Aristotle's Vision of Nature* (posthumous), ed. John H. Randall Jr. (New York: Columbia University Press).

Philosophical Implications of Sense Realism

A Response to Daniel Wagner[1]

James D. Capehart, Ph.D.
Sacred Heart Apostolic School
Rolling Prairie, IN

In his essay "The Logical Terms of Sense Realism: A Thomistic-Aristotelian & Phenomenological Defense" Daniel Wagner addresses the problem of universals and specifically the problem of the Nominalist solution to it in both a refreshingly new and yet *traditional* fashion. It is "new" in that it foregoes the genetic account of human knowing—at least for the time being—in making the case for realism. It is "traditional" in tying it into Aristotle's logical account of how we form our notions of *secondary substance*—genus, species, and difference—and how we predicate these notions of secondary substance of *primary substances*—i.e., individuals. Furthermore, in confronting Nominalism by means of examining how we think and speak about individuals, Wagner takes a common ground approach for the starting point of this debate. No matter what form of Nominalism is invoked, a given Nominalist philosopher is thinking and predicating about things even when he denies the reality of universals as corresponding to real essences existing within things. Bracketing this phenomenon of how we encounter in sensation, think about, and name things not only as individuals but as *kinds of things* provides a framework for discussion which I believe the Nominalist must accept at least implicitly because he makes use of it in science and in everyday life. With this in mind, Wagner proceeds to provide a most profitable treatment of Aristotle's account of predication and definition first in the *Topics,* then in the *Categories*, followed by a *reductio ad absurdum* argument for realism, all founded upon a Thomistic-Aristotelian-Avicennian account of form.

In the following commentary, I will proceed in two phases: first, I will provide a general summary of Wagner's key points; second, I will suggest two areas for further development, one which can map this treatment more explicitly onto St. Thomas' position as found in *De Ente et Essentia* and another which will connect

---

[1] Correspondence to editors@realityjournal.org.

and emphasize the anthropological and moral philosophical implications of Wagner's—I believe successful—defense of moderate realism.

In his introduction Wagner makes the case that the genetic "defense" for a doctrine of realism should be delayed for after a presentation of the logical account for realism. As he explains, "It is a methodological error to think that the genetic account comes first in the realist approach to knowledge because, objectively speaking, human beings are already regularly engaged in thinking and speaking acts characteristic of a realist attitude using concepts *as though* they signify what things in the world *really* are."[2] Thus, while a given nominalist might reject a given realist's genetic account for the process of human knowing—honestly, is that not precisely the problem?—he still makes use of concepts, predicating them of things. The nominalist may say that all that is common between things of a given genus or species is their name—hence "nominalism" for *nomen, nominis*, name—but Wagner is seeking to examine the logical foundations of that process which even the nominalist uses, precisely because he is human. While the focus of the essay is on human language and thought, it will establish anthropological, natural, metaphysical, and ethical foundations for a thoroughly realist philosophy.

Proceeding into the body of the essay, Wagner begins with a treatment of predication in *Topics*. This is helpful for the reader who is not as familiar with the textual Aristotle for its presentation of the *predicables*—definition, property, genus, difference, and accident—and their relation to the *categories*—"what it is"/"definition," quantity, quality, relation, place, time, position, possession, action, and passion.[3] If a categorical term tells what something is or tells the kind of thing it is, like a genus, species, property, or difference, then that categorical term is regarded to be *definitive* of the subject. If it is non-definitive, but merely states what the subject happens to have but might not have, the term is just an *accident*. Thus, as Wagner explains, for Aristotle, "...knowledge pursued in rational discourse is a matter of determining how various categorical predicates are connected to the subject of inquiry, either as definitive (genus, species, difference), or as accidental (accident)."[4] Aristotle's logic is firmly rooted in a realism of coming to know what is constitutive of the essences of things, of what is merely accidental of them, and predicating in either case accurately.

---

[2] Wagner 2019: "The Logical Terms of Sense Realism: A Thomistic-Aristotelian and Phenomenological Defense", 21.

[3] Cf. Wagner 2019: "The Logical Terms of Sense Realism", 27-28.

[4] Ibid, 28.

Wagner then proceeds to a detailed explication of predication in the *Categories*. As has been hinted at already, both works according to Wagner should be treated not only as logical but as simultaneously logical and ontological. This becomes especially clear through Wagner's presentation of *equivocal* and *univocal predication* in the *Categories*. Terms are equivocal when while the term itself is common the "'account of the being [i.e., the definition] in accord with the name is different.'"[5] Thus, for a *term* to be used *equivocally*, the actual definitional account of what is referred to in the world differs in each usage despite the commonality in pronunciation of a given term—like the "bat" that hits a ball or the "bat" that flies around at night. However, in a case of *univocal predication*, "a term and the content of the definition attached to it are applied identically to a set of individual existing beings."[6] In other words, *univocal predication* occurs when the same *term* as well as the *same definitional account* is applied to a set of singular, particular things. "Apple" can only be said univocally of two or more things, if by that term one means that the things share a common account of what it means to be an "apple." But does not science and real life depend upon the ability to predicate "apple" of things which share in that meaning, "honey bee" of buzzing things of that same meaning, or "peanuts" of shelled legumes of that same meaning?[7]

> The identity between primary and secondary being is the principle of form. This allows us to explain the phenomenon of defining, already given to us in common experience. Univocal predication is possible because **1)** the form captured by the definition in the intellect is identical to that existing in the individual—though we must say, following Avicenna and St. Thomas Aquinas, in a different mode of being—and, **2)** because each particular primary being that is defined possesses a species/form identical to that of the other members of its class.
>
> *Wagner, "The Logical Terms of Sense Realism" [p.56-57].*

---

[5] Ibid, 29, quoting *Categories*, 1 (1a1-3).

[6] Wagner 2019: "The Logical Terms of Sense Realism", 30.

[7] N.B.: farmers, entomologists, and people with severe allergies sure do hope so.

Thus, Wagner shows that *univocal predication* is the foundation of sense realism and is really the key to the problem at hand. In fact, through his detailed textual account of Aristotle, Wagner explains that the root of realism is in the *univocal predication* of *secondary ousia*—genus and species—of *primary ousia*—individually existing particulars. *Primary ousia* has ontological priority over those terms which are predicated of it, as *secondary ousia* and the other nine categories are either *said of* primary beings as *subjects*—as in the case of predicating *secondary ousia* of an individual—or are *in them* as in subjects—as in the case of the predication of accidents of an individual.[8] This ontological priority asserts itself by the fact that universals—i.e., concepts—are formed in the intellect based upon an encounter with a set of individuals through sensation. As Wagner clarifies, "Since universals are formed in the intellect by a collection of what is common to a set of individual primary beings given first to sensation, it follows that the non-existence of an essential feature in the primary beings will result in its non-existence as a secondary being, i.e., as genus or species."[9] Thus, as rooted in really existing individuals, the concepts we form of them are true only to the degree that they express what the individuals really have or what they really are essentially, and deny what they really lack. Secondary being then is expressive of real, essential commonalities of things of like kind and because of this is truly said *univocally* of the individuals of which they are predicated.[10]

After making his case for the logical foundations of realism within Aristotle's logic, Wagner proceeds to present a short history of the Problem of Universals and Nominalism as it developed in the Middle Ages and came to its "perfection" in Ockham's Nominalism. This is followed by a *reductio ad absurdum* argument against said Nominalism in the fashion of Aristotle's defense of the Principle of Contradiction in the *Metaphysics*.[11] For the Nominalist, there can be no *univocal predication* of terms and their definitions to particular beings, as they argue that there is no shared, common nature within particulars to ground such predication. Nevertheless, such assertions entail truth claims about how *secondary ousia* relates to particulars, but also entails that some sense of common definitional account of particulars is necessary not only for science but for ordinary, everyday life. How could one be expected to "buy an apple" or "take out the trash" if someone didn't know the meaning of "apple" or "trash" but also of the human actions "buy" and "take out?" Thus, predication of a

---

[8] Cf. Wagner 2019: "The Logical Terms of Sense Realism", 39-42.

[9] Ibid, 41.

[10] Cf. ibid, 47.

[11] Cf. ibid, 47-52.

definition to an individual presupposes an identity between the meaning of the definition and the individual. It also entails a relation between primary beings of like kind as having a shared essence. The nominalist must make use of this framework of these relations even in the midst of attempting to deny them, but also in the attempt at any kind of meaningful philosophy, science, and human life.[12]

This brings me to mention a minor point of development and also, I think, a major one. Wagner has presented this as an Aristotelian-Avicennian-Thomistic-Phenomenological defense of realism. This was a large task to draw from all four traditions in one essay, even if Thomas and Avicenna are themselves from within the Aristotelian tradition. Still, Wagner concludes his treatment with a very brief explanation of the principle at root for this identity between *secondary ousia* and *primary ousia*, viz. *form*. In short, the Avicennian/Thomistic account of the modes of existence of *essence* or *form* within the mind as known and within material things themselves are presented as a kind of metaphysical grounding for the epistemological/logical account that he has given. Without in any way suggesting Wagner's essay to be incomplete in what it was attempting and I think successfully did, any follow up essay would do well to tie in this previous account to a more developed treatment of St. Thomas' own explicit doctrine on the problem of universals as presented in *De Ente et Essentia,* III.[13] Wagner had already indicated that the more *genetic account* of the problem of universals should come after his logically rooted treatment, so Thomas' more detailed explanation for how *form* exists in singulars and in the mind would map on quite profitably either in an extended version of this essay or as a follow up.[14]

Regarding the point of major development, I have alluded to it already when I noted that the ability to "buy an apple" or "take out the trash" entailed not only a universal meaning to be applicable to "apples" and "trash" but also to "buy" and "take out." While Nominalism can easily be shown to have laid waste to perennial natural philosophy and metaphysics, it has also contributed to the rejection of an objective ethics rooted in knowing what human beings are, what actions are in accord with that nature and bring about flourishing, and what actions do violence to that nature and thwart flourishing. Nominalism taken in its fullness would not only reject the intrinsic commonality of essences within things of like kind but also of a common essentiality to human actions of like

[12] Cf. ibid, 52-53.

[13] However, this text is cited, as well as is its Avicennian counterpart, at 57n81.

[14] See Kreeger 2019: "Aquinas On Suppositum, Essence & Universals", *Reality: a journal for philosophical discourse* online at https://realityjournal.org.

kind. The specification of human actions as intrinsically evil in kind according to a knowable formal object of the act becomes unintelligible with such an epistemological, metaphysical, and physical worldview. Consequently, Wagner's defense of realism through our modes of thought and speech has significant implications for philosophical anthropology and ethics as a counter to Ethical Nominalism. In short, to make a case for an objective ethics depends upon knowing what human beings are and what is the *human good*—that is, having a definitional account of what human beings are and what constitutes *the good* for them as this type of being. Also, such an ethics entails that human actions have common natures which can be known and specified as good or evil in kind. Wagner's essay establishes a launching point, then, for what I think can be extremely valuable further philosophical discussion and development. But neither of these points should be regarded as deficiencies within the essay itself, as every good essay should succeed in a specifically stated purpose and should point toward the next avenues for discussion. Wagner's treatment of the logical terms of Aristotle's sense realism has done just that.

References Historically Layered

KREEGER, Seth.

2019. "Aquinas on Suppositum, Essence & Universals", *Reality: a journal for philosophical discourse*, online: <https://realityjournal.org/2020/02/05/article-aquinas-on-suppositum-essence-universals/>. Retrieved 25 February 2020.

WAGNER, Daniel C.

2019. "The Logical Terms of Sense Realism: A Thomistic-Aristotelian & Phenomenological Defense", *Reality: a journal for philosophical discourse*, 1.1 (2020): 19-67.

Signs and Reality

An Advocation for Semiotic Realism[1]

Brian Kemple, PhD
Continuum Philosophical Insight
Executive Editor, REALITY

The world today has a "meaning" problem. That is: while the attainment of "meaning" poses a perennial difficulty common to every human life in every human age, our lives in this age have a problem with attaining meaning—indeed, a twofold problem. First, the problem being that we do not know, precisely, to what the term "meaning" refers; and second, the problem being that even if we recognize one aspect or more of the term's referent, we do not

---

[1] Correspondence to kemple@realityjournal.org.

Table of Contents

Note that this article presupposes some knowledge: namely, a Thomistic account of the human person, as a body-soul composite with faculties of sensation (*sensus exteriores*), faculties of perception (*sensus interiores*), and faculties of intellection (*intellectus agens et possibilis*), as well as appetitive faculties following both perceptual and intellectual cognition.

understand how it can be resolved into a coherent whole, for we lack the requisite principles.

Among the obstacles preventing both the attainment of the meaning of "meaning" and its coherent resolution are myriad misunderstandings of what it means to say that we "know reality"; misunderstandings which not only fall short but miss the mark entirely. More must be done in order to explain both how realism is possible and just what falls into the reality which realism is said to make known.

At the heart of the struggle for realism is the question of to what extent and in what regard the cognitive means of knowing are the same as the object known. This question is especially central to the Thomistic tradition, for Thomas often refers to the *species intelligibilis* as a *similitudo* of the object known. Various misinterpretations and muddy explanations of this reference have hindered an understanding of how the human intellect knows its object.

To resolve this Thomistic problem and the problems of meaning, we propose a **semiotic realism**, a realism that structures its doctrines in accord with the nature of signs and that accordingly understands the *species intelligibilis* as fragmentary, incomplete, and in need of continual deliberate interpretational refinement in order that we attain a better grasp on the truth of the real.

I. Introduction

The world today has a "meaning" problem. That is: while the attainment of "meaning" poses a perennial difficulty shared by every human life in every human age, *our* lives in *this* age have a *problem* with attaining meaning—indeed, a twofold problem.[2] The first aspect of this problem is that we do not precisely know to what the term "meaning" refers. This confusion stems—in a lengthy and convoluted history that we cannot here discuss—from a commonly adopted and implicitly nominalistic perspective that identifies "meaning" with a **referential** construct.[3] In other words and put succinctly, "meaning" is said

---

[2] All problems are difficulties but not all difficulties are problems: that is, a problem is a difficulty that has a solution, a way of being resolved such that it is *fixed*. All mathematical problems, for instance, have (at least) one solution which works always in all cases. But some difficulties, do not necessarily have a determinate solution: such as maintaining a relationship (which may have problems in need of solutions, but which solutions do not maintain the relationship, only prevent its dissipation), being virtuous, or discovering meaning.

[3] Cf. John Deely 2001: *Four Ages of Understanding*, 487-607 for the history of modern philosophy, the root from which the current problem springs; though to fully understand

either as pertaining to someone's personal interests ("I always feel safe here; this house means 'safety' to me...") or to the conventional definition as one might find in a dictionary ("The meaning of 'charisma' according to Merriam-Webster..."). The realist objection to this reduction of meaning to referential contexts—namely, that "meaning" belongs first and foremost to *things*, to the realities as they have a cognition-independent existence not circumscribed by referential contexts and thus that prior to referential meaning stands **intelligible** meaning—today requires a clearer articulation.

This need follows, for the second aspect of our problem with meaning is that, even if we recognize this multimodality of the word "meaning", we do not understand how the various modes can be resolved into a coherent whole, as we lack the requisite principles. Can one and the same object—meaning, an intelligibility precisely as it is in relation to a cognitive power[4]—have a cognition-independent intelligible meaning *and* a cognition-dependent[5] referentially-contextual meaning? Do these two senses of meaning conflict with one another, or limit one another? Can the intelligible really be accessed without carrying along the referential—that is, can we really escape the limitations of our own referential context?

Moreover, implicit in both "intelligible" and "referential" uses of "meaning" is a third sense: the sense of importance, or the **teleological** meaning—that is, "This is meaningful to me because..."—the kind of meaning we generally associate with fulfillment or attainment of purpose. While the realist, particularly if reared in the tradition of Aristotle and Thomas Aquinas, has at least an implicit understanding of the causal, hierarchical relations between these senses of meaning, the unconsciously nominalist world at large is at a loss, and the semi-conscious nominalist belief of many in the academy has taken all three senses of

---

the constriction of meaning to reference, one would have to examine in greater depth the 20th century nominalisms and relativisms.

[4] See John Deely 2009: *Purely Objective Reality*, 8-15 for an explanation of the terms "object" and "objective". In short, their meaning in the conventional contemporary vernacular is precisely opposite that which they held at their inception; and the concept they signify has no other single-term signifier in present-day English.

[5] I use these two terms—that is, cognition-dependent and cognition-independent—as translations of the Latin *ens rationis* and *ens naturae* or *res rationis* and *res naturae*. This is ***not*** to suggest an ontological priority of cognitive action, but only a categorization of how we experience objects insofar as we are cognitive agents.

"meaning" to be circumscribed by the referential, such that there is no "intelligible in itself" but only "intelligible as referred to this or that mind".[6]

Thus, chief among all the obstacles preventing both the attainment of the meaning of "meaning" and its coherent resolution are the myriad misunderstandings of what it means to say that we "know reality"; some misunderstandings only falling short,[7] while others miss the mark entirely, leaving us with vague and unresolved concepts of "reality".[8] More must be done in order to explain both how realism is possible—that is, how the intelligible sense of meaning is not only something which we may attain, but which is

---

[6] Cf. Jesper Hoffmeyer 2010: "God and the world of signs" in *Zygon* 45.2, 386-87; Niklas Luhmann 1997: *Die Gesellschaft der Gesellschaft*, 18; Jacques Derrida 1967: *Of Grammatology*, 4. Calvin Schrag 1986: *Communicative Praxis and the Space of Subjectivity*, 57.

[7] Gilson falls short, for instance, in holding (1965: *Le Thomisme*, 268) that human concept-formation is "naturally unerring" and that the "intellect conceives essences as hearing perceives sounds and sight colors". This error stems from mistakenly thinking that the sensed object contributes the whole of our conceptual content (1939: *Thomist Realism*, 183: "nothing is in the understanding unless it has first been in the senses"), rather than that all our knowledge *begins* from sensation (Aquinas i.1259/65: *SCG*, lib.2, c.37, n.2 "omnis nostra cognitio a sensu *incipit*", emphasis added); see Kemple 2017: *Ens Primum Cognitum* 104-10 for more. Conversely, someone like Karl Popper entirely misses the mark, as holding that (1934: *Logik der Forschung*, 8): "there is no such thing as a logical method of having new ideas, or a logical reconstruction of this process. My view may be expressed by saying that every discover contains 'an irrational element', or a 'creative intuition', in Bergson's sense."

I will not address any variety of so-called "analytic" arguments against realism, such as the model-theoretic argument advanced by Hilary Putnam (1977: "Realism and Reason", 1981: *Reason, Truth and History*, etc.), for the reason that they are—generally speaking, though there may be exceptions—fundamentally flawed in holding the correspondences between thought and the world as between properly-composed representational or informational psychological or logical quanta and their correlates "outside the mind" (also found in, e.g., Jürgen Habermas 1981: *The Theory of Communicative Action: Volume One: Reason and the Rationalization of Society*, 9: "A judgment can be objective if it is undertaken on the basis of a transsubjective validity claim that has the same meaning for observers and nonparticipants as it has for the acting subject himself."). At best, a quasi-problem and at worst, an absurdity, it is resolved either way by considering the *relational* and *semiotic* nature (rather than representational) of cognitive action.

[8] Resolution is inherently twofold: for there is a resolution to what is more primordial in the order of cognition, to the *per se nota quoad nos* and to what is more primordial in the order of existence, to the *per se nota quoad se*.

primary for us as human beings—and just what falls into the reality which realism is said to make known.

At the heart of the struggle for realism is the question of *to what extent* and *in what regard* the **cognitive means of knowing** are *the same* as the **object known**. In other words, if the starting point for realism is Aristotle's assertion that "the soul is in *some way* all things", then we need to develop an understanding not only of the "all things" but also of the "some way". This question concerning the nature of our knowledge is especially central to the Thomistic tradition, for Thomas often refers to the *species intelligibilis* or the "intelligible specification" whereby we know (the *quo*) as a *similitudo* of the object known (the *quod*).[9] In other words, the intellect naturally is all things *in potency*, but is any of them *in act* only by the reception of some specifying or presentative form. Some have taken this claim to indicate that the intellect knows the intelligible species directly and thereby knows the object only indirectly, as what is "reflected" in the intelligible species; such that we know a thing outside the mind by knowing its similitude inside the mind.[10] Others have taken the *similitudo* to signify that the received species (or *species impressa*) forms the functional whole of the expressed species (*species expressa*), and so the reality of knowledge has a consistent and complete intelligibility from object sensed, to object perceived, to object understood; in other words, that the intention of the knower towards the known by means of a concept entails no interpretational input from the knower, but is instead an immediate sign of the object.[11] Both views are poorly

---

[9] E.g., i.1259/65: *SCG*, lib.1, c.53, n.2; 1266-68: *ST* Ia, q.79, a.6, c.; q.84, a.3, c; a.4, c; q.85, a.1, ad.4; a.2, c; ad.1, ad.2; and in many other texts. The phantasm is referred to as a *similitudo rei particulars* (1266-68: *ST* Ia, q.84, a.7, ad.2; q.85, a.1, ad.3, etc.).

[10] Cf. Robert Sokolowski 2008: *Phenomenology of the Human Person*, 294-96. Or see the frequent language of *representation* being used in, e.g., Fernand van Steenberg 1947: *Epistemologie*, 130-38. See Gilson 1939: *Thomist Realism and the Critique of Knowledge* for more on the problem.

[11] Worse than Gilson's error above—Gilson admitting the reality of the *species expressa* albeit with such caveats as to misconstrue badly its nature—is that interpretation denying there is any such thing as a *species expressa*, perhaps because such a term is not found explicitly in the text of Aquinas, or that the *verbum mentis* (easily grasped by any perspicacious interpreter as a synonym for the *species expressa*) is in no way distinct from the intellect's act of understanding itself (see O'Callaghan 2010: "Concepts, Mirrors, and Signification: Response to Deely", *ACPQ* 84.1: 133-62). Against this, read Deely's original review (2008: "How to Go Nowhere with Language: Remarks on John

supported by the texts of Thomas himself.[12] More poignantly, they are incompatible with what reflection upon experience unveils for us: namely, that the means of our knowledge are fragmentary, incomplete, and in need of continual deliberate interpretational refinement in order that we attain a better grasp on the truth of the real.

By drawing on Aquinas, John Poinsot, and John Deely, we might grab the tools needed to engage in such a reflection upon our experience—namely, upon the process of forming and collating percepts, and from those percepts, forming and elaborating our concepts. The result of this process, the direction of the knower back to the known, is the accomplishment of a semiotic relation: by a sign-vehicle (either a percept or a concept, or in any actual case of a concept, both a concept *and* a percept), our minds are directed back towards the object that is made known. The nature of our knowledge follows from the nature of the relations whereby it is possessed; so too, therefore, our access to reality. Since these relations are constituted by signs, I propose a **semiotic realism**: a realism that structures its doctrines in accordance with the nature of signs.[13]

Signs, it must be noted, are never perfect signifiers of their objects signified. In other words, a sign-vehicle[14] never presents the full reality of the object, partly due to its own nature as a mediator and partly due to the limitations of whatever the sign-vehicle effects.[15] Moreover, because *cognitive* signs, percepts and

---

O'Callaghan, *Thomist Realism and the Linguistic Turn*", *ACPQ* 82.2: 337-59) and his response to the response (2012: "Analytic Philosophy and the Doctrine of Signs: Semiotics or Semantics: What Difference Does It Make?", *TAJS* 28.3-4: 325-63) to get a fuller understanding of the error.

[12] Cf. Maritain 1959: *Degrees of Knowledge*, 119-21, 393-96 (especially 393n2).

[13] As Deely writes in 2012: "Analytic Philosophy and the Doctrine of Signs", 348: "'Scholastic realism' is, indeed, as Peirce said, essential to but not sufficient to constitute semiotics on its proper terms as a perspective that already transcends the modern oppositions of realism to idealism, and of language to all other systems of signification." The realism we need to truly move beyond modernity is not simply a recovery of the scholasticism of Aquinas and his school (nor of Bonaventure, Scotus, or any other scholastic of merit), but rather to recover the truth found in that realism and go beyond it.

[14] See below, n.39.

[15] Peirce indicated this disparity (1906/7: "Prolegomena to an Apology for Pragmatism", *CP*.4.536) between the sign-vehicle's signifying and the object by a twofold consideration of the latter: that is, of the *immediate object* and the *dynamic object*, the first being the

concepts, are both expressed forms whereby the mind is actually directed back towards the object through mental operations of collation and elaboration, the **terminal object** (the object as known) may include meanings not found directly in the **stimulative object**[16] (the object as effecting the knower): and these meanings present in the terminal object may or may not be fitting to the stimulative object. In other words, they may enhance *or* impede our knowledge; these "added meanings" may give us a better understanding of the thing than derived from the thing itself, or they may mislead us into believing falsehoods about the thing.

This semiotic realism does not result in a *narrowed* access to the real, nor does it simply mask the real with fabricated objects of interpretation, but rather opens the door to understanding how it is that we truly access the real at all, including but not limited to the realities of *ens naturae*—as well as the ways in which we *fail* to access the real.

2. The Nature of Reality

To say the word "real" in any pre-philosophical context is to suggest the corporeal: what has weight, substance, and an existence independent of opinion. This suggestion is the provenance both of a "common sense" preference derived from our own corporeal nature and of the common reception of the empiricist tradition. That is: both our own experience and our largely unconscious intellectual heritage suggest to us a primacy of things that we can touch, feel, heft, push against, see, hear, smell, and taste. The table is more real to us than the idea of the table, and the person whose hand we hold

---

object in the precise manner the sign-vehicle relates it, and the second the object as more than presented in that specific sign relation. For instance, if I write "John Deely's *Four Ages of Understanding* is a history of philosophy", the predicate "history of philosophy" specifies an immediate object to you, the reader; but beyond that particular specification, others can yet be made, as the dynamic object is not exhausted. I can add, "It is focused on semiotics and how the sign has been treated throughout history", or "It claims the essential difference between the third and the fourth ages is the recovery of *signum*", and so on; I could go on about this or that physical copy ("The spine has taken a beating") or about the pattern of words as a whole which constitutes any copy ("It is quite long and will generally run over 1000 pages"), nearly *ad infinitum*.

[16] This phrase, "stimulative object", is a translation of the ubiquitously-used phrase in both Aquinas and Poinsot, *obiectum movens*.

more real than the one about whom we only read. We may question whether insults slung our way should really hurt, but there is little doubt that rocks slung by our enemies may do real harm. There is a fitting and easily grasped proportion between ourselves, as embodied knowers, and material things, as bodily-knowns.[17]

We thus slide unconsciously into a materialism that excludes much of *what is* from the conceptual objectivization of "the real". No doubt, some blame may be placed upon René Descartes, for it was in reaction to his *dubium sensorium* that Locke and others identified the real with the sensible—while unquestioningly accepting the idealism that was the real danger of the Cartesian revolution—but blame belongs to all who have let continue this narrowing of "reality".

Even Thomistic authors lapse into a linguistic division between the extramental real, expressed in terms that suggest a primacy of the corporeal, and the mentally fictitious or unreal.[18] This division effaces the essential continuity between the sensible and intelligible real by diminishing the role of relation in the constitution of reality. In other words, if we unconsciously take to speaking in terminology suggesting that reality resides in the corporeal, materialists and nominalists[19] alike gain an insurmountable advantage—an often-unconscious

---

[17] Gilson i.1931-32: *The Spirit of Medieval Philosophy*, 249: "There is… a natural relation, an essential proportion, between the human intellect and the nature of material things".

[18] It is unclear, for instance, when the term *ens reale* came into use; it is found in Duns Scotus (e.g., i.1298-1300: *Quaestiones super libros Metaphysicorum Aristotelis, Libri VI-IX*, lib.7, q.13, 64 [10], p.240); the unknown author of the *Summa totius Logicae Aristotelis*; Godfrey of Fontaines (see John Wippel 1981: *The Metaphysical Thought of Godfrey of Fontaines*, 85n123); Thomas Cajetan (c.1493/95: *In de ente et essentia*, 24-25/66-68); William of Ockham (see Armand Maurer 1999: *The Philosophy of William of Ockham*, 75n184); and countless other scholastic authors.

But it is also found among many modern Thomists. See for example Josephus Gredt 1899: *Elementa Philosophiae Aristotelico-Thomisticae*; Peter Coffey 1914: *Ontology, or the Theory of Being*, 42-43; 1917: *Epistemology, or the Theory of Knowledge*: 121; Fernand van Steenberg, 1947: *Epistemologie, in passim*; 1952: *Ontologie*, 24; George Klubertanz 1955: *Introduction to the Philosophy of Being*, 190-92; Joseph Owens 1963: *An Elementary Christian Metaphysics*, 38-39; ubiquitously in Deely, and so on.

[19] Though many definitions of nominalism have been proposed throughout the centuries, perhaps the one which best comprises all its many manifestations is this: the denial that relations as such possess an ontological status independently of the mind, or,

adoption of their preferred framework not only linguistically, but also conceptually—in every discussion.[20]

> Yet, for scholastics, the domain of cognition-dependent reality generally is a kind of *terra non-considerata*. To put it another way, it is *non-being*, given that "real being" for so many scholastics is *ens naturae*, being considered precisively as separate from the domain of knowledge, technical craft, and moral freedom. All of these "realities" are *entia rationis* or, to take a telling remark from Antoine Goudin, O.P. (1639-1695), *umbra entis*, the shadow of being. Here, we have the cyclopean tendency sadly followed by a man who was well aware of many of the issues at play (especially when it came to matters of *ens morale*). Scholastics too often treat "realism" as meaning "natural realism." Without always seeing the implications of their position (and most certainly against their own intentions), their account of reality is quite cramped in comparison with the vistas of reality in which they actually live. I have written about this at length elsewhere, so I will spare the reader my meandering thoughts on this point. But the point remains: dear scholastics, you who are the heirs of the single most powerful conceptual apparatus for metaphysical speculation, there is more to reality than in your *ens naturae*!
>
> *Minerd, "The Analogy of* Res-*ality" [p.126].*

---

being effectively the same thing, if they do exist they cannot be known. Cf. Poinsot 1632: *Tractatus de Signis*, 80/12-20.

[20] In his 1935 *Methodical Realism*, Gilson notes that idealism lays out a problem that is (p.21) "posed in terms which, of necessity, imply idealism itself as a solution." Attempting to muster a challenge to idealism on its own terms already commits one to failure. With similar self-awareness, we must both free ourselves from terminology which implies materialism as the answer and further prevent ourselves from again lapsing into it.

2.1. *Res* as a transcendental

To restore what this division effaces and open wider the doors of reality, two realizations are necessary. First, it must be noted that the phrase "*ens reale*" never once appears in Aquinas' oeuvre, despite its frequency in the authors of the Thomist school.[21] Certainly, there is the omnipresent notion of "being independent of cognition" as what is opposed to "being dependent on cognition"; mentions of *res extra animam* are frequent, and the phrase *in re* usually indicates what exists in a being independent of cognition. But rather than call this cognition-independent being *ens reale*, Aquinas' preferred nomenclature is *ens naturae*[22] or the pairing of *res rationis* and *res naturae*.[23] Since *reale* derives from *res*, it would therefore seem odd to oppose *res rationis* by the phrases of either *ens* or *res reale*. This would result in *res* having not merely an analogical valence but an equivocal rupture.

Second, we readily oppose "real things" to "mental things", and often read Aquinas this way, as though his was the same opposition. In other words, I think there has been a tendency to read backwards into Aquinas our own contemporary presuppositions about "reality" and thus by extension into the meaning of the term *res*.[24] This reading is illegitimate for two reasons: **1)** first that this was never the meaning of the term *res* as Aquinas understood it, as we will see immediately below; and **2)** second, to be addressed in the following section, the "reality" of an object consists not only in its independent existence, but also in its ability to affect what independently exists.

---

[21] See n.18 above.

[22] E.g., i.1256-59: *DV*, q.21, a.2, ad.7; 1270/71: *In Metaphysicae*, lib.4, lec.2, n.13; ibid, lec.4, n.5.

[23] E.g., 1252/56: *In Sent*, lib.2, d.37, q,1, a.1, c.; i.1256-59: *DV*, q.29, a.4, ad.12; 1266-68: *ST* Ia, q.13, a.7, c., to give just a few examples of many.

[24] A tendency that began centuries ago—the slide into a certain privileging of the sensibly-real being common to our human nature. In John Poinsot, for instance, although "res" is acknowledged as pertaining to non-corporeal realities, the overwhelmingly ordinary usage is reference to cognition-independent beings. Gilson advocated trusting most of all in the *verba ipsissima* of Aquinas; and yet not only is *ens reale* anachronistically read back into his work, but words the usage of which he would not even recognize, such as "objective" (e.g., Robert Brennan 1942: "Troubadour of Truth" in *Essays in Thomism*, 7); and although it is a defensible practice to argue the coherence of such terminological insistencies (which one might do with *ens reale*), it is another altogether to uncritically presume their fittingness. Cf. Deely 2008: *Descartes & Poinsot*, 31.

If we suspend our prejudices, apprehending the meaning of *res* in Aquinas should not be difficult: for there are exceptionally clear and consistent texts explaining its use. We will look here at three, that together illustrate the primary purpose of *res* as signifying that which has an intelligibility. The first is taken from the *Commentary on the Sentences*:[25]

> It must be said that, according to Avicenna, as mentioned above (d.2, q.1, .a3), these nouns "being" [*ens*] and "thing" [*res*] differ insofar as there are two objects of consideration in a thing [*in re*], namely the quiddity or intelligible rationale of it, and the existence of it; and it is from the quiddity that the noun "thing" [*res*] is taken. And because the quiddity is able to have existence, both in the singular existent which is outside the soul and in the soul, insofar as it is apprehended by the intellect, therefore the noun "thing" [*res*] is related to each: both to that which is in the soul, insofar as it is said to be the thing of thought, and to that which is outside the soul, insofar as a thing is said to be as established and firmed in nature. But the noun "being" [*ens*] is taken from the existence of the thing...

There is a bit of circuitousness at work in this passage: for Aquinas must use a term before distinguishing it, in asserting that there are two objects of consideration "in a thing [*in re*]": the quiddity and the existence. Both objects may be signified by *res*. In other words, *res* may be used indiscriminately and

---

[25] c.1252/56: *In Sent.*, lib.1, d.25, q.1, a.4, c.: "Respondeo dicendum, quod secundum Avicennam, ut supra dictum est, dist. 2, qu. 1, art. 3, hoc nomen ens et res differunt secundum quod est duo considerare in re, scilicet quidditatem et rationem ejus, et esse ipsius; et a quidditate sumitur hoc nomen res. Et quia quidditas potest habere esse, et in singulari quod est extra animam et in anima, secundum quod est apprehensa ab intellectu; ideo nomen rei ad utrumque se habet: et ad id quod est in anima, prout res dicitur a reor reris, et ad id quod est extra animam, prout res dicitur quasi aliquid ratum et firmum in natura. Sed nomen entis sumitur ab esse rei..." Cf. i.1256-59: *DV*, q.1, a.1, c.: "Non autem invenitur aliquid affirmative dictum absolute quod possit accipi in omni ente, nisi essentia eius, secundum quam esse dicitur; et sic imponitur hoc nomen res, quod in hoc differt ab ente, secundum Avicennam in principio Metaphys., quod ens sumitur ab actu essendi, sed nomen rei exprimit quidditatem vel essentiam entis." We may speak of a being with an eye towards its intelligible dimension: which is to say, in consideration of its resolubility to *ens primum cognitum*; or with an eye towards its existential dimension: as resoluble to *ens inquantum ens* and from there, to *ipsum esse subsistens* as the first cause of it. This is the twofold resolution of *ens* to which too few Thomistic thinkers have attended carefully. Cf. Kemple 2017: *Ens Primum Cognitum in Thomas Aquinas and the Tradition*, 241-46. It is worth noting that, in the same text of *De veritate*, the meaning of *aliquid*, "something", is explained as what signifies "some other *what*", *aliud quid*.

thus implicitly signifying both objects, or it may be used discriminately in principally signifying one and only consignifying the other. The principal imposition of the noun (its establishment in language for the purpose of communicating something) is from the quiddity or the intelligible meaning; thus, *res* only consignifies the existence of the thing—which signification belongs properly to *ens*—but principally and properly signifies the fact that it may be known and defined.

The second text, taken from the *Commentary on the Metaphysics*, confirms and clarifies this interpretation of *res* as principally signifying the intelligible dimension of a being by including a consideration of *res* between *ens* and *unum*:[26]

> It is clear from the previously given reason, not only that these [terms, *ens* and *unum*] are one thing [*unum re*], but that they differ by their intelligible rationale. For if they do not differ by rationale, they would be wholly synonymous, and thus there would be no reason to say, "human being" and "one human". Thus it must be known that the noun "human" is imposed from the quiddity or the nature of humans; and the word "thing" [*res*] is imposed from the quiddity only; while the word "being" [*ens*] is imposed from the act of existing; and the word "one" [*unum*] from the order or indivision. For "one" [*unum*] is "being undivided [*ens indivisum*]". What has an essence and quiddity through that essence, and what is in itself undivided, is the same. Whence these three—"thing" [*res*], "being" [*ens*], and "one" [*unum*]—in all ways signify the same object, but according to diverse rationales.

Here, we see the same points made about the significance of *res*, but with the added emphasis that *res* is imposed "from the quiddity **only**". The existence of the being does not factor into the determination of the noun at all, which signification is left rather to *ens*; indeed, if the principal signification of *res* was

---

[26] 1270/71: *In Metaphysicae*, lib.4, lec.2, n.6: "Patet autem ex praedicta ratione, non solum quod sunt unum re, sed quod differunt ratione. Nam si non differrent ratione, essent penitus synonyma; et sic nugatio esset cum dicitur, ens homo et unus homo. Sciendum est enim quod hoc nomen homo, imponitur a quidditate, sive a natura hominis; et hoc nomen res imponitur a quidditate tantum; hoc vero nomen ens, imponitur ab actu essendi: et hoc nomen unum, ab ordine vel indivisione. Est enim unum ens indivisum. Idem autem est quod habet essentiam et quidditatem per illam essentiam, et quod est in se indivisum. Unde ista tria, res, ens, unum, significant omnino idem, sed secundum diversas rationes."

to be the existential dimension, then it would be entirely redundant to have both terms, *res* and *ens*.

And the third and final text here considered is taken from the *Summa theologiae*:[27]

> To the third it must be said that this noun "thing" [*res*] belongs among the transcendentals. Whence, insofar as it pertains to relation, it is predicated plurally of the divine, but insofar as it pertains to the substance, it is singularly predicated. Whence Augustine says, in the same place, that "the same Trinity is the highest of things."

Thus, not only is the term *res* not confined to the concrete and existing, it is also not bound by the order of the substantial (*esse in*). Rather, as a transcendental, the extension of *res* comprises also that which exists within the order of the relational (*esse ad*). In other words, there may be a "relational thing", not only because some relations may be "real"— a relation wherein each fundament has an effect on the other as a terminus—but because **relations themselves** are *res*, having unique intelligible dimensions.

Thomas indicates this intelligibility of relations when he says:[28] "some relative [names] are imposed for signifying the very relative habitudes themselves, such as 'lord', 'servant', 'father', and 'son', and other such things of this kind, and these are called relatives according to the existence of relation [*relativa secundum esse*]."[29] As Poinsot argues, the distinction between *relationes reales* and *rationis* consists not in anything having to do with the relation itself (*secundum esse*), but in that *relationes rationis* lack the conditions necessary for being *relationes reales*.[30]

We cannot, therefore, understand the full extent of what is signified by "reality" unless we understand the full significance of *res*—not only the substantial and

---

[27] 1266-68: *ST* Ia, q.39, a.3, ad.3: "Ad tertium dicendum quod hoc nomen res est de transcendentibus. Unde, secundum quod pertinet ad relationem, pluraliter praedicatur in divinis, secundum vero quod pertinet ad substantiam, singulariter praedicatur. Unde Augustinus dicit ibidem quod eadem Trinitas quaedam summa res est."

[28] 1266-68: *ST* Ia, q.13, a.7, ad.1: "relativa quaedam sunt imposita ad significandum ipsas habitudines relativas, ut dominus, servus, pater et filius, et huiusmodi, et haec dicuntur relativa secundum esse".

[29] For more on the *relativa secundum esse* and *relativa secundum dici*, see Kemple 2017: *Ens Primum Cognitum*, 282-320 or Deely 2010: *Medieval Philosophy Redefined*, 96-104.

[30] Poinsot 1632: *TDS*, 90-91.

not only the cognition-independent, but the relational and the cognition-dependent, as well; for relation is equiprimordial[31] with substance in our experience of reality, and relation in and of itself as an intelligible *res* is indifferent to cognition-independence.[32]

2.2. The twofold importance of relations

This is not to say that cognition-dependent relations are realities, in a strict interpretation of that term; they do not have the "reality" found in absolute beings. It is, however, to say, that there is something real *concerning* or *about* these relations; namely, the effects they may have on the cognitive agents who perceive them. In other words, cognition-dependent relations may have real effects on cognitive agents.

To understand this, we need to see the specific nature of sign-relations' causality. Causation between two distinct things is always located in the *terminus* of their relation; that is, in the place where the effect occurs. Now, not all real relations have an effect—as two corporeal things may be related through a formal similitude even though they have no corporeal contact (as the doors to the Cathedral at Amiens are really larger than the door to my bedroom)—but only those which are through the categories of action and passion. These relations are affected through the confluence of efficient, formal, and material causality: as when the stamp is pressed into the seal, leaving a similitude of itself in the wax, the one stamping is an efficient cause (and the stamp an instrumental efficient cause), the wax is the material cause, and the retained shape the adventitious formal cause resulting in the consequent similarity.

In such cases, the foundation of the relation is the acting of the agent (the one stamping), the terminus is the reception by the patient (the wax being stamped), and the relation itself—the *relativum secundum esse*—is the action (the transitive act of stamping): the action brings the one stamping and the thing stamped into a relation of efficient cause and material recipient of the effect. It

[31] That is, in a way that both occur equally at the very beginning, such that if there exists one there necessarily exists the other. The genesis of this idea is found through Heidegger's 1927: *Sein und Zeit*, but the precise formulation is found best in Ratzinger's 1970: *Introduction to Christianity*, 132: "the undivided sway of thinking in terms of substance is ended; relation is discovered as an equally valid primordial mode of reality".
[32] Deely 2007: *Intentionality and Semiotics*, 115-36.

is by formal properties in the agent (putting in act the capacity to stamp) and the instrument (the shape and hardness) that a change is affected in the matter (the wax). But this is not the only way change is affected through a relation. In fact, any cause extrinsic to the substance of its effect is clearly a cause through a relation.[33]

Among those causes, the most important for understanding the reality of relations and the meaning of *res* is the **objective** or **specifying cause**. This causality belongs to an object, which is a *res*, either *naturae* or *rationis*, precisely as it is the foundation of a relation with a cognitive faculty. This functioning of an object in acting as a specifying cause is distinct from the way in which an object may terminate a cognitive relation; that is, objects may have two distinct relations with cognitive faculties: one as *stimulative* and the other as *terminal*.[34]

The stimulative relation is that relation whereby the object determines a faculty to receive an impression of the object as some specific *what*. To give several simplified examples: the wavelength oscillation of visible light at ~635-700nm specifies the normally-functioning human eye as seeing the color red; a pit bull's growl specifies the perceptual faculties of the cat (most likely) to perceive a threat; and a child's avoiding eye contact, stuttering, and fidgeting while explaining to a parent how the window was broken may specify the parent's intellect to grasp a falsehood.[35] Thus, the specificative objects are the particularly oscillating wavelengths, the growling, and the body language. Conversely, the terminal objectivity is the object as known by the cognitive agent; thus, in these examples, *this red thing* (say, a stop sign), *this threatening dog*, and *this false story being told by the child*.

Most important for our purposes, however, is that the interpretatively-constituted terminal object may become itself a further stimulus of **both**

---

[33] For a concise explanation of the different kinds of causes, see Kemple 2019: *Introduction to Philosophical Principles*, 45-62.

[34] Poinsot 1632: *TDS*, 25/19-26/1: "Obiectum est res, quae movet vel ad quam tendit cognitio, ut cum video lapidem vel hominem" – "An object is a thing, which either moves or towards which cognition tends, as when I see a stone or a human."

[35] 1259/65: *SCG*, lib.2, c.73, n.36 [n.38 in the English translation]. Aquinas frequently speaks of the *obiectum movens* specifically in regard to the appetitive powers as well, albeit such stimulation always being preceded by apprehension (cf. 1256-59: *DV*, q.5, a.10, c.; 1259/65: *SCG*, lib.3, c.140, n.6; 1271: *ST* Ia-IIae, q.9, a.1, c.; ibid q.10, a.2, c.; 1271-72: *ST* IIa-IIae, q.145, a.2, ad.1, etc.).

apprehension and appetition. In other words, the relationship between a cognitive agent and its object is a recursive one. Thus, the stimulative object of future apprehensions is not simply the *res naturae*, but the *res naturae* together with a judgment about it.

This is not the explicit teaching of Thomas Aquinas; but neither is it adverse to his teaching, for in discussing the nature of relation, he makes very clear that what does not belong to an *ens naturae* may have a real effect on a cognitive agent:[36]

> But there are some relations in which one extreme is a thing of nature [*res naturae*], and the other is only a cognition-dependent thing [*res rationis*]. And this occurs whenever the two extremes are not of one order. As sensation and knowledge are referred to the sensible and the knowable, which—insofar as they are certain things existing in a natural act of being—are outside the order of sensible and intelligible acts of being, therefore in knowledge and sensation there is a real relation [*relation realis*], insofar as they are ordered to the known and the sensible things; but these things themselves, considered in themselves, are outside these kinds of order. Whence in those things there is not a relation really towards the one knowing and the one sensing, but according to a cognition-dependent being only [*rationem tantum*], insofar as the intellect apprehends them as the terminus of the relations of knowledge and sense.[37] Whence the philosopher says, in Metaphysics V, that those things are not called relative because they themselves are referred to others, but because the others

---

[36] 1266-68: *ST* Ia, q.13, a.7, c.: "Quandoque vero relatio in uno extremorum est res naturae, et in altero est res rationis tantum. Et hoc contingit quandocumque duo extrema non sunt unius ordinis. Sicut sensus et scientia referuntur ad sensibile et scibile, quae quidem, inquantum sunt res quaedam in esse naturali existentes, sunt extra ordinem esse sensibilis et intelligibilis, et ideo in scientia quidem et sensu est relatio realis, secundum quod ordinantur ad sciendum vel sentiendum res; sed res ipsae in se consideratae, sunt extra ordinem huiusmodi. Unde in eis non est aliqua relatio realiter ad scientiam et sensum; sed secundum rationem tantum, inquantum intellectus apprehendit ea ut terminos relationum scientiae et sensus. Unde philosophus dicit, in V Metaphys., quod non dicuntur relative eo quod ipsa referantur ad alia, sed quia alia referuntur ad ipsa. Et similiter dextrum non dicitur de columna, nisi inquantum ponitur animali ad dextram, unde huiusmodi relatio non est realiter in columna, sed in animali."

[37] Note here the *recursivity*—as they are apprehended by the intellect as the termini of these relations *after* being known and being sensed. Thus, being sensible and knowable they are stimuli; being sensed and known they are termini; being apprehended as termini of sensing and knowing, they are again stimuli (and potentially *ad infinitum* as the intellect may reflect on its reflection on its knowing, and reflect on that reflection, etc.).

> are referred to them. And similarly "to the right" is not said of the column, except insofar as it is posited to be to the right of an animal, whence a relation of this kind is not really in the column but is really in the animal.

Just as "to the right" is not really in the column, "aggressive" might not really be in the dog, or "lying" really in the child's actions—perhaps because he is afraid of being punished, either by the parent or by someone else—and so on with any other judgment we may make, some of which may be true and others false. Yet because these judgments form a part of the terminal object, they become part of the recursively-considered stimulative object, and therefore have reality not *in themselves* but *by their relational effects*. Being known is not anything in the object known, but it is to the one knowing; so, too, is being believed, being desired, and so on. Something need not be either absolutely true or unqualifiedly good in order that it produce by relation a real effect on a cognitive agent.

2.3. The complexity of the real

No one should be surprised by the claim that what in itself is "unreal" can have real effects—we often react in very real ways to falsehoods and fictions. But, understandably, many may be taken back by the claim that we can and often do in some way make the "unreal" *relationally* real. In other words, when the in-itself-unreal is made a terminal object of some cognitive act, it may further become a stimulative object such that, as recursively perceived or understood by the cognitive agent, it "contains" something other than what belongs to the *ens naturae*.

This intentional constitution does not replace or diminish the *entia naturae*, nor does it displace the intelligible meaningfulness of *entia naturae* into *entia rationis* or a merely referential frame. Rather, it shows that our understanding of *entia naturae* and *entia rationis* is continuous, complex, and potentially complementary. The *entia naturae* remain always primary, for their possession of existence independent of cognition marks a far greater actuality; yet the attendant *entia rationis*, though entirely dependent upon cognition for their existence, may enter into the suprasubjective cognition-dependent realm we call culture.

To understand how this complexification of the real occurs, we need to understand the nature of the sign, for it is the uniquely-human experience with signs that makes possible all that complexity: not only the development of culture, but its perversion; not only the revelation of truth but the diffusion of falsehood.

3. The Nature of Signs

The potential for falsity in the semiosic relations[38] whereby cognitive agents are ordered towards terminal objects follows in that these relations are not merely dyadic (involving two things), as between the object and the cognitive agent, but triadic (involving three), such that the presentation of the object to the cognitive agent is mediated by some third. Historically, this third has been called a "sign", but is more accurately called a "sign-vehicle".[39] To give an example of why this is a more accurate name: in seeing a picture of St. Patrick's Cathedral in New York City, my attention is directed by the photo to the cathedral as it actually stands. This directed attention might occur in any number of ways: I might think of my visit in 2016, or of the attempt someone evidently made to set it ablaze in April 2019 (shortly after the Cathedral of Notre Dame in Paris caught on fire), or even of associated memories, such as the sculpture of Atlas directly across the street, or the expensive shops up and down Fifth Avenue. But to someone who has never been to New York City, or to Fifth Avenue, or to St. Patrick's Cathedral, the picture might simply evoke a notion of a church—perhaps not even with any notion of its Catholic identity.

---

[38] The terms "semiosic" and "semiotic" may be confusing: "semiosic" refers to the ability of a living creature to make use of a sign, such that goals of the creature are pursued through the interpretation of signs (and thus, all animals are semiosic, but vegetative living creatures are not; though the precise line of delineation between animal and vegetation is unclear). In contrast, "semiotic"—used as an adjective—refers to the human cognitive ability to not only use signs, but to have an awareness of signs themselves, to grasp signs *as signs*, from which follows a host of cognitive abilities not shared by any non-human animals, including language (as possessing semantic depth pertinent to the cognition-independent being of objects and thus as opposed to mere vocalization or speech).

[39] Peirce, at times, would use the term "representamen"—sometimes indicating that a representamen is a genus of which sign-vehicle is a species (a representamen requiring a mind), but at other times this distinction seems to fade. Conventionally, in semiotics literature, the two are now mostly used as synonyms (although "sign" is still often conflated with "sign-vehicle"). See Nathan Houser 2010: "Representamen/Sign" in *The Routledge Companion to Semiotics*, 307.

Show the same picture to a member of the isolated tribes of North Sentinel Island, and he or she would not even recognize it for that much.

In other words, for the vehicle to function as a sign, the cognitive agent to whom the vehicle presents the object must have the capacity for recognizing the vehicle's relation to the object. The vehicle does not *actually* signify unless the mind can be actually related to the object, for signification is a *relating* and if the relating is not accomplished, then neither is the signification. Showing a picture of St. Patrick's to a rock will signify nothing at all; showing it to a dog will signify only shapes and light (and whatever else the dog might sense, like the smell of the photograph).

In every sign, therefore, there must be a stimulative object (the significate) which is the fundament of the relation, a vehicle (the signifier) which is an intermediary of the relation, and an "interpretant" (to whom the object is signified) which is the terminus of the relation.[40] We can see this in the inverse direction as well, as that by some vehicle, the interpretant becomes the foundation of a relation to the object as a terminus. We therefore **define the sign** as the irreducibly triadic relation accomplished through a vehicle between a fundament and a terminus; that is, not one thing standing for or in relation to another, but the completed actuality of relating between two beings through a third.[41]

Put otherwise, the sign consists in the relation between an object and an interpretant accomplished through some vehicle: as the smoke (vehicle) seen by the animal (interpretant) indicates fire (object); or the stop sign (vehicle) signifies the law (stopping and ceding the right of way to other traffic before proceeding) to a driver (interpretant); or the word "Imprimatur" on the publication data page of a book (vehicle) signifies to a reader (interpretant) the approval of a Church authority (object). While each of these examples has the same essential tripartite structure, each vehicle is connected with its object in a

---

[40] Peirce coined this term, "interpretant" (as opposed to "interpreter") to expand the possibilities of semiosis beyond cognitive agents, so as to include plants and even inorganic being. See Kemple 2019: *The Intersection of Semiotics and Phenomenology*, 154-55; 166-68; 186-90.

[41] This definition purposefully retains an ambiguity, in that it names neither object nor interpretant as the fundament or the terminus; for both object and interpretant are, whether we are considering the object as stimulative or as terminative, capable of being either fundament or terminus.

different way. The smoke relates to the fire by nature; the word "imprimatur" with the Church's approval by stipulation; and the stop sign with the law by custom. While the distinction between natural and "artificial" (a word with unfortunate connotations) has often been made, this threefold distinction—by nature, by stipulation, and by custom—is more accurate.[42]

3.1. Signs by nature

The universe is perfused with signs, Charles Peirce once said;[43] that is, everything is at least *virtually* a sign, signifying something other than itself. From this fact, implicitly recognized if seldom appreciated, arises all our curiosity about the natural world; and from our recognition of natural objects as signifying, we discover the truth about the natural world. By our sense perception, we discover entities independent of our cognitive activity. But through that sense perception—which is more than the merely passive reception of our sense organs, but an active consideration—we recognize a *something more* than the merely sensed; we perceive *relations*, both fulfilled and unfulfilled. Seeking fulfillment of the latter drives our inquiries into these cognition-independent activities: whether they are laws of physics, tendencies in evolution, or animal behavior.

Thus signification may occur through cognition, life, or even the inorganic; the dance of the spider signifies its desire to mate, the flowering of a plant signifies its fertility, and the rising of the tide signifies the gravitational pull of the moon orbiting the near side of the earth.

3.2. Cultural signs: stipulation and custom

Most of the signs with which we humans deal in our day-to-day operations, however, are *not* signs by nature, or, more accurately, not signs *purely* by nature. Rather, especially today in the electric, digital age, our lives are perfused by cultural signs, where the imposed signification follows a volitional act: in other words, someone—or more likely, a group—chooses to make such a vehicle stand for such an object. These are signs therefore either by stipulation (*ad placitum*)

---

[42] Cf. Poinsot 1632: *TDS*, 269-283.

[43] Peirce 1906: "Issues of Pragmatism" in *CP*.5.448n.

or by custom (*ex consuetudine*). Included among these cultural signs are all symbols, including all words.

A stipulated sign requires a voluntary agent: that is, a being capable of imposing on some vehicle the function of signifying a particular object. Such an imposition follows from the vehicle not having such a significance by its nature. Rather, the stipulated sign receives its order from an extrinsic denomination. For instance, every neologism—while it may draw upon etymology or previous works, or comparable words in different languages—is an attempt at creating a stipulated sign, as are any assignments of variables in mathematical proofs ("let X stand for…"), ciphers, and all signs we have accepted from some or another authority.[44]

Many more signs in our experience, however, are by custom:[45]

> custom either can be the cause of a sign, as, for example, if a people by their customs introduce and propose some sound for signifying; or it can function as an effect which leads us to know its cause, as, for example, a dog frequently seen accompanying someone manifests that that person is its master, and the custom of eating with napkins manifests to us a meal when we see napkins set out, and universally almost every induction is founded on the frequency and custom whereby we see something often happen.

Customs establish signs by "the use and consensus of a people",[46] unlike stipulated signs which come from an individual (and specifically one possessing the authority[47] to impose an extrinsic denomination), and therefore require a frequency of use among a multitude. Slang words, for instance, tend to come from custom rather than stipulation; no one says, "We're going to use 'sweet' to

---

[44] As an example of this latter, Poinsot frequently references the Sacraments.

[45] Poinsot 1632: *TDS*, 278/19-29: "consuetudo vel potest esse causa signi, sicut si populus consuetudine sua introducat et proponat aliquam vocem ad significandum; vel potest se habere ut effectus, qui nos manuducit ad cognoscendam suam causam, sicut canis frequenter visus comitari aliquem manifestat, quod sit dominus eius, et consuetudo comedendi in mappis manifestat nobis prandium, quando mappas videmus appositas, et in universum fere omnis induction fundatur in frequential et consuetudine, qua videmus aliquid saepe fieri."

[46] Poinsot 1632: *TDS*, 279/20: "secundum usum et consensum populi".

[47] Who possesses such authority, and how, is another matter altogether, more suited to questions of education and politics.

mean 'cool' from now on," but one person begins doing it, others follow, and it quickly becomes a customary signification.

Something different occurs, however, in a custom arising as an effect that signifies its cause. For in such a case, the signification is itself something by nature: namely, that *every* effect signifies its cause. The wind blowing causes the vane to change direction, just as the messiness of eating causes the usage (and thus the placement) of napkins; "signification arising from custom is founded on something natural, to wit, on the procession of an effect from its cause and on its coincidence with that cause. Therefore custom as an effect founding signification is reduced to a natural cause."[48] But here, just as within the *purely* natural signs, we may be deceived: as someone might associate, for instance, someone having many books with that person being intelligent or well-read when in fact they are only wealthy.

> Given the poor grandeur of the human intellect, we only come to know more recondite realities on the basis of our knowledge of what is more familiar to us. Therefore, a robust doctrine of cultural signs is very important even for us to fully articulate a general theory of signs. Too often, Deely and his students seem to present these matters as something coming *after* the general doctrine of signs. This is akin to the general scholastic approach, which too often tries to present a doctrine *in facto esse* instead of presenting it, so to speak, *in fieri*. Yes, we need to be careful not to confuse the part (practical signs) for the whole (signs as such). However, our poor human knowledge requires this first *becoming* in order that such knowledge may, in fact, *be*. The ladder must be built up to our philosophical synthesis; it does not descend from the heavens already completed.

---

[48] Poinsot 1632: *TDS*, 279/33-38: "talis signifcatio fundatur in aliquo naturali, scilicet in processu effectus a sua cause et covenientia cum illa. Ergo consuetudo ut effectus fundans significationem reducitur ad causam naturalem."

Likewise, even in free human actions which result in the establishment of customary signs, but still entails a certain naturalness: namely, the naturalness of habituation following frequently repeated acts. That the customary sign signifies as it does follows by nature. Since culture is constituted primarily by customary signs—stipulated signs retaining their cultural efficacy *only* when they become adopted customarily—the reduction of customary significations to a natural principle demonstrates that culture and nature are ***not*** separated essentially, but rather that culture as a potentially ever-growing suprasubjective web spanning not only multiple individuals but multiple generations develops on the basis of a natural property of the mind to discern patterns, both cognition-independent and cognition-dependent.

3.3. Pure signs

In all of the above instances, there is some cognition-independent thing which must itself first be grasped by a receptive power of the interpretant in order to accomplish a significant relation to the object: the blind see neither smoke nor stop sign, and the deaf do not hear insults, for the vehicles are imperceptible to them. Often, such sign-vehicles have been called *instrumental* signs, as opposed to *formal* or *pure* signs,[49] which are not grasped as objects themselves that intermediate between the interpretant and the object, but immediately accomplish the relation; which are, namely, the psychological states or cognitive means of percepts and concepts. These cognitive signs are *also* cognition-independently existing things—considered as accidents of the cognitive agent—but which need **not** be grasped in their cognition-independent being in order to signify.[50]

As John Deely demonstrates in many of his works, it is a mistake common to modern philosophy that they believed our psychological states not to be pure signs, but instrumental ones. Rather, as was the common understanding of the scholastics, especially in the Thomistic tradition and most especially John Poinsot

[49] We must keep in mind that such nomenclature refers less properly to the sign as a whole and more to the sign-vehicle

[50] Deely 2009: *Augustine & Poinsot*, 44n20.

(and recovered by Charles Peirce),[51] all our thinking is by means of signs. Thus, the question when it comes to the sameness of our cognitive means and the objects known by them—that question, I said earlier, which stands at the heart of the struggle for realism—is a question of how a sign can be the same as what it signifies.

What follows is an abbreviated answer to that question.

4. Cognitive Signs

There are two questions to be answered in this section: first, how are our cognitive signs formed? And second, what do these cognitive signs make known? In order to relate these questions to the proposal of semiotic realism as the solution to our problem of meaning, we will consider not only intellectual cognitive signs, but also the perceptual. Only thus can we get at the meaning of "meaning".[52] For, as Aquinas rightly claims in many places, the proper object of the human intellect is the *quidditas rei materialis*—the quiddity of a material thing.[53] Were it not for sensation and perception, we could not get any hold of material things at all; hence it comes as a prerequisite to arriving at an understanding of how we arrive at the quiddity, that we first arrive at an understanding of our relation to the material thing (which, as what is singular, cannot be known by the intellect).[54]

---

[51] Cf. 1868: "Questions Concerning Certain Faculties Claimed for Man" in *EP*.1.23-24.

[52] Few topics, arguably, have received less attention but needed them more within Thomistic philosophy than the interior sense powers, or the faculties of perception as I prefer to call them. While some attention has turned there recently (e.g., Anthony Lisska 2016: *Aquinas's Theory of Perception*; Daniel De Haan 2014: "Perception and the Vis Cogitativa: A Thomistic Analysis of Aspectual, Actional, and Affectional Percepts" in *ACPQ*, 88.3: 397-437; 2010: "Linguistic Apprehension as Incidental Sensation in Thomas Aquinas" in *Proceedings of the ACPA*, vol.84: 179-96, and some others), by and large the question of perception has been treated as little more than a necessary stepping stone between sensation and intellection, bypassing all the many nuances which have a profound impact on both the human intellectual and sensitive operations.

[53] 1266-68: *ST* Ia, q.85, a.5, ad.3; ibid, a.8, c.; ibid, q.86, a.2, c.; ibid, q.88, a.2, c. ibid, a.3, c.; i.1256-59: *DV*, q.18, a.5, ad.6; c.1265-66: *Quaestiones disputatae de anima*, a.16; or *natura rei materialis*, 1266-68: *ST* Ia, q.87, a.2, ad.2; a.3, c., and ad.2. See Kemple 2017: *Ens Primum Cognitum* 163-70 for discussion.

[54] i.1259/65: *SCG*, lib.1, c.65, n.9.

4.1. Perceptual signs

Beyond the conventionally-identified exterior senses (sight, hearing, smell, taste, and touch), the impressed specification of a perceptual cognition requires what Aquinas calls the *sensus communis*, but which I interpretively translate as the "integrating sense".[55] It is through this sense that the sensations of the exterior sense faculties are first collated into an objective whole—a perceptual *species impressa* or phantasm—which the interior senses subsequently form into a percept.[56] It is the percept which serves as the foundation of the relation by which we are cognitively united to the sensible things in our environments as terminal objects.

When we consider all the objects of the exterior sense faculties which may be collated into this whole—not just of particular things, but of the whole situational context in which that thing may appear—we realize that the perceptual objectivization is potentially infinitely complex. But more than this, the perceptual object includes intentions which stem purely from its particular relations to the cognitive agent. For instance, in perceiving a book on my desk, I not only perceive its shape, colors, parts, text, cover image (and all the countless details visible in that image, David Roberts' 1859 *Interior of the Cathedral, Pisa*), but also its positioning—on the desk, to the left of *this* notebook, to the right of *that* pen, at a slight angle from the desk's edge (and so on, potentially with regard to every other item sensibly present), how it reflects the light from three distinct sources—not to mention a vague sense of the time of day at which I perceive it, of the room in which it is perceived, of my own posture while perceiving it, and so on; as well as the tinge of guilt at not having yet read as much of it as I wish (compounded by the guilt of all the other books treated with the same neglect).

An obvious shift occurs with this last—the guilt—for this seems wholly interior; nothing having to do with the book itself at all, but only with my relation to the

[55] Cf. Kemple 2019: *Introduction to Philosophical Principles*, 76-77; 156-58.

[56] We here use the term "phantasm" as a generic term, including but not limited to the collated percept (which is a *species expressa*).

book.[57] The percept on the basis of which the book is perceived involves in its constitution a contribution from earlier experiences extrinsic to the book itself; something more than the mere *species impressa* as given to me by the object itself. The object, then, includes in its terminal objective constitution that which it receives *only* by my relating to it. Considered in retrospect however, *all* of the aspects in which the thing perceptually appears to me, both as a whole in itself comprising many parts and as itself a part of a greater context, rely upon relations, both of each part to all the others and of all the parts to myself.

When a phantasm is impressed upon us, therefore, it is impressed with a potential (and often actual) myriad of relations to other objects likewise impressed upon us. The formation of our perceptually mediated lives is not by an atomistic collocation of sensible object after sensible object, but a continual and multifaceted impression in which we attend to particular objects with varying degrees of awareness of their related objects, irregularly alternating between attending to parts and wholes. This attention to phantasmal objects includes not only the relations among the sensibles, but also the relations constituted by our own perceptual interpretation, i.e., by the collation of new and old perceptual objects through which we render our particular judgments.

This shows that all perceptual collation is discursive: which is to say that it moves from a prior to a posterior, and thus from something better known to oneself to something lesser known to oneself.[58] What, precisely is being collated at the level of perceptual cognition, how, and for what purpose are questions on which we could dwell for countless pages. To answer succinctly, however: we collate individual intentions for the sake of the operative good of ourselves. In other words, we discursively combine, separate, and evaluate both retained (in

---

[57] It is this grasp of oneself constitutes in part the meaning of an object that Heidegger denotes "phenomenological construction" as the intermediate stage in the application of the phenomenological method (1927: *Die Grundprobleme der Phänomenologie*, 26-23/19-23; cf. 1923: *Ontologie: Hermeneutik der Faktizität*, 90-91/69 and 99/76 for an example of this in practice).

[58] 1266-68: *ST* Ia, q.58, a.3, ad.1: "discursus quendam motum nominat. Omnis autem motus est de uno priori in aliud posterius. Unde discursiva cognitio attenditur secundum quod ex aliquo prius noto devenitur in cognitionem alterius posterius noti, quod prius erat ignotum" – "'discursion' names a certain motion. For every motion is from one prior to another posterior. Thus, discursive cognition occurs insofar as from something known prior one is brought to cognition of something known posterior, which was previously unknown."

memory) and present (in sense) stimulative perceptual objects to form terminal perceptual objects upon which we may act: pursuing them, avoiding them, or ignoring them.

Through a variety of sign-mediated specifications of stimulative objects impressed upon the receptive perceptual faculties, and by means of collative operations belonging to the cogitative faculties, we form expressed specifications, *species expressae*, whereby we are ordered towards terminal objects which differ from the impressed specifications on account of those collative operations. We perceive as a terminal object not just the dog, but the threatening-dog-to-flee; not just the food, but the appetizing-food-to-consume. Through the composition of this expressed specification is worked out a **referentially-meaningful** terminal object.[59] By this phrase, "referentially-meaningful", we indicate that the object's meaning is constituted by its reference to the cognitive animal.[60] A piece of raw meat, for instance, has a different meaning as referred to a dog and to a human being, and a different meaning as referred to a meat-eating human and to a vegan, just as the crucifix has a different meaning to the Catholic than it does to the Buddhist. Referential meaning as such, though it may be perfused with a significance provenating[61] from the intellect, is determined by the relation or set of relations between the cognitive agent and the object.

---

[59] Aquinas holds this view as concern human beings, but not other animals, whom he considered to be moved in their operations purely by "instinct" (cf. 1266-68: *ST* Ia, q.82, a.2, ad.3). Greater observation of animal behavior has since revealed that animals have a discursive and collative consideration of the objects of their perception. Animals are nevertheless still determined in their "reasoning" operations, insofar as they are bound to pursue objectives according to a self-referential context of meaning, i.e., "what is good for me", and never to the intelligible meaning of the good itself.

[60] Cf. Deely 2009: *Augustine & Poinsot*, 82-83: "Simultaneously with but logically posterior to the action of the stimulus revealing something of the physical surroundings (that is to say, partially objectifying them), the animal responds to this nascent objectification by adding to it relations based now not on the stimulating source as a part of the physical surroundings but based rather on the organism's own nature and past experience."

[61] Cf. Deely 2010: *Semiotic Animal*, xiii for the origin of this word.

Because non-human animals and their cognitive objects are always materially individuated particulars,[62] referential meaning is therefore always indeterminate—since both fundament and terminus of the relations constituting it are material—and thus subject to change. Not only may new impressions be made, that is, but so too the expressed specification given a new interpretation. Referential meaning for human beings, however, is permeated by meaning which originates with a different and subsequent impression, namely, the intellectual.

But the intelligible meaning grasped by the intellect does not appear *ex nihilo*. Rather, it comes from the objects that we sense and perceive, and the percepts we form of them. Thus, the *species expressae* of the perceptual faculties serve a twofold function: not only do they direct our cognition back towards objects as having a referential meaning but they may also allow us to discover the intelligible meanings of those objects. Provisionally, we can say that it consists fundamentally in the realization of meaning belonging to the object itself, beyond what is grasped referentially, such that the intelligible meaning of the object is irreducible to its referential meaning.[63] This intelligible meaning is what Aquinas designates in calling an object a "*res*", a thing.

We must note that the percept or phantasm is considered, as the result of perceptual cognition, the "matter of the cause"[64] for the operation of the *intellectus agens* whereby the object is rendered intelligibly meaningful and thus

---

[62] Notably, *particulars* but not *singulars*. There is generality and abstraction at the level of perceptual cognition, as evidenced in animals generalizing about singulars based upon particular characteristics (such as skin color, sex, height, etc.).

[63] In his description of [intellectual] "abductive inference", Peirce states that (1903: "Pragmatism as the Logic of Abduction" *EP*.2.227) it "shades into perceptual judgment without any sharp line of demarcation between them". That is, the two are so closely bound together in our experience that there are abductive inferences which seem very much like perceptual judgments, and vice versa, for very often we comingle intelligible and referential meanings—for better or worse. Entering into the nuances suggested by Peirce—and the struggle to interpret Peirce—is far beyond this article. See Kemple 2019: *The Intersection of Semiotics and Phenomenology*, 204-10.

[64] 1266-68: *ST* Ia, q.84, a.6, c.: "non potest dici quod sensibilis cognitio sit totalis et perfecta causa intellectualis cognitionis, sed magis quodammodo est materia causae" – "It cannot be said that the cognition of sensible things is the total and perfect cause of intellectual cognition, but rather in a certain way is the matter of the cause."

as the *obiectum movens* or specifying cause for the *intellectus possibilis*.[65] In other words, the phantasm from which the intellect grasps meaning must be one which is potentially intelligible, such that, once meaning has been grasped, the phantasm is adequate for the intelligible meaning to be realized as belonging to the object that phantasm signifies, either in itself or by analogy.

To take a very simple example, consider the intelligible meaning of a "cube": a shape possessing six flat equally sized sides, with eight vertices, and twelve edges. A single instance of perceiving a cube—quickly, with minimal examination—would not likely divulge the full intelligibility of a cube, of the "cubeness" of it. One must, rather, examine it from many sides, turn it over, approximately compare the sides to one another, the corners, the angles, the size of the various aspects, until finally the percept is such that it may be grasped as what it is; a process which may occur quickly for some, but slower for others. To give a more complex example, consider the percept of both a single animal and of animals in general: naïve thinkers, like Descartes, look quickly at their operations and claim that they do not feel pain. An experientially-rich perceptual observation of animals leads us to grasp the truth—that they *do* feel pain—and moreover that they have particular reasoning and judgment about the objects in their environment, but only as to referential meaning.

The threshold of distinctively human curiosity—which goes far beyond the mere curiosity in pursuit of referential meaning found in other animals—is crossed at ages likely before our recollection: namely when first we recognize that the

---

[65] i.1259/65: *SCG*, lib.2, c.73, n.36: "Alio ergo modo se habet intellectus possibilis ad phantasma quo indiget, ante speciem intelligibilem: et alio modo postquam recepit speciem intelligibilem. Ante enim, indiget eo ut ab eo accipiat speciem intelligibilem: unde se habet ad intellectum possibilem ut obiectum movens" – "Therefore the first mode by which the *intellectus possibilis* has a relation of need to the phantasm is as prior to the intelligible specification and the second mode is after the reception of the intelligible specification. Before, it needs the phantasm as that by which it receives the intelligible specification; and thus the phantasm is related to the *intellectus possibilis* as a stimulative object." Cf. Deely 1994: *New Beginnings*, 161: "This is the 'causality', that is to say, the dependency in being, that knowledge as such has upon the object known. The object *specifies* the knowledge as being of this rather than of that." And 170: "This is the causality that enables the sign to achieve its distinctive function of making present what the sign-vehicle itself is not, regardless of whether the object signified enjoys a physical existence apart from the signification."

objects we encounter are not mere objects, but things having a being all their own, beyond their practical relevance to ourselves.[66]

4.2. Intellectual signs

The operation of the intellect—the *intellectus agens*—whereby this conceptual formation begins is twofold: *illuminare*, the illumination of the material object such that its form may be discovered in the light of intelligibility, and *abstrahere*, or the distinguishing of the specifically-intelligible form from the material whole in which it is found. This twofold operation results in the impression of an intellectual specification, a *species impressa intelligibilis*.[67] Upon this impressed specification, the intellect operates by composition and division and thereby constitutes a *distinct* intelligible specification, the *species expressa intelligibilis*.[68] This latter—and *this latter only*—is the concept properly speaking. Though our concepts begin relatively simply, as habitually retained means of knowledge pertaining both to intelligible *and* referential meaning, over time they become increasingly complex, both in their own constitution and in their relations.

Just as the perceptual objectivization is at first the grasp of a referential meaning not yet-worked-out, so too the intellectual objectivization is initially the grasp of some intelligible meaning made present through what is in perception[69]—which

---

[66] That is, while the primacy of *ens* as the object of our intellectual cognition is a persistent truth—such that every intellectual realization has *ens* as the fundamental object in which all others are realized (1266-68: *ST* Ia, q.5, a.2, c.: "ens est proprium obiectum intellectus, et sic est primum intelligibile, sicut sonus est primum audibile" – "being is the proper object of the intellect, and is thus the first intelligible, just as sound is the first audible")—there must also be some moment in time in the ontogenetic development of the individual human when *being* is first cognitively grasped.

[67] i.1256-59: *DV*, q.11, a.1, ad.16: "intellectus agens imprimit species intelligibiles in intellectum possibilem" – "the *intellectus agens* impresses the intelligible species in the *intellectus possibilis*".

[68] This phrase—"*species expressa*"—does not appear in Aquinas, though it is common in the tradition by the time of Poinsot. Thomas, rather, speaks of the *verbum mentis* or the *intentio intellecta*. See Kemple 2017: *Ens Primum Cognitum*, 248-76 for a detailed discussion of the *species expressa*, as well as Maritain 1959: *Degrees of Knowledge*, 387-417.

[69] Cf. c.1252/56: *Super Sent.*, lib.2 d.20, q.2, a.2, ad.2: "perfectio intellectus possibilis est per receptionem objecti sui, quod est species intelligibilis in actu. Sicut autem in objecto

is as limited as is the prepared phantasm—and which has likewise not yet been worked out as to how it should be understood. It is that through which first contact with the intelligible meaning of the object has been made.

One should not therefore be lulled into believing there exists within the material, corporeal, mutable objects of sense perception an invisible albeit positively-self-existing intelligibility, which needs only to be extracted from the muddled concrete realities in which it is found; as though, within the "fleshy" reality of the natural world there exists an ethereal "skeleton" of intelligibility, made visible through an x-ray-like light of the *intellectus agens' illuminatio* and separated out into the *intellectus possibilis* by *abstrahere*.[70] Rather, it is through the agency of the intellect that these objects are rendered intelligible at all; for their actual existence is not a hypostatic intersection of the intelligible and the sensorial-perceptible, of the immaterial and material, but is an actual confused existence of form and matter, such that the existence of the form necessitates simultaneous co-existence of the matter.

In other words, the intellectual discovery of intelligible meaning is the impression of the perceptual sign-vehicle of a stimulative object's meaning *without* its material potentiality; it is through such receptivity that the soul is somehow *all* things, for while the collated percept involves an abstraction from *this* or *that* particular sensed individual (at the very least from the *hinc et nunc* moment of the sense observation), the impressed specification of the

---

visus est aliquid quasi materiale, quod accipitur ex parte lucis, quae facit visibile in potentia esse visibile in actu: ita etiam objectum intellectus quasi materialiter administratur vel offertur a virtute imaginativa; sed in esse formali intelligibili completur ex lumine intellectus agentis, et secundum hanc formam habet quod sit perfectio in actu intellectus possibilis" – "The perfection of the *intellectus possibilis* is through the reception of its object, which is the *species intelligibilis* in act. Just as in the object of sight there is something as the material, which is received from the intervention of light, which makes the potentially visible to be visible in act, likewise there is in the object of the intellect something as materially conducted or offered by the perceptual faculties [*a virtute imaginativa* – see below]; but the formal intelligibility [of this offering] is completed in existence from the light of the *intellectus agens*, and it is on account of this form that the *intellectus possibilis* has what is perfection in act". Note that *vis imaginativa* here, as is often the case, is used as a generic term for the entirety of the perceptual faculties (the *vires imaginativa, memorativa, et cogitativa*).

[70] We see among Thomists a frequent struggle with the meaning of illumination and abstraction and the nature of their result; see Kemple 2017: *Ens Primum Cognitum*, 171-88 and 198-203.

intellectually-stimulative object abstracts from *all* particularity, except insofar as that particularity may be a condition on the intelligibility of the object.

In other words, perceptual signs make the soul *some* things, which is to say that the reception of the *species impressa intelligibilis* makes present the essential *what* of the object but does **not** produce the concept whereby it is actually understood. The impressed specification is indeed how the cognitive means and the stimulative object as it is known have a sameness; for the impression is an immaterial likeness of that object's intelligible meaning. But, while it is accurate to say—as many Thomists of the 20th century did, in repudiating the nominalist philosophies of modernism and drawing on Thomas himself[71]—that the *species impressa* is a *quo*, or "that by which" the intellect knows a *quod*, "that which", the *species impressa* alone is insufficient for explaining the full process of how the intellect is directed towards an object as the **terminus** of a cognitive relation. This terminal objectivization requires a **concept**, which itself requires *some* composition, which is to say a working-out of the meaning beyond what is made intelligible through any singular impressed specification of intelligibility.

That is, every concept is formed through the operations of composition and division, with the sole exception of the primordial concept of *ens*:[72] the realization of the irreducibility of objects to their precise objectivization, the "something more" of the object which unveils its being as a cognition-independent intelligible thing. This initial realization is the very light of intelligibility: the *illuminare* of the *intellectus agens* whereby all other objects are realizable as having a being beyond their referentially-meaningful constitution as related to the self. Thus illumined, as beings of a potential supra-referential significance, their specific intelligibility may be discovered as distinct from their unintelligible concrete mode of existence;[73] and the act of this discovery is what is signified by *abstrahere*. In that discovery is established a

---

[71] Most especially 1266-68: *ST* Ia, q.85, a.1-2; see also i.1259/65: *SCG*, lib.1, c.53, n.2.

[72] Kemple 2017: *Ens Primum Cognitum*, 248-36, especially 258-59; cf. Deely 2001: *Four Ages of Understanding*, 355-57.

[73] Some might fear that this gives rise to a nominalism: that the universal known by the intellect is not really in the thing. But this is a modal confusion; for the universal is really in the thing, only it is not in the thing in the same precise mode as it has in the intellect. To believe it is would be to confuse the causal principles at work: for there is a kind of equivocal causation that occurs in intellectual cognition, the power of the *intellectus agens* in forming the *species impressa intelligibilis* being in a more eminent mode than the matter upon which it works, such that its effect supersedes that from which it causes.

relation between the *intellectus possibilis*, as that-into-which the *species* is received, and the stimulative object, the percept, as that-from-which the *species* is derived. Subsequently, the *species impressa intelligibilis* is composed at the very least with the concept of *ens*, such that the "*quid*" is the "irreducibly intelligible *quid*", a "what" beyond the referentially-estimated operative good. Only thus can the intelligible species—as elaborated by being composed with at least the notion of *ens*—result in a comportment of the *intellectus possibilis* (or, speaking more properly, the whole human person) back towards the object, for without such a composition, the intellect grasps only a *what*. This elaboration is the formation of an intellectual *species expressa*.[74]

> However, let me issue what I think are worthwhile scholastic words of warning. Kemple is correct that "composition and division" and discursivity play roles in all of our knowing. However, in stricter sense, composition and division are involved in the second operation of the intellect, which forms its own kind of expressed *species* in the form of a nexus of subject and predicate. Likewise, discursive knowledge is the purview of the third operation of the intellect, which also produces an expressed *species*, one that is still an enunciation or judgment, though modified because of the mediate knowledge involved in the third operation of the intellect. In the intellect's first operation, a definition is not so much a kind of "composition" as it is a *concentrating act*

[74] This intellectual *species expressa* requires some perceptual *species expressa*, which need not be the same perceptual *species expressa* from which the *species intelligibilis* was discovered but could be an entirely new one formed for the explicit purpose of giving a concrete realization to the intelligible meaning. See i.1259/65: *SCG*, lib.2, c.73, n.36: "Sed post speciem in eo receptam, indiget eo quasi instrumento sive fundamento suae speciei: unde se habet ad phantasmata sicut causa efficiens; secundum enim imperium intellectus formatur in imaginatione phantasma conveniens tali speciei intelligibili, in quo resplendet species intelligibilis sicut exemplar in exemplato sive in imagine" – "But after the *species* is received in it, the *intellectus possibilis* needs the phantasm as an instrument or fundament for its *species*; and thus it is related to the phantasm as an efficient cause, for the intellect commands the phantasm to be formed in the perceptual faculties to be fitting to the specific intelligible specification in which the intelligible specification is reflected as the light in a mirror, as the exemplar in the example or image."

> whereby the specific differences—often drawn from common and proper accidents as we seek after essential definitions, to the degree that these are even attainable—help to focus our basic knowledge into more distinct articulations.
>
> This is a point of no small importance for understanding the nature of intellectual activity and the way that the human mind slowly progresses from the known to the (heretofore) unknown. Indeed, too often, in my opinion, when Aristotelians and Thomists speak about such progress from the known to the (heretofore) unknown, the discussion at hand is unduly restricted to the intellect's third operation—the domain of discursivity properly so called. No doubt, this is based on the fact that Aristotle himself addresses this problem, born of Plato's *Meno*, in the *Posterior Analytics*, the portion of the *Organon* devoted to the discursivity of the intellect in constituting science. Yet, even in the *Posterior Analytics*, we have a profound witness to the activity of the intellect in a non-discursive domain of pivotal importance: the work of defining middle terms, on which scientific demonstration hinges for all of its strength. Without properly defined middle terms, one's *objectively inferential* drawing of conclusions will be of little use. Indeed, the very abstraction of the sciences (and, hence, their distinction) depends upon the mode of defining.
>
> *Minerd, "The Analogy of Res-ality" [p.136-37].*

But most of our intellectual elaborations do not end merely with a single act of composition between a simple *quid* and *ens*; just as the perceptual collation may proceed potentially *ad infinitum*, as there are always more perceptual intentions by which the object may be considered, so too conceptual elaboration has no definitive point of cessation. On the one hand, that is, we may have a relatively simple concept possessing few notes within its elaborated construction, such that it signifies only vaguely.[75] On the other hand, we may have a concept with a very distinct, refined signification which may signify either broadly or narrowly but in either case precisely.

These elaborations, however—particularly as left vague—may suffer incoherencies. Someone may compose or divide what should not be composed or divided: as a concept of the human intellect which recognizes that it deals with apprehension and judgment of things in the world, but without noting the distinguishing mark of its recognition of the cognition-independent, and thus leaving the concept of "intellect" open to both human and non-human animals. On the one hand, this is a failure to compose the "apprehension of objects in a cognition-independent dimension of intelligibility" with that of "intellect", and on the other, a failure to divide the "cognition-dependent limitations of non-human animal cognition" from that of "intellect". Both possibilities, here, involve the attribution of something vaguely understood to an object with which it is irreconcilable.

It is this irreconcilability between the intention and the object as a thing that renders the conceptual sign false.[76] For the falsehood follows not simply from the fact that the terminal object comprises more than was found in the stimulative object; on the contrary, the elaboration of the intellect in composing and dividing may add in its consideration something to the object which does not belong to it from itself alone, but which is nevertheless fitting and true. All functions which do not spring into existence apart from the cognitive operations of human beings, from which operations culture is constituted, consist in such additions: the designation of offices and duties (judges, police officers, professors, students), contracts, neutral laws, the categorization of specific relationships, fictional characters, tales, myths, and so on. Whether such cognition-dependent designations do or do not cohere with the stimulative objects must be worked out by the labor of the mind: seeking not only to

---

[75] Consider the order of proceeding given by Cardinal Cajetan c.1493/95: *In de ente et essentia*, 3/41, from confused to distinct and virtual to actual. Cf. Kemple 2017: *Ens Primum Cognitum*, 33-37.

[76] This is the distinction between a concept and an enunciation; an enunciation may signify a false composition, as a composition or division without assent, whereas a concept properly speaking presents an object as the terminus of an intentional relation of being.

compose or divide, but in so doing, to resolve what it composes or divides with the cognition-independent reality.

4.3. Signs of meaning

The *species expressa intelligibilis*, which Aquinas names either the *verbum mentis*, *verbum interius*, or the *intentio intellecta*,[77] and which we call the concept, is a sign of intelligible meaning shaped by the intellect to which it signifies that meaning. The *species impressa intelligibilis* is the principle of this *intentio intellecta* and thus the *species expressa* necessarily has some similitude to whatever thing has been impressed upon the intellect,[78] but this similitude

---

[77] i.1259/65: *SCG*, lib.1, c.53, n.3: "Ulterius autem considerandum quod intellectus, per speciem rei formatus, intelligendo format in seipso quandum intentionem rei intellectae, quae est ratio ipsius, quam significat definitio. Et hoc quidem necessarium est: eo quod intellectus intelligit indifferenter rem absentem et praesentem, in quo cum intellectu imaginatio convenit; sed intellectus hoc amplius habet, quod etiam intelligit rem ut separatam a conditionibus materialibus, sine quibus in rerum natura non existit; et hoc non posset esse nisi intellectus sibi intentionem praedictam formaret" – "It must further be considered that the intellect—through the *species* of the thing by which it has been informed—by the act of understanding forms in itself a certain intention of the thing understood, which is the intelligible rationale of it, and which the definition signifies. And this is necessary: for the intellect indifferently understands a thing as absent or present, in which the imagination agrees with the intellect; but the intellect has this, moreover, that it understands the thing as separate from material conditions, without which [the object] does not exist in the nature of things; and this is not able to be unless the intellect forms for itself the aforesaid intention." That the *verbum interius* and *intentio intellecta* are synonyms can be found ibid, lib.4, c.11, n.6.

[78] i.1259/65: *SCG*, lib.1, c.53, n.4: "Haec autem intentio intellecta, cum sit quasi terminus intelligibilis operationis, est aliud a specie intelligibili quae facit intellectum in actu, quam oportet considerari ut intelligibilis operationis principium: licet utrumque sit rei intellectae similitudo. Per hoc enim quod species intelligibilis quae est forma intellectus et intelligendi principium, est similitudo rei exteriorirs, sequitur quod intellectus intentionem formet illi rei similem: quia *quale est unumquodque, talia operatur*. Et ex hoc quod intentio intellecta est similis alicui rei, sequitur quod intellectus, formando huiusmodi intentionem, rem illam intelligat" – "This understood intention, since it is as though a terminus of the intelligible operation, is other than the intelligible specification which makes the intellect in act, which it is necessary to consider as a principle of the intelligible operation; although each is a similitude of the thing understood. Through this that the intelligible specification which is the form of the intellect and principle of understanding is a similitude of the exterior thing, it follows that the intention the

does not form the whole of its signification—which is clear, since there is no error in the intellect's reception of an intelligibility, while the definition which signifies the *species expressa* may be false.[79]

Notably, this potential falsity of *species expressae* is common both to those of the intellect and of the perceptual faculties. Our perceptual judgments are deceived regularly; a distinction, perhaps, that would have saved Descartes from some of his philosophical errors, for the senses are *not* deceived, but only the perception. Thus, we may by default trust the senses, the point of contact with the "exterior world" but need continual re-examination of our own evaluations of what is received by sense, just as we need to re-examine our compositions and divisions of what is received by the intellect.

We need to consider, therefore, precisely what the *species expressae* of the intellect is doing, and how: namely, signifying and, in signifying, attempting delivery to us of the meaning of the objects it signifies. It is a *pure sign*, which is to say, a sign that signifies without first itself being known as an object. It signifies the stimulative object which produced the *species impressa*, but as somehow composed or divided from other objects previously encountered and known through distinct *species impressae*; as, at the very least (as mentioned above), every specific intelligibility—which is to say, any intelligibility delimited against other intelligibilities and thus at least implicitly not only some *quid* but distinct as *non-aliquid*, "not some other 'what'"—must be combined with the universal intelligibility of *ens primum cognitum*, being conceived as irreducible to meanings constituted by reference back to oneself. Ordinarily though, we compose and divide a multitude of specific intelligibilities beyond this basic combination. Let us very briefly consider three examples, one of a purely natural object, one of an object purely objective, and another of a mixed object, that is, part naturally-constituted and part objectively-constituted.

For a purely natural object, let us consider a sea creature. It is long and tubular, with no flippers and at least one dorsal fin. One might, therefore, think it is an eel; but closer investigation reveals that the fin is not spiny and there is no jaw, but concentric rows of teeth in a suction-like mouth. Thus, it is recognized as a

---

intellect forms likewise is of that thing: because *such as each thing is, so are the works it does*. And from this that the understood intention is like some thing, it follows that the intellect, in forming an intention of such kind, understands that thing."

[79] 1266-68: *ST* Ia, q.85, a.6.

lamprey; but how should this creature be classified? Lacking a jaw, it is not of the same family as eels—its evolutionary lineage is different. At some point in its life, it has a notochord, dorsal neural tube, and a few other characteristics in common that identify it as part of the phylum chordata. It has a skull (like the hagfish) and vertebrae (unlike the hagfish). Yet its classification remains disputed, and so the *species expressa* by which we know it remains yet vague; but what is signified to us is definitely this animal, the chordate phylum, of the disputed subphyla craniata and vertebrata (that is: it is disputed whether these are proper classifications, not whether the lamprey has a skull and vertebrae). Thus, even without direct experience of a lamprey, we may form a concept of it, signified by the word "lamprey", which signifies to us this eel-like fish with a variety of distinct characteristics, not only known positively (e.g., dorsal fin) but also negatively (e.g., lacking a jaw).

For a purely objective object, let us consider a fictional character; say, Fyodor Dostoevsky's Rodion Romanovich Raskolnikov. He is intelligent, handsome, impoverished, isolated, dedicated to his sister and mother, driven to a moment of madness by the theory—resounded in Nietzsche's Übermensch—of a man above all concerns, and consumed by guilt after committing a crime in the name of this theory. We picture a man gaunt and approaching emaciation, with perhaps active but wild eyes, dressed poorly, his hair perhaps a mess (psychological disturbance often inducing hands-in-hair activity). Or one might picture him as portrayed in several film adaptations (John Hurt, John Simms, or Crispin Glover, say—none of which fit the image I have myself). Though the particulars of the phantasm may vary from individual to individual, the *intelligibility* signified by the name Raskolnikov is the same. That the character is not a real person allows various irreconcilable images nevertheless reconcilable to the same signified intelligible meaning. In other words, while there is a definite pattern of characteristics and behaviors which constitute the character of Raskolnikov—such that, portraying him as a French dandy interested in chasing girls and partying would be entirely unfitting, and thus, not really a portrayal of Dostoevsky's character at all—because the constitution is *purely objective*, meaning that it exists *only on the basis* of the *species expressae* held by a mind or several minds, there is a greater degree of indeterminacy in its ontological constitution than there is in that of a natural being.

Allow me to climb back onto my hobby horse for one moment. I encourage Dr. Kemple to reflect on the role of *signa practica* even more fully. There is such a fertile domain here that we must develop. Too often, the language coming from Deely speaks of the practical domain (and the culturally-constituted, action-oriented domain) without engaging more fully in this topic. This is odd, given that the issue of *signa practica* comes up in an essay that was dear to him: Maritain's "Sign and Symbol." We have much work to do here, and I suspect it was underdeveloped by scholastics because it seemed to be a fearful "subjectivist" domain. Yet, there are precious clues in their theology of the sacraments. Let us turn there, as well as to the Baroque discussions of political and legal realities / fictions. Let us not get lost in the topics of "cognitional metaphysics" (or, to take that phrase from the youthful Simon, "L'ontologie du connaître") which defined much of the era that formed Deely's own thought. We absolutely must not leave aside the topics which Kemple has so intelligently unpacked. But we also must push further on. Intellection is practical as well as speculative. The same can be said about signs as well. Semiotics alone can articulate the great and inventive domain wherein the human person takes up and manipulates the relations among things and actions precisely because of the infinite amplitude of the intellect and quasi-creative power of the will. Finally, let me set aside the ramifications of all this for the levels of ontology below that of man.

Minerd, "The Analogy of Res-ality" [p.128].

Finally, for a mixed object, one that is part natural and part objective, let us consider a professor. Here, without naming names, I am considering a real person under whom I studied as an undergraduate. Male, in his 60s, round glasses, goatee—always wore nice suits and favored the color purple—very talkative, giving lectures I often found murky, not because his explanations were unclear but because they always led into greater mysteries. But while these characteristics belong to the person, the nature of the relationship, of student to professor, retained a formality; I never called him by his first name, but always "Doctor ______". I did not grade his work, but he graded mine. I did not give him assignments, but the other way around. I did what he told me, in the courses, for, as he said, the syllabus was a kind of contract between us. None of these aspects—titles, obligations, the recognition of authority or of contractual restrictions and rights—exist purely in nature (however much they might be *based* on things existing in nature, such as his superior knowledge, experience, and so on), but require an addition; such that my concept of the human person is joined to the concept of the pattern which makes someone a professor, whereby I know an individual as not merely what he is naturally, but also objectively.

Worth mentioning again is the necessity for actually understanding the conceptual intelligibility signified by each *species expressa intelligibilis* of a perceptual *species expressa*, as a congeries of sensible qualities in which we see the intelligibly-meaningful exemplar particularly exemplified. To exemplify the intelligible meaning I need something which is referentially-meaningful to me as well, something encountered in a context of action in the world. Thus, by a confluence of signs—concept and percept together—the meaning of the real may become an object; not only terminative, but through the ever-recursive process of understanding, also stimulative. Even the natural object of the lamprey is not understood, unless precissively, in its pure nature alone, but in a relational and even referential context. That is: we naturally think of the lamprey not only as a chordate and so on, but as quite an ugly creature—the thing of nightmares, that is unlikely to but may attack a human being. These relationally-constituted objects are the **real**; that is, a reality which includes but reduces neither to its referential nor its intelligible meanings, but welds both together.

5. Conclusion: Semiotic Realism

In a certain regard, the referential context of our worldly experience is such that it includes intelligible meanings as objects for it. It is not that we escape our specifically human frame of reference—that we attain something like a God's eye view of so-called "objective" reality—but rather that our frame of reference is *inherently* dynamic; that we do not need to transcend the self because the constitution of the self—as a cognitive agent semiotically united to the world—is through a dynamic relation to the world.

But this world is not merely the world of physical things, *res naturae*. It receives its constitution also in part from the cognitive actions of human beings. Our reality is not only the things we can touch and see and hear, but also the titles and offices and traditions elaborated between us all in the pattern of relations we call culture. Our ability to use signs, semiosis, in its specifically-human capacity as *aware* of that ability, as semiotic animals, results in the possibility of an ever-expanding objective constitution of our lives' experience. To quote Deely:[80]

> "Reality" is more than a word, but it is also more than hardcore reality as well. In fact, "reality", even in the hardcore sense [i.e., *ens naturae*], would not be accessible at all in awareness were it not for purely objective relations necessary for animals to orientate themselves in the environment, objective relations which provide, just as did the intersubjective relations of the physical environment in the first place, that further interface whereby semiosis in the human animal becomes conscious of itself, and semiotics begins to exist as a postmodern perspective on "reality" as involving social construction, yes, but involving the hardcore elements of the physical universe as well. This is the awareness that enables the semiotic animal to expand the objective world to the infinite, in a semiosis asymptotically assimilating the whole of reality to the level of human understanding, a "reality" wherein truth is an accomplishment, not a given, and where the human responsibility for finding what is true and making what is true go together.
>
> The physical universe may exist in advance of the human animal, but the objective world as open to intelligibility and infinite semiosis does not. For the semiotic animal, once it has become conscious of semiosis, responsibility for the human shaping of that objective world within which the physical environment forms a part becomes inescapable, according to the saying of Aquinas that speculative understanding of being becomes practical by extension [1266-68: *ST* Ia, q.76, a.11, s.c.].

If we are to have a living, thriving realism, therefore, it must be a realism capable of dealing with the entirety of the real; not just the reality we engage directly through our senses, but the reality we experience perceptually and intellectually as well, a reality comprising the relations and *especially* the sign-relations which constitute so much of our experience. Only thus can we discover not only the

[80] 2009: *Purely Objective Reality*, 118.

intelligible meaning of the *entia naturae* constituting the physical world, but also the intelligibility of the referential context of our cultural world, and through both, discover, improve, and defend the teleological meaning of human life. In the words of John Deely, "We need, in short, at the outset of the postmodern era, a specifically semiotic notion of reality."[81]

[81] 2002: *What Distinguishes Human Understanding*, 63.

References Historically Layered

AQUINAS, Thomas (1225—1274).

All references to the digital editions of Aquinas' works stored on <www.corpusthomisticum.org>.

1252/56. *Scriptum super libros Sententiarum* (*In Sent.*)

i.1256-59. *Quaestiones disputatae de veritate* (*DV*)

i.1259/65. *Summa Contra Gentiles* (*SCG*)

c.1265-66. *Quaestio disputata de anima*

1266-68. *Summa theologiae, prima pars* (*ST* Ia)

1270/71. *Sententia super Metaphysicam* (*In Metaphysicae*)

1271. *Summa theologiae, prima secundae* (*ST* Ia-IIae)

1271-72. *Summa theologiae, secunda secundae* (*ST* IIa-IIae)

BRENNAN, Robert Edward (1897—1975).

1942. "Troubadour of Truth" in Robert Edward Brennan (ed.), *Essays in Thomism* (New York: Sheed & Ward, Inc.): 1-24.

CAJETAN, Tommaso de Vio (1469—1534).

c.1493/95. *Commentaria in De Ente et Essentia*, ed. M.H. Laurent (Turin, Italy: Marietti, 1934).

COFFEY, Peter (1876—1943).

1914. *Ontology; or the Theory of Being: An Introduction to General Metaphysics* (New York: Longmans, Green, and Co.). References are to a reprinted edition published by Forgotten Books, 2012.

1917. *Epistemology; or the Theory of Knowledge: An Introduction to General Metaphysics* (New York: Longmans, Green, and Co.), 2 volumes. References are to a reprinted edition published by Forgotten Books, 2012.

DE HAAN, Daniel

2010. "Linguistic Apprehension as Incidental Sensation in Thomas Aquinas" in *Proceedings of the ACPA*, 84: 179-96.

2014. "Perception and the Vis Cogitativa: A Thomistic Analysis of Aspectual, Actional, and Affectional Percepts" in *American Catholic Philosophical Quarterly*, 88.3: 397-437.

DEELY, John (26 April 1942—2017 January 7).

1994. *New Beginnings: Early Modern Philosophy and Postmodern Thought* (Toronto: University of Toronto Press).

2001. *Four Ages of Understanding: the first postmodern survey of philosophy from ancient times to the turn of the 20th century*. Toronto: University of Toronto Press.

2002. *What Distinguishes Human Understanding* (South Bend, IN: St. Augustine's Press).

2007. *Intentionality and Semiotics: A Story of Mutual Fecundation* (Chicago: Scranton University Press).

2008. *Descartes & Poinsot: The Crossroad of Signs and Ideas* (Scranton, PA: Scranton University Press).

2008. "How to Go Nowhere with Language: Remarks on John O'Callaghan, *Thomist Realism and the Linguistic Turn*", *American Catholic Philosophical Quarterly*, 82.2: 337-59

2009. *Purely Objective Reality* (Berlin: Mouton De Gruyter).

2009. *Augustine & Poinsot: The Protosemiotic Development* (Chicago: Scranton University Press).

2010. *Medieval Philosophy Redefined: The Development of Cenoscopic Science, AD354 to 1644 (From the Birth of Augustine to the Death of Poinsot*) (Chicago: Scranton University Press).

2010. *Semiotic Animal: A Postmodern Definition of "Human Being" Transcending Patriarchy and Feminism* (South Bend, IN: St. Augustine's Press).

2012. "Analytic Philosophy and the Doctrine of Signs: Semiotics or Semantics: What Difference Does It Make?", *The American Journal of Semiotics*, 28.3-4: 325-63.

DERRIDA, Jacques (15 July 1930—2004 October 9).

1967. *De la Grammatologie* (Paris: Les Editions de Minuit). Reference to the English translation by Gayatri Chakravorty Spivak, *Of Grammatology* (Baltimore: The Johns Hopkins University Press, 1976).

GILSON, Étienne (13 June 1884—1978 September 19).

i.1931-32. *L'espirit de la philosophie medievale* (Paris: Librairie Philosophique J. Vrin). References are to the English translation by A.H.C. Downes, *The Spirit of Medieval Philosophy* (Notre Dame, IN: University of Notre Dame Press, 1991).

1935. *Le réalisme méthodique* (Paris: Librairie Philosophique J. Vrin). References are to the English translation by Philip Trower, *Methodical Realism: a handbook for beginning realists* (San Francisco: Ignatius Press, 2011).

1939. *Réalisme thomiste et critique de la connaissance* (Paris: Librairie Philosophique J. Vrin). References are to the English translation by Mark A. Wauck, *Thomist Realism and the Critique of Knowledge* (San Francisco: Ignatius Press, 2012).

1965. *Le Thomisme* (6th ed.: Paris: J. Vrin). References are to the English translation by Lawrence K. Shook and Armand Maurer, *Thomism: The Philosophy of Thomas Aquinas* (Toronto: Pontifical Institute of Mediaeval Studies, 2002).

GREDT, Josephus (1863—1940).

1899. *Elementa Philosophiae Aristotelico-Thomisticae*, two volumes, 12th edition (Barcelona, Spain: Editorial Herder, 1958).

HABERMAS, Jürgen (1929—).

1981. *Theorie des Kommunikativen Handelns, Band I, Handlungsrationalität und gesellschaftliche Rationalisierung* (Frankfurt am Main: Suhrkamp Verlag). Reference to the English translation by Thomas McCarthy, *The Theory of Communicative Action: Volume One: Reason and the Rationalization of Society* (Boston: Beacon Press, 1984).

HEIDEGGER, Martin (26 September 1889—1976 May 26).

1923. *Ontologie (Hermeneutik der Faktizität)* (Frankfurt am Main: Vittorio Klostermann, 1988). English translation by John van Buren, *Ontology – The Hermeneutics of Facticity* (Indianapolis: Indiana University Press, 1999).

1927. *Sein und Zeit* (Tübingen: Max Niemeyer Verlag, 2006), originally published in the *Jahrbuch fur Phänomenologie und phänomenologische Forschung*, ed. E. Husserl. English translation by John Macquarrie and Edward Robinson, *Being and Time* (New York: Harper and Row, 1963).

1927. *Die Grundprobleme der Phänomenologie*. References are to the 1982 English translation by Albert Hofstadter, *The Basic Problems of Phenomenology* (Bloomington, IN: Indiana University Press, 1988).

HOFFMEYER, Jesper (1942—).

2010. "God and the world of signs: semiotics and the emergence of life: a biosemiotic approach to the question of meaning" in *Zygon* 45.2: 367-90.

HOUSER, Nathan (1944—).

2010. "Representamen/Sign" in *The Routledge Companion to Semiotics*: 307.

LUHMANN, Niklas (8 December 1927—1998 November6).

1997. *Die Gesellschaft der Gesellschaft* (Frankfurt am Main: Suhrkamp Verlag). Reference to the English translation by Rhodes Barrett, *Theory of Society* (Stanford, CA: Stanford University Press, 2012).

KEMPLE, Brian

2017. *Ens Primum Cognitum in Thomas Aquinas and the Tradition: The Philosophy of Being as First Known* (Boston: Brill | Rodopi).

2019. *The Intersection of Semiotics and Phenomenology: Peirce and Heidegger in Dialogue* (Boston: Mouton de Gruyter).

2019. *Introduction to Philosophical Principles* (Self-Published: Amazon CreateSpace).

KLUBERTANZ, George, S.J. (29 June 1912—1972 July 5).

1952. *Introduction to the Philosophy of Being* (New York: Appleton-Century-Crofts, Inc., 1955).

LISSKA, Anthony

2016. *Aquinas's Theory of Perception: An Analytic Reconstruction* (Oxford: Oxford University Press).

MARITAIN, Jacques (18 November 1882—1973 April 28).

1959. *Distinguish to Unite, or the Degrees of Knowledge*, trans. from the 4th French ed. of original 1932 edition, *Distinguer pour unir: ou, Les degrés du savoir* (Paris: Desclée de Brouwer), under the supervision of Gerald B. Phelan (New York: Scribner's).

MAURER, Armand (21 January 1915—2008 March 22).

1999. *The Philosophy of William of Ockham: In the Light of Its Principles* (Toronto: Pontifical Institute of Medieval Studies).

O'CALLAGHAN, John

2010. "Concepts, Mirrors, and Signification: Response to Deely", *American Catholic Philosophical Quarterly*, 84.1: 133-62

OWENS, Joseph, C.S.B. (17 April 1908—2005 October 30).

1963. *An Elementary Christian Metaphysics* (Milwaukee, WI: Bruce Publishing Co.). References are to the University of St. Thomas Center for Thomistic Studies edition reprinted in 1985 (South Bend, IN: University of Notre Dame Press).

PEIRCE, Charles Sanders (10 September 1839-1914 April 19).

Note. References of Charles Sanders Peirce are to two distinct editions of collected works: *CP* refers to Peirce, Charles Sanders, *Collected Papers*, vols. 1-6 edited by Charles Hartshorne and Paul Weiss; vols. 7-8 edited by A.W. Burks (Cambridge: Belknap Press of Harvard University Press, 1958-1966). This is also available in a digital edition, located on the InteLex Past Masters Online Catalog <www.nlx.com>. Citations of the format *CP*.1.100 refer to the edition, volume, and paragraph number, respectively.

EP refers to the two-volume set of the Peirce Edition Project, *The Essential Peirce*, where *EP*.1 covers 1867-1892 and *EP*.2 covers 1893-1913 (Bloomington, IN: Indiana University Press, 1992 and 1998). References of the format *EP*.2: 260-62 refer to edition, volume, and page numbers, respectively.

1868. "Questions Concerning Certain Faculties Claimed for Man" in *EP*.1: 11-27.

1903. "Pragmatism as the Logic of Abduction" in *EP*.2: 226-41

1906. "Issues of Pragmatism" in *CP*.5: 438-52.

1906/7. "Prolegomena to an Apology for Pragmatism", *CP*.4.536

POINSOT, John [of St. Thomas] (1589—1644).

1632. *Ars Logicae Prima Pars*, in the edition prepared by John Deely, *Tractatus De Signis*, 2nd edition (South Bend, IN: St. Augustine's Press, 2013).

POPPER, Karl (28 July 1902—1994 September 17).

1934. *Logik der Forschung* (Vienna: Verlag von Julius Springer). Reference is to the English translation by Karl Popper with the assistance of Julius and Lan Freed, *The Logic of Scientific Discovery* (New York: Routledge, 2002).

PUTNAM, Hilary (31 July 1926—2016 March 13).

1977. "Realism and Reason" in *Proceedings and Addresses of the American Philosophical Association*, 50.6: 483-98.

1981. *Reason, Truth and History* (Cambridge: Cambridge University Press).

RATZINGER, Joseph (16 March 1927—).

1970. *Introduction to Christianity* (New York: Herder and Herder).

SCHRAG, Calvin (4 May 1928—).

1986. *Communicative Praxis and the Space of Subjectivity* (Bloomington, IN: Indiana University Press).

SCOTUS, John Duns (1266—1308 November 8).

i.1298-1300. *Quaestiones super libros Metaphysicorum Aristotelis, Libri VI-IX*, edited by Andrews et al. (St. Bonaventure, NY: The Franciscan Institute at St. Bonaventure University, 1997).

SOKOLOWSKI, Robert (3 May 1934—).

2008. *Phenomenology of the Human Person* (New York: Cambridge University Press).

VAN STEENBERGEN, Fernand (1904—1993).

1946. *Ontologie* (Paris: Louvain Éditions de l'Institut Supérieur de Philosophie). References to the English translation by Martin J. Flynn, *Ontology* (New York: Joseph B. Wagner, Inc., 1952).

1947. *Épistémologie* (Paris: Louvain Éditions de l'Institut Supérieur de Philosophie). References to the English translation by Martin J. Flynn, *Epistemology* (New York: Joseph B. Wagner, Inc., 1949).

WIPPEL, John F. (1933—).

1981. *The Metaphysical Thought of Godfrey of Fontaines: A Study in Late Thirteenth-Century Philosophy* (Washington, D.C.: Catholic University of America Press).

The Analogy of *Res*-ality

Reflections in Response to Brian Kemple[1]

Matthew K. Minerd, Ph.D.
Byzantine Catholic Seminary of
Ss. Cyril and Methodius
Pittsburgh, PA

I have been asked to write a response to Dr. Brian Kemple's essay, "Signs and Reality: An Advocation for Semiotic Realism." What follows will be a kind of "rough and ready critical glance" over this worthy reflection by the final doctoral student of Dr. John Deely, a man for whom I have great personal affection. We are fortunate to have before us for discussion a work in semiotics by someone trained in detail in the scholastic tradition that was so central to Deely's own work. If semiotics is not to risk becoming a philosophical *mélange*, it needs scholastic rigor like what we find in Kemple's thought-provoking essay.

Indeed, when I say that my remarks are "critical," this word is meant in the semi-classical sense espoused by latter-day Thomists: a reflective consideration of a body of knowledge, heeding *above all* the principles operative therein.[2] Kemple and I share a great deal, both in vocabulary and in intellectual lineage. Therefore, this article will perhaps be somewhat "insider baseball" for those who are new to this domain of discussions. However, stick along for the ride, for I think that there is much good to come from heeding a bit of dialogue, especially when one's dialogue partner makes an argument of such importance.

---

[1] Correspondence to editors@realityjournal.org.
Table of Contents

[2] One might refer to relevant works by Garrigou-Lagrange, Maritain, Maquart, Gredt, and Woodbury to get an overall context for my use of the term.

I. General Remarks

Although my plan below is to trace Kemple's article, allow me several general remarks. Above all else, let us indeed take heed of this article's summons to understand the truly transcendental scope of the transcendental notion *res*. This is a matter of great importance for the structure of metaphysics itself, enunciated quite well by Kemple:[3]

> We cannot, therefore, understand the full extent of what is signified by "reality" unless we understand the full significance of *res*—not only the substantial and not only the cognition-independent, but the relational and the cognition-dependent, as well; for relation is equiprimordial with substance in our experience of reality, and relation in and of itself as an intelligible *res* is indifferent to cognition-independence.

A kind of cyclopean philosophical outlook is indeed interested in the fact that all beings, in whatever predicament/category, are not only apt to exist (and hence, are quite appropriately called *beings*) but, simultaneously have an essential constitution (and hence, are called *things*, *res*, with equal propriety). Yet, the *realitas* involved in being a *res* is of much broader scope, precisely because of the *perseity* that exists in many domains, be they mind-independent or mind-dependent. Wherever there is *perseity*,[4] we have an essence. And wherever we have an essence, we have a being which exists according to its given mode of being, even if that being is "purely objective."[5] And where we have a being, we have a *res*. Reality is everywhere that being can be found, whatever sort of being that may be. (One need only think of the notion of moral objects and circumstances. This is merely an analogical case of the *per se* and the *per accidens*—analogical and, hence, quite different from the case of "natural essences," yet not wholly so.)

Indeed, the scope of the notion *res* or *aliquid* (or, in Greek, *ti*) tempted certain thinkers, for example, certain Stoics, to hold that *res* is the highest "metaphysical" notion, not *being*. According to a materialistic worldview we could indeed say that there are many *things* that are not *beings*: time, space, the

---

[3] Kemple 2019: "Signs and Reality" in *Reality: a journal for philosophical discourse* 1.1 (2020): 87-88.

[4] That is, wherever there is an essential distinction which can be contrasted to that which is accidental.

[5] My sense is, of course, that of the late scholastic tenor familiar to the readers of Deely. See Deely's excellent, late-career work John Deely 2009: *Purely Objective Reality*.

void, *things spoken* (*lekta* in contrast to the physical words), goatstags, and many other such things. If we might use the Baroque scholastic term *ontology* as a synonym for *being-directed metaphysics*, we could say that such thinkers looked to articulate a *tinology*, a *thinghood-directed-metaphysics*.[6]

Yet, for scholastics, the domain of cognition-dependent reality generally is a kind of *terra non-considerata*.[7] To put it another way, it is *non-being*, given that "real being" for so many scholastics is *ens naturae*, being considered precisively as separate from the domain of knowledge, technical craft, and moral freedom. All of these "realities" are *entia rationis* or, to take a telling remark from Antoine Goudin, O.P. (1639-1695), *umbra entis*, the shadow of being. Here, we have the cyclopean tendency sadly followed by a man who was well aware of many of the issues at play (especially when it came to matters of *ens morale*). Scholastics too often treat "realism" as meaning "natural realism." Without always seeing the implications of their position (and most certainly against their own intentions), their account of reality is quite cramped in comparison with the vistas of reality in which they actually live. I have written about this at length elsewhere, so I will spare the reader my meandering thoughts on this point.[8] But the point remains: dear scholastics, you who are the heirs of the single most powerful conceptual apparatus for metaphysical speculation, there is more to reality than in your *ens naturae*!

This main principle is of such great importance: reality is more than the sum of *res naturae*. Today, while driving to pick up my wife from her office, I looked down the stretch of highway (which is itself placed near a mall). One is *bombarded* with so many realities which are cognition-dependent that it is almost impossible to see anything else. Yes, there are "signs," that is, the foundational elements on the basis of which I then interpretively am aware of the surrounding businesses: "here is Pep Boys," "here is Kentucky Fried Chicken," "here is a Jeep dealership," etc., etc. However, there are many other such signs as well, so very many *practical signs*, indicating to me actions taken

---

[6] For all of this, see John P. Doyle 2012: "Sprouts from Greek Gardens: Antisthenes, Plato, Aristotle, and the Stoics," in Victor Salas (ed.), *On the Borders of Being and Knowing: Some Late Scholastic Thoughts on Supertranscendental Being*: 1-17.

[7] See John Deely 1982: *Introducing Semiotic: Its History and Its Doctrine*, 26.

[8] See Matthew Minerd 2017: "Beyond Non-Being: Thomistic Metaphysics on Second Intentions, *Ens morale*, and *Ens artificiale*," *American Catholic Philosophical Quarterly*, 91.3: 353-79 and 2019: "Thomism and the Formal Object of Logic," *American Catholic Philosophical Quarterly* 93.3: 411-44.

by others or actions I perhaps should take: brake lights indicating that I should perhaps slow down; political bumper stickers which (hopefully) bolster my own communal participation in the political order through a kind of common sentiment; small dashes on the ground indicating the entire legal-rule structure for lane usage. Indeed, even the edge of the road, something made up of a particular (naturally accidental) configuration of various elements, itself has a cognition-dependent meaning: *don't pass beyond this point if driving!*

All of this is *real*. Just because it may be a *res rationis*, it is not a *non-res*. It is all a *res*.

Non-being, umbra entis—no! All of this *reality* is of such great importance. Without this insight, the world becomes dust in one's hands, an uninhabitable domain in which we do not see the human in the midst of the *merely natural* to which we would thereby reduce all things. One is reminded of the nominalist position regarding the sacraments in Christian theology: these aren't in any category; they are just heaps of things, words, actions, etc. But, the Thomists (and others too) said quite differently: they are signs; indeed, they are customary signs, *entia rationis*! And yet what a central place the sacraments play in Christian theology (at least in its Catholic and Orthodox forms)! Relation could be thought of as being the glue that binds together these disparate realities. They are *many* in *ens naturae*; they are one in *ens ordinis sacramentalis*.

The same can be said of all the reality that we concern ourselves with every day. There is a great deal of development needed here, and I mean only to sketch out some initial reflections. But let us take great heed that the domain of *res* includes many *objects* which themselves have an intrinsic constitution, an essence giving them a *per se* character. This is of great importance in many philosophical problems (not the least of which is the very reality of truth).

But, let us be clear again and indeed emphasize this great insight of Kemple by repeating his own words:[9]

> We cannot, therefore, understand the full extent of what is signified by "reality" unless we understand the full significance of *res*—not only the substantial and not only the cognition-independent, but the relational and the cognition-dependent, as well; for relation is equiprimordial with substance in our

[9] Kemple 2019: "Signs and Reality", 87-88.

experience of reality, and relation in and of itself as an intelligible *res* is indifferent to cognition-independence.

In other words: let us take the analogical scope of *res* very seriously indeed!

Allow me to climb back onto my hobby horse for one moment. I encourage Dr. Kemple to reflect on the role of *signa practica* even more fully. There is such a fertile domain here that we must develop. Too often, the language coming from Deely speaks of the practical domain (and the culturally-constituted, action-oriented domain) without engaging more fully in this topic. This is odd, given that the issue of *signa practica* comes up in an essay that was dear to him: Maritain's "Sign and Symbol." We have much work to do here, and I suspect it was underdeveloped by scholastics because it seemed to be a fearful "subjectivist" domain. Yet, there are precious clues in their theology of the sacraments. Let us turn there, as well as to the Baroque discussions of political and legal realities / fictions. Let us not get lost in the topics of "cognitional metaphysics" (or, to take that phrase from the youthful Simon, "L'ontologie du connaître") which defined much of the era that formed Deely's own thought. We absolutely must not leave aside the topics which Kemple has so intelligently unpacked. But we also must push further on. Intellection is practical as well as speculative. The same can be said about signs as well. Semiotics alone can articulate the great and inventive domain wherein the human person takes up and manipulates the relations among things and actions precisely because of the infinite amplitude of the intellect and quasi-creative power of the will. Finally, let me set aside the ramifications of all this for the levels of ontology below that of man.[10] That is, however, a topic for another day. It is one of great importance, however, if we are to understand man in his incarnate condition.

2. Particular Remarks in Sequence

I will now turn to my particular remarks. Given limits of space, I will merely march through the text from start to finish, only noting the most important points in Kemple's essay and reflecting on their significance.

First, in his introduction, Kemple summarizes well the issue facing the whole of the modern and contemporary outlook: "What is objectivity?" This issue is not always well formulated by the said outlook. Properly formulated, the question

[10] Namely in the domains of biosemiotics, phytosemiotics, and physiosemiotics.

should be taken to mean: "What is the nature of the nexus of cognition-independent and cognition-dependent meaning involved the knower's vital relationship with known realities?" This question is not merely a repetition of one more introductory philosophical problem familiar to all undergraduate majors in philosophy. Rather, it is a question that is highly technical: the question of *objectivity* as such, i.e., a particular way of being which is more intimate than the union of matter and form (for, as Cardinal Cajetan noted well, following Averroes, because *it is* the known, the knower is more intimately united to the known than matter is united to the form which it *receives*). Wherever there is objective reception, we find a whole *new and unique way of being*.

As a way of being lived by finite (indeed, materially-bound) beings, the order of objectivity for humans must itself be progressive in character. There is a kind of *becoming* in our knowledge, a becoming which is expressed in the conceptual elaboration whereby the confused becomes more distinct, the simple becomes the enunciated, and the enunciated enters into the framework of discursive bodies of knowledge whereby we slowly but surely build up the sciences, ever attenuating our articulations, gathering *in the objective domain of knowledge*, these partial views of reality which we slowly form from generation to generation. And this says nothing of the whole domain of culture wherein our practical objectivity exists: the domains of moral being and artistic being.

If we fail to see this as a problem, we miss a part of reality, as Kemple states so well in the closing remarks to his introduction. And as he remarks quite correctly too, semiotics, as presented by both Johns (Poinsot and Deely), attempts to articulate that without which objectivity would be impossible: signs.

As he opens the second section, Kemple signals the covert reductivism often afoot even in Thomists' minds. The distinction between *ens reale* and *ens rationis*, a distinction that would better be articulated (as Kemple himself notes) as that of *ens naturae* in contrast to *ens rationis*, often turns aside the Thomist's attention from the particular mode of being befalling the cognitional as such: objectivity. But, I've beaten this horse well up to this point and therefore will merely note my pleasure that this is a major structural point in Kemple's essay.

Modernity is the intellectual domain of dualisms: matter and spirit (or mind), matter and ideas, the sensible *vs.* the intelligible, inorganic *vs.* organic, knowers *vs.* non-knowers, nature *vs.* culture, etc. However, through an articulation of the unique role played by relation in reality as such, it is much easier to see how these domains are not hermetically sealed off from each other. Indeed, because of its particular "towardness," relation remains indifferent to *ens naturae* and *ens rationis*. In either domain, it remains a relation. Moreover, through all the levels of reality, we find ourselves faced with the analogical interplay of extrinsic formal causality and signs, through which *communication* is indeed possible, structured in terms of multiform levels of act and potency, this latter being, in the end (as Deely saw well at the start of his career), the primary structural notion in metaphysics (and not, categoriality limited to so-called "ens reale").

In Section 2.1, Kemple provides brief but important remarks on the little transcendental *res*, which I discussed above. The *res-ality* of relations, even when they are "*relationes rationis*," gives a true density to the domain of the objective *as objective*. This topic deserves lengthier reflection, though I think primarily from a phenomenological perspective. Here Kemple understandably draws upon a few texts from Aquinas. However, more than a detailed textual study, my hope would be next to unpack the properly proportional structure of the transcendental *res*, enabling us to articulate the dependencies and distinctions between things in the domain of *ens naturae* and things in the various domains contained within *ens "rationis."*

> ...we readily oppose "real things" to "mental things", and often read Aquinas this way, as though his was the same opposition. In other words, I think there has been a tendency to read backwards into Aquinas our own contemporary presuppositions about "reality" and thus by extension into the meaning of the term *res*. This reading is illegitimate for two reasons: **1)** first that this was never the meaning of the term *res* as Aquinas understood it, as we will see immediately below; and **2)** second, to be addressed in the following section, the "reality" of an object consists not only in its independent existence, but also in its ability to affect what independently exists.
>
> *Kemple, "Signs and Reality" [p.84].*

Let me note here again something I hinted at above in my own introductory remarks. It is precisely by articulating how there can be such "cognition-dependent *things*" that the articulation of *truth* is assured for domains such as morality (but in many other domains of culture too). (Let us note, though, that cognition-dependent beings are a mixture of things and objects precisely because they are cognition-dependent.) The "things" existing according to *ens morale* are not things in the sense of what exists according to *ens naturae*. They are not unrelated, of course, and only a kind of Kantian dualism would separate the moral from the "brute (Newtonian) physical." However, much of the ink spilled among Thomists would be better applied if they saw that the very reality of moral notions is concerned with *things* that are only *analogically* the same as the *things* studied in purely speculative knowledge concerned with *ens naturae*.

For our purposes, this realization enables one to explain how there are *things* such as virtues (which are not merely psychological-subjective states but, rather, are objective formalities which *measure human acts in ens morale*) as well as *art forms, political bodies, institutions*, etc. In light of what has been written by Maritain, Deely, and Cahalan (though, remotely based on remarks found in Garrigou-Lagrange's own *Sens commun*), truth involves the union of two *objects* in one and the same *thing*, that is, one *reality having its own stable, essential structure*, though compositely considered in terms of various formalities which articulate its structure through the intellect's second and third operations of judgment and reasoning respectively. However, much must be done to articulate this matter—reflections of grave importance but great difficulty too. Still, I wanted to note that this theme espied by Kemple, here concerning *res rationis*, shows that the tradition is open to such developments. Like Deely and his astute disciple, I feel that it is ever important that we forge forward by noting the continuity in our own tradition.

Among the comments made in section 2.2, I would like to draw attention to Kemple's important observation that, "Among those causes, the most important for understanding the reality of relations and the meaning of *res* is the **objective** or **specifying cause**."[11] This is a topic of great importance; indeed, I would only like to push him to consider in even greater detail the importance of extrinsic formal causality *as a whole*. I suspect that his own engagement with Deely's work will lead to some clarifications that will help slightly more hide-bound Thomists as myself articulate these points more carefully. The practical

---

[11] Kemple 2019: "Signs and Reality", 89.

constituting of signs involves exemplar causality (which has important relations with our volitional capacities, something not always focused on by Thomists, out of fear of being called voluntarists). However, on the basis of such exemplarity, something takes on a new objectivity as well (or at least I suspect this is one way to speak of the matter). In any case, when it comes to the issue of what we call "specifying causes," I would note that we need to be careful to distinguish objective specificative causality from signative causality, which is a kind of objective causality, though through the vicegerancy of signs.[12]

I think that the students of Deely would do a great service to Thomists if they would declare from on high the role of extrinsic formal causality in great detail. Too many cyclopean Thomists underrate the importance of this topic, which in fact, structures all of reality. Granted, Thomists piously note its role as regards the exemplar causality of the Divine Ideas, but the good metaphysician knows that such lofty analogates can only be expressed on the basis of our more down-to-earth knowledge of such causality, which sadly is underrated despite its ubiquity. We need a lengthy *Tractatus de causalitate exemplaris*, dealing at length (and with great phenomenological precision) with *all of the* analogates of all the various types of exemplar causality. Let the semioticians provide this for us!

And all of this is real causality—*real*, not in the reductionistic sense of *ens reale* but *real* as in the sense that much of the warp and woof of being would not exist without this causality. As Kemple says, drawing on Aquinas: "what does not belong to an *ens naturae* may have a real effect on a cognitive agent."[13] We must push this point to the maximum in order to draw out all of the sap within it. This whole domain of relational effects is of such importance that we cannot articulate our experience of reality without articulating this point. The language of semiotics alone can do this—but only if this language robustly builds itself on the central insights of someone like Deely, who was so sensitive to the domain of *relationes secundum esse*.

---

[12] The point is discussed in thinkers like Woodbury and Maquart (on whose texts Woodbury bases his own). These texts are available through Deely's bequest to St. Vincent College, Latrobe PA. and may provide some insights on what the best of the Thomist tradition said in articulating these matters concerning extrinsic formal causality.
[13] Kemple 2019: "Signs and Reality", 90.

> To understand how this complexification of the real occurs, we need to understand the nature of the sign, for it is the uniquely-human experience with signs that makes possible all that complexity: not only the development of culture, but its perversion; not only the revelation of truth but the diffusion of falsehood.
>
> *Kemple, "Signs and Reality" [p.91-92].*

As he closes his comments in section 2, Kemple uses an expression which I found striking: "the complexification of the real." He then connects this immediately to the nature of relation (the great insight of the Thomist school, really, is here clearly seeing the *ad esse* at the heart of relation, making it quite distinct within the Aristotelian-Thomist metaphysic). And let us not forget, however, that such complexification of the real is involved throughout all of reality, and not merely in the relationship between "nature" and culture. For example, the very notion of "nutrition" is relational, for it is only because of the formal causality of vegetative life that something becomes nutrition *for* something else.

However, that being said, I would like to draw attention to section 3.2 ("Cultural signs: stipulation and culture"), a section which I would have liked to have been much longer, given its importance, at least in my opinion. One of Deely's great strengths was the fact that he provided us with a general doctrine of signs. Indeed, without this general doctrine, we would be blind to the fact that semiotics is a question of being as being (and, hence, of *reality as real*), and not merely a question of human knowledge and "subjectivity" (in the modern sense of the word). However, that being said, the domain of semiotic reality most familiar to us is the domain of our own making, the one that we inherit culturally and ourselves actively bear into the future.

Given the poor grandeur of the human intellect, we only come to know more recondite realities on the basis of our knowledge of what is more familiar to us. Therefore, a robust doctrine of cultural signs is very important even for us to fully articulate a general theory of signs. Too often, Deely and his students seem to present these matters as something coming *after* the general doctrine of signs. This is akin to the general scholastic approach, which too often tries to present a doctrine *in facto esse* instead of presenting it, so to speak, *in fieri*. Yes, we need to be careful not to confuse the part (practical signs) for the whole (signs as such). However, our poor human knowledge requires this first *becoming* in order that such knowledge may, in fact, *be*. The ladder must be built up to our philosophical synthesis; it does not descend from the heavens already completed. (I recall Fr. Garrigou-Lagrange once stating that this was the great merit of Aristotle's treatment of definition in the second book of the *Posterior Analytics*: in this text, we get to witness the great philosopher in the midst of discovering this very doctrine, on which he likely had meditated for decades during his days with Plato. It is, thus, far livelier than in the ready-made presentations of formal logic written by Aristotle's very able Scholastic disciples.)

Our most proximate experiential basis of semiosis is found precisely in this domain of stipulation and culture. The task of the semiotician, I think, is to show the *foundational realism* implied by this very experience. Perhaps a fear lingers that a focus on culture will end in shipwreck upon the idealistic shoals of modernity (as well in a form of bondage to "post-modernist" semiotics, which in fact is not *post*-modern but, instead, a kind of apotheosis of modern epistemological trends). In any case, I wish that we had much lengthier reflection, from the very start of semiotic discussions, on the phenomenon of stipulated signs. One must be careful not to get trapped here and lose the overall (and utterly general) character of semiotic activity which structures all of reality. Nonetheless, this is the domain we know best, and that is where we must humbly begin.

A detailed conceptual articulation of these points, however, will require a great deal of expertise on the part of the semiotician who is looking to be careful. Above all, it will require much more attention to be paid to the question of *signa practica*. This is very difficult to do from within the scholastic tradition in which all followers of Deely (rightly) rejoice to live their intellectual lives—but it is only there that it can be done indeed. The scholastics of Poinsot's day were quite taken up with this topic in the domain of the sacraments. Yes, we must also turn to the secular treatments of these topics where they can be found in those who were influenced by scholasticism, especially in the world of German scholasticism, at least from what I have uncovered in my own research up to this day.[14] However, in order to be fully forearmed, we must master that very difficult space that is found in the discussions of the reality and causality of the

---

[14] I would add, too, it is important to consider the debates over so-called intentional causality proposed by Fr. Cardinal Louis Billot, S.J.

sacraments. The followers of Deely would do well to consult, here, the text of Poinsot, which remains strikingly developed in comparison with many others of his era (though, the text that we have, solely in the Vivès edition, is less likely to be fully his own, from what I recall as I write these remarks). Moreover, the clearest articulation of the position taken by Poinsot can be found both in Maritain's remarks in "Sign and Symbol," as well as in the work of Fr. Emmanuel Doronzo, who is a faithful and well-informed articulator of the Thomist school, a man whose work should be better known than it is.

Though this is something that will require a great deal of work, I think it is a point of pressing importance, one that I wish more of the followers of Deely would emphasize. John himself seemed to miss this point, alas, because of the methodological limitations he placed upon himself (something that his wife, Brooke, has made abundantly clear to me on this particular topic). I think that the treatment of the semiotics of practical intellection could change the face of Thomism, if only it is done right. I want to encourage Kemple, who is well armed for this fight, to play his role in this conquest.

As I quickly move to my conclusion, I would merely like to focus on some things in section 4.2 which are of great importance. It has been my experience that many Thomists who are vaguely aware of Deely's work in semiotics do not understand the importance of what he says regarding the *species expressa intellecta* (or "internal word," concept, or whatever other term one wishes to use). Thomists are rightly jeered when they come off as treating intellection as a kind of "spotlight" (or, alas, x-ray) aimed by the agent intellect at potential intelligibilities actualized by intellection. They do not reflect on how this beam works! (I have heard this critique registered even by thinkers who are disposed positively toward Thomism.) Kemple's reflections on this topic are quite important, and the reader should pay heed to them.

> That is, every concept is formed through the operations of composition and division, with the sole exception of the primordial concept of *ens*: the realization of the irreducibility of objects to their precise objectivization, the "something more" of the object which unveils its being as a cognition-independent intelligible thing. This initial realization is the very light of intelligibility: the *illuminare* of the *intellectus agens* whereby all other objects are realizable as having a

being beyond their referentially-meaningful constitution as related to the self.

Kemple, "Signs and Reality" [p.106].

However, let me issue what I think are worthwhile scholastic words of warning. Kemple is correct that "composition and division" and discursivity play roles in all of our knowing. However, in stricter sense, composition and division are involved in the second operation of the intellect, which forms its own kind of expressed *species* in the form of a nexus of subject and predicate. Likewise, discursive knowledge is the purview of the third operation of the intellect, which also produces an expressed *species*, one that is still an enunciation or judgment, though modified because of the mediate knowledge involved in the third operation of the intellect. In the intellect's first operation, a definition is not so much a kind of "composition" as it is a *concentrating act* whereby the specific differences—often drawn from common and proper accidents as we seek after essential definitions, to the degree that these are even attainable— help to focus our basic knowledge into more distinct articulations.

This is a point of no small importance for understanding the nature of intellectual activity and the way that the human mind slowly progresses from the known to the (heretofore) unknown. Indeed, too often, in my opinion, when Aristotelians and Thomists speak about such progress from the known to the (heretofore) unknown, the discussion at hand is unduly restricted to the intellect's third operation—the domain of discursivity properly so called. No doubt, this is based on the fact that Aristotle himself addresses this problem, born of Plato's *Meno*, in the *Posterior Analytics*, the portion of the *Organon* devoted to the discursivity of the intellect in constituting science. Yet, even in the *Posterior Analytics*, we have a profound witness to the activity of the intellect in a non-discursive domain of pivotal importance: the work of defining middle terms, on which scientific demonstration hinges for all of its strength. Without properly defined middle terms, one's *objectively inferential* drawing of conclusions will be of little use.[15] Indeed, the very abstraction of the sciences (and, hence, their distinction) depends upon the mode of defining.[16]

The first operation of the human intellect is of great importance.[17] Here, in the search for definitions, we have a true operation of νους ("direct intellectual

---

[15] On objectively inferential syllogistic inference—which is not the only sort of inference that one can draw—see the lengthy explanatory note in Reginald Garrigou-Lagrange 1934: *The Sense of Mystery*, 28-9n41-42.

[16] See Poinsot 1632: *The Material Logic of John of St. Thomas* [*Cursus philosophicus, ars logica*, pt. 2], q.27, a.1 (p. 558-59): "But, if immateriality is the root of intelligibility, and if, consequently, diverse immateriality is the root of diverse intelligibility, it plainly follows that the root and principle of diverse scientific knowability is diverse immateriality and abstraction, considered not absolutely and apart from all complexity, but in its movement from premises to conclusions. In sciences, the premises and the instruments of proof are the first principles and their definitions, for it is by the first principles and the definitions that the properties are demonstrated of the subject. These definitions and principles are diverse insofar as they use diverse ways of defining or explaining quiddities; this is the same as to involve diverse kinds of immateriality. Indeed, if what renders a thing intelligible is immateriality, and if diverse ways of understanding are caused by diversity in immateriality, and if diverse ways of understanding are caused by diversity in immateriality, diverse immateriality causes also diversity in understanding the quiddity, in other words, diversity in defining. Thus, diversity in the way of defining or understanding the quiddity is the same as diverse immateriality. But where there is diversity in the way of defining, there is also, consequently, diversity in the way of demonstrating, since the principles by which demonstration is effected in the sciences are definitions." The whole article bears reading.

[17] And, this holds, in my opinion, for the case of analogy. The Thomist school's position concerning the analogy of proper proportionality, especially as explained by John of St. Thomas and Yves Simon seems to be pregnant with implications regarding the interactions of the various acts of the intellect. The so-called imperfect abstraction (by which a given analogous notion is only quasi-abstracted from its analogates) indicates a kind of vital concourse between the three operations of the intellect. Thus, there is a quasi-definition of properly proportional analogous terms as well—though, such quasi-definitions are not by way of genus and species but, rather, by way of order among their analogates. Read in light of certain comments in the article by Fr. Garrigou-Lagrange cited in the next note, I believe that Yves Simon's work on this topic can be developed in this direction to great benefit. Once more, this great domain of intellectual activity bears witness to what Kemple acknowledges in his article. See Yves Simon 1970: "On Order in Analogical Sets,", 135–71.

Great illumination here could be drawn from reflections offered by Deely, who importantly notes the role of language in the process of analogy. The presupposed

insight")[18] pushing onward as the intellect seeks to define the terms that it uses. Beginning with the dim light of a confused and vague concept, we have a true task before us: the expression of one and the same concept, though through genus and specific difference, by which we express the same notion more clearly and distinctly. The product of the first operation of the intellect is an intellectual word by which we express to ourselves this defined "insight" into the reality in question. Certainly, a great deal of reasoning is needed to tease out the various accidents, properties, genera, and species involved. Indeed, to this end, I suspect all of us who hold Aristotle dear would gain much by reflecting at much greater length on the *Topics*, which provides us a kind of organized guide for such a search for the various "predicables" involved in a definition.[19] Yet such reasoning merely opens the door to the basic insights which themselves are not

---

analogical noetic and linguistic elements interweave in important ways. See John N. Deely 2002: "The Absence of Analogy," *The Review of Metaphysics* 55.3: 521–50. In particular, see his summary remarks on p. 548: "Analogy is but secondarily a class of terms within language. Primarily and essentially, analogy is rather a process within language, the process whereby two terms come to be understood through the meaning of a common third, and so a part of the larger process whereby language is a living reality, wherein, by a variety of often unexpected, simple chance events, the meaning of one linguistic element enters into and modifies the meaning of another previously unrelated term." While there is a sense of "real" analogy among beings in a mind-independent fashion (without which our knowledge would be unfounded), we should always remember that analogical unity is first of all something contrasted to other kinds of unity in the domain of knowledge and language. Analogicity is a second intentional relationship. Yet, that is a topic for a much broader and more nuanced discussion!

[18] See ibid, 23n31: "It is understanding, νους, that progressively passes from the first vague [confuse] intellectual apprehension (before any judgement or reasoning) to distinct intellectual apprehension. To accomplish this, it uses as its instruments (in a sense inferior to it) ascending comparative induction and descending division. However, these are only instruments for it, and the real definition attained by this process exceeds these instruments." Moreover, see Reginald Garrigou-Lagrange 1935: "De Investigatione definitionum secundum Aristotelem et S. Thomam. Ex posteriorum Analyt. L. II, C. 12-14; L. 13-19 Commentarii S. Thomae," *Acta Pont. Academiae Romanae S. Thomae Aq. et Religionis Catholicae* 2: 193-201. This essay will be included in a volume to be published by Cluny Media in December 2019. For interesting parallels in the domain of a kind of Aristotelianized phenomenology, see Sokolowski 1992: "Making Distinctions," in *Pictures, Quotations, and Distinctions: Fourteen Essays in Phenomenology*: 55–91.

[19] For reflection on this point see Régis 1935: *L'Opinion selon Aristote*; Gardeil 1911: "La certitude probable," *Revue des Sciences philosophiques et théologiques* 5: 237-66, 441-85; 1911: "La topicité," *Revue des Sciences philosophiques et théologiques* 5: 750-57.

proven.[20] I have not said everything necessary here, but these remarks suffice for laying out the basic point about the first operation of the intellect.

There is a different sort of intellectual word formed by the intellect's second operation. This operation involves the interconnecting of two notions into a complex nexus, an *enunciable statement*, on which a judgment is rendered.[21] A statement presupposes its terms: "Virtues are *habitus*" is not the same thing as "Virtue: an elicitive habitus." The latter merely defines, the former combines the two in a new kind of relation. This is why there are new logical second intentions involved in the second operation of the intellect. Think of the square of opposition from introductory logic courses. All of these relationships among statements are various *relationes rationis* belonging the domain of the second operation of the intellect. Our mind is doing something different than defining here. It is a new sort of intellection, and for this reason, a new kind of *verbum* is psychologically formed by the intellect.[22]

Our language itself indicates the direction that our intellect is inclined, however, as it seeks to reach its perfection. By a bit of terminological sloppiness, we tend to refer to statements as "propositions." However, propositions *precisely as such* belong only to the domain of syllogistic reasoning. By entering into chains of reasoning, statements become propositions, the causes of our drawing of conclusions, and in these conclusions, we have a new sort of knowledge. In the light of the major premise, "Virtues are *habitus*," and the minor premise, "*Habitus* are enduring states of character," we draw the (bland but true) conclusion, "Virtues are enduring states of character." The conclusion is known mediately, for it is only known through the *discursus* of reason. This is why John of St. Thomas held that the third operation of the intellect produces an altered

---

[20] Although, yes, one definition can be proven by another, as when an essential definition is proven through a definition drawn from final causality. Not everything can be discussed here, though, in a review, so I ask the reader to mercifully consider the limitations of the genre.

[21] Regarding the distinction between enunciation and judgment see Maritain 1933: *Elements de philosophie, tome 2: L'ordre des concepts*, in the English translation by Imelda Choquette, *An Introduction to Logic*, 84–98; and Simon 1934: *Introduction à l'ontologie du connaître*, in the English translation by Vukan Kuic and Richard J. Thompson, *Introduction to Metaphysics of Knowledge*, 136–58.

[22] On the earlier history of this point, see de Muralt 1991: "La doctrine médiéviale de l'esse obiectivum" in *L'enjeu de la philosphie médiévale: études thomistes, scotistes, occamiennes*: 90-167 (esp. 127ff). Also see the next note.

kind of derivative product that is akin to what is produced by the second operation of the intellect. (It does not, note well, produce a wholly new kind of *verbum*, however.)[23]

Much more could be said about this third operation of the intellect. Here we have the whole domain of rhetorical, "poetical," non-demonstrative ("topical"), and demonstrative reasoning. Indeed, the final domain of reasoning is itself sub-differentiated into that which is science and that which is wisdom, and as I argue elsewhere, the latter two ought not to be generically collapsed into each other.[24] However, what I have said suffices for making quite clear that the activity of intellection is great Imagine, likewise, then, what must be added when we consider that *practical* intellection involves the entire domain of imperative discourse as well—an imperative discourse that involves appetite!

I should add, in passing, that this entire presupposed noetic shows that there cannot be a simplistic meeting of contemporary logic with traditional, Aristotelian logic. The presupposed ontology and phenomenology of mental acts is quite different, and any attempt to dress up Aristotelian logic in contemporary, nominalistic garb will in fact bring about a substantial change in the Aristotelian schema. Alas, such a meeting of systems will take much more work than many realize, perhaps above all, those who style themselves Analytic Thomists. But progress forward cannot be made by merely ignoring the significant presuppositions of the Aristotelian position itself. There is much to be learned from the Baroque logicians in this regard, but such a task is quite

---

[23] For John of St. Thomas's own position, see *Cursus philosophicus thomisticus*, ed. Beatus Reiser, vol. 3 (*Naturalis philosophiae*, vol. 2), q.11, a.3 (esp. 372a7-373b17). He concludes: "And thus, I concede that the third operation has a distinct verbum since it is a distinct operation. *However, it is modally, not really, distinct from what is represented in its own propositions*. But, when one proceeds from a simple apprehension to a composite manifestation, a distinct object shines forth in the quiddity or truth to be manifested. And thus, discourse according to causality (i.e., according to illation) presupposes discourse according to succession (i.e., according to many succeeding propositions), as St. Thomas says in 1266-68: *ST* Ia, q.14, a.7. *However, it does not make one* [*concept / verbum*] *out of many propositions*" (my translation, italics added)

[24] This is the subject of a lengthy study entitled "Wisdom be Attentive: The Noetic Structure of Sapiential Knowledge" to appear in *Nova et Vetera*. For an insightful study noting the distinction between the notion of science and wisdom, see Muñiz 1958: *The Work of Theology*.

daunting. One understands why Maritain abandoned his attempt to write a contemporary material logic![25]

> In a certain regard, the referential context of our worldly experience is such that it includes intelligible meanings as objects for it. It is not that we escape our specifically human frame of reference—that we attain something like a God's eye view of so-called "objective" reality—but rather that our frame of reference is *inherently* dynamic; that we do not need to transcend the self because the constitution of the self—as a cognitive agent semiotically united to the world—is through a dynamic relation to the world.
>
> But this world is not merely the world of physical things, *res naturae*. It receives its constitution also in part from the cognitive actions of human beings. Our reality is not only the things we can touch and see and hear, but also the titles and offices and traditions elaborated between us all in the pattern of relations we call culture. Our ability to use signs, semiosis, in its specifically-human capacity as *aware* of that ability, as semiotic animals, results in the possibility of an ever-expanding objective constitution of our lives' experience.
>
> *Kemple, "Signs and Reality" [p.114-15].*

Now, having said all of this, Kemple's thematic point is of great importance. Human knowledge is achieved through a lengthy (and, technically, unending) process of articulation, improvement, and interrelating of concepts. (Indeed, it is shot through with this as a kind of historicity which at once freights and enables it *qua human*.) Kemple is right to tease out this point. I hope to see much more from him in the future on this important topic. However, I believe that such reflections must be undertaken in continuity with the later Thomist

[25] See Maritain i.1920-40: "Grande logique, ou Logique de la raison vraie," in *Oevres complètes*, vol. 2: 667-763.

school's treatment of these matters. Great strides can be made in this regard, once more showing that the semiotic outlook can incorporate the truths of the past while striding forward confidently.

Finally, I want to put a "plug" in here, also, for the topic dear to Deely's students and noted by Kemple, namely, the way that such expression is also involved in the estimative sense / cogitative power. From the perspective of psychology, this is very important, and we could add the same regarding memory and even the non-active imagination. (Sometimes, at least among Arab Aristotelians if I recall correctly, the estimative sense was referred to as the active imagination.) However, I have no further thematic point to make in this regard for our purposes in this review article.

3. Conclusion

Temporal constraints prevent me from going on at greater length concerning this excellent article. Kemple has provided us with a worthy advocation for a semiotic form of realism. We can only hope that he and others will continue to develop these themes at greater length. If at times I have expressed my frustrations with "Thomists," this is only because I share similar frustrations to those felt by John Deely: they do not embrace the full vitality of their patrimony. Everything that the modern person has desired to articulate regarding the true grandeur of the human person—a finite grandeur, no doubt, indeed one which ultimately will not find fulfillment except by receiving it from an order that is higher than nature—can be articulated by the vocabulary of the Thomist school, if only its adherents listen, however, to its members who advocate on behalf of the "way of signs."

References Historically Layered

AQUINAS, Thomas (1225—1274).

1266-68. *Summa theologiae, prima pars* (*ST* Ia).

DEELY, John (26 April 1942—2017 January 7).

1982. *Introducing Semiotic: Its History and Its Doctrine* (Bloomington, IN: Indiana University Press, 1984).

2002. "The Absence of Analogy," *The Review of Metaphysics*, 55.3: 521-50.

2009. *Purely Objective Reality* (Berlin: Mouton de Gruyter).

DE MURALT, André (1931 September 1—).

1991. "La doctrine médiéviale de l'esse obiectivum" in *L'enjeu de la philosphie médiévale: études thomistes, scotistes, occamiennes* (Leiden: E.J. Brill, 1991), 90-167.

DOYLE, John P.

2012. "Sprouts from Greek Gardens: Antisthenes, Plato, Aristotle, and the Stoics," in *On the Borders of Being and Knowing: Some Late Scholastic Thoughts on Supertranscendental Being*, ed. Victor M. Salas (Leuven: Leuven University Press, 2012), 1-17.

GARDEIL, Ambroise (29 March 1859—1931 October 2).

1911. "La certitude probable," *Revue des Sciences philosophiques et théologiques*, 5: 237-66, 441-85.

1911. "La topicité," *Revue des Sciences philosophiques et théologiques*, 5: 750-57.

GARRIGOU-LAGRANGE, Reginald (21 February 1877—1964 February 15).

1934. *Le Sens du mystère et le clair-obscur intellectuel* (Paris: Desclée de Brouwer, 1934); *The Sense of Mystery*, trans. Matthew K. Minerd (Steubenville, OH: Emmaus Academic, 2017).

1935. "De Investigatione definitionum secundum Aristotelem et S. Thomam. Ex posteriorum Analyt. L. II, C. 12-14; L. 13-19 Commentarii S. Thomae." *Acta Pont. Academiae Romanae S. Thomae Aq. et Religionis Catholicae*, 2: 193-201.

MARITAIN, Jacques (18 November 1882—1973 April 28).

1933. *Elements de philosophie, tome 2: L'ordre des concepts (I. Petite logique / logique formelle)* (Paris: Téqui, 1933); *An Introduction to Logic*, trans. Imelda Choquette (London: Sheed & Ward, 1946).

i.1920-40. "Grande logique, ou Logique de la raison vraie," in *Oevres complètes*, vol. 2 (Fribourg, CH: Éditions Universitaires, 1987): 667-763.

MINERD, Matthew

2017. "Beyond Non-Being: Thomistic Metaphysics on Second Intentions, *Ens morale*, and *Ens artificiale*," *American Catholic Philosophical Quarterly*, 91.3: 353-79.

2019. "Thomism and the Formal Object of Logic," *American Catholic Philosophical Quarterly*, 93.3: 411-44.

MUÑIZ, Francisco P.

1958. *The Work of Theology*, trans. John P. Reid (Washington, D.C.: The Thomist Press, 1958).

POINSOT, John [of St. Thomas] (1589—1644).

1632. *Ars Logica, Secunda Pars* in the English translation by Yves R. Simon, John J. Glanville, and G. Donald Hollenhorst, *The Material Logic of John of St. Thomas* (Chicago: University of Chicago Press, 1955).

1634. *Naturalis Philosophiae, Quarta Pars* in Beatus Reiser, (ed.) *Cursus philosophicus Thomisticus*, vol.3 (Turin: Marietti, 1930).

RÉGIS, Louis-Marie (8 December 1903—1988 February 2)

1935. *L'Opinion selon Aristote* (Paris: Vrin).

SIMON, Yves R. (14 March 1903—1961 May 11).

1934. *Introduction à l'ontologie du connaître* (Paris: Desclée de Brouwer, 1934); English trans. by Vukan Kuic and Richard J. Thompson, *An Introduction to Metaphysics of Knowledge* (New York: Fordham University Press, 1990).

1960. "On Order in Analogical Sets." New Scholasticism 34.1: 1-42; included in Yves R. Simon, *Philosopher at Work: Essays*, ed. Anthony O. Simon (Lanham. MD: Roman & Littlefield, 1999): 135-71.

SOKOLOWSKI, Robert (3 May 1934—).

1979. "Making Distinctions," *Review of Metaphysics* 32: 639-76; included in Robert Sokolowski, *Pictures, Quotations, and Distinctions: Fourteen Essays in Phenomenology* (Notre Dame, IN: University of Notre Dame Press, 1992): 55-91.

Reality and the Meaning of Evil

On the Moral Causality of Signs[1]

Kirk Kanzelberger, PhD
Franciscan University, Steubenville, OH

ABSTRACT: "Evil is *really* only a privation." This philosophical commonplace reflects an ancient solution to the problem of theodicy in one of its dimensions: is evil of such a nature that it must have God as its author? Stated in this particular way, it also reflects the commonplace identification of the *real* with natural being—the realm of what exists independently of human thought and perspectives—as opposed to all that is termed, by comparison, "merely subjective" and "unreal". If we stick with this way of construing the meaning of "reality", then by the excellent arguments of the tradition we are also stuck with defending the sufficiency of privation as a response to what evil "really is".

---

[1] Correspondence to editors@realityjournal.org

Table of Contents

In this article, we argue against both ways of being stuck. We argue, first, that a one-sided focus upon the being of nature blocks an adequate understanding of the world we actually live in: the semiotically constituted lifeworld that is the proper locus of human realities, including moral evil. We argue, second, that the positivity of moral evil consists not only, nor even primarily, in the positivity of "action" as such, but in structures of objectivity engendered by creative reason that oppose the due end, and that involve a specific genus of pure object which we call a *mystical daydream.* Like any objects, these objects are communicable and formative in relation to the lifeworld, within which they in turn engender further interpretants for both those who do and those who suffer evil, thanks to the causality of signs.

I. Introduction

As philosophical topics go, evil is better than most at cocktail parties. One can even find ordinary people at cocktail parties who have heard something of a philosophical theory about evil, namely, that evil is in itself no positive thing, but a privation, "the lack of a good that should be there". Let us imagine a dialogue at a cocktail party between a graduate student in philosophy (GS) of a "neo-Thomistic" bent, and a friendly interlocutor (IN).

IN: "I've heard that evil is supposed to be just a lack of goodness. Is that right? Is that what you think?"

GS (*pleased*): "Yeah—technically, it's a *privation*, the lack of a good that should be there. For example, the ability to fly is a particular good, a particular 'perfection' of being that some creatures have and some creatures don't. The lack of an ability to fly, though, isn't a privation or an evil for moles, but—excluding the ostrich and a few others—it *is* for birds, since the bird as a whole is structured for a life that depends naturally on that ability. So if a bird lacks the ability to fly, or to fly as well as it needs to, *this* is an evil, a privation — the lack of a good that should be in this being, this subject."

IN (*musing*): "Yes, an ostrich could just kick the life out of a would-be predator. But if it's a sparrow, that lack of an ability to fly comes from somewhere, doesn't it? I mean, if the poor thing has an injured or deformed wing, something made the wing to be that way. Isn't that something evil, too?"

GS: "Well, no. 'There's the rub' with nature, as Hamlet might say. You're right on target with your mention of would-be predators. In nature there are a practically infinite variety of natural agencies, each doing their own thing. The result is that, just by being what it is and doing what it does, something can end up causing injury, death, or a mutation in something else's DNA. Thomas Aquinas—though he knew nothing about DNA, obviously—argued that this sort of occurrence is inherent in a universe of corporeal beings continually coming into being and passing away, and even feeding off each other. The death of the ass is the life of the lion: what is bad for one creature is good for some other, and all of this contributes to the common good of the whole universe."

IN (*after a few seconds*): "I'm sorry—did you answer my question somewhere in there?"

GS: "I thought I did. In hunting and killing the ass, the lion causes a loss, a privation—an evil, that is to say—relative to the ass, which is no longer. But even though it causes this evil for the ass, the lion isn't evil—it's acting in accordance with its own nature and its natural interests. This is good for the individual lion and the propagation of its species, and also good for the universe as a whole. It just doesn't happen to be good for that particular ass. It's the same with whatever would-be predator or mutating agency caused the deformity of the sparrow's wing, poor thing."

IN: "What if it was a human who tortured the sparrow and left it that way?"

GS (*after a few seconds*): "Oh, I'm sorry. Okay, that's not what we call natural evil or the 'evil in nature', but rather moral evil, which is a bit different."

IN: "Actually, that's what I was thinking about all along. Not prey and predators and congenital deformities and that kind of thing, but wickedness."

GS: "Right, gotcha."

IN: "So moral evil is a bit different, you say?"

GS: "Yes and no. It's different, in that the evil person who tortures the sparrow is *not* acting in accordance with his or her nature. Not at all. The nature of a person, a moral being, is to do what is morally good. So the cause of the bird's injury in *that* case is indeed something that is *already* evil, the person and his or her morally bad action."

IN: "So in that case, evil isn't a privation, it's an action. I'm relieved—thanks!"

GS (*not losing a second*): "I said, yes *and no*. Moral evil is *still* a privation, just like natural evil. The morally evil action is evil *because* it lacks something that should be there."

IN: "You just said the action itself was evil. Or rather, 'bad'. Is there a difference?"

GS: "No, that's right, the action *is* evil, and this is exactly what's evil about it: it lacks the moral goodness that a human action ought to have. Evil or privation is always *in* something positive, an existing thing or action that is good insofar as it has being. Evil is always *in* a positive subject, but if we insist on asking about 'evil itself', or 'evil insofar as it is evil', this is nothing but a privation."

IN: "But this evil itself, this wickedness, is... real."

GS: "Of course it is. A privation is real—it makes a difference, in this case a big one! But it's the difference made by a lack or a loss, not the difference made by something positive, as if there were some positive quality or flavor of being called 'evil'."

IN (*her brow furrowing*): "I don't think I follow you. This human being is not just *lacking* a good; he is *attacking* a good. He is taking what is good, what is intact, what is perfect, and deliberately bringing it to ruin. It's as if this goodness itself, the goodness of this perfect little sparrow, nauseates him. Or, it pleases him to annihilate it. Or, both the one and the other."

GS (*beginning to shift weight between the balls of his feet*): "Yes, well, that's the trouble. It's the wrong thing that pleases him and/or nauseates him. Or, it's the wrong thing that appears useful to him for some reason. In any event, it's the wrong thing that appears good to him. That's why his action *lacks* the ordering to a truly good end that it ought to have."

IN (*staring directly into his pupils*): "So... you're saying that wickedness *is* this `lack of ordering to a truly good end'?"

GS (*feet moving like a ballet dancer*): "Insofar as `wickedness' means the evil itself *of* a wicked action, yes. (*rolling the dice*) Let me ask you this, begging your pardon in advance: do you believe in God?"

IN (*slightly taken aback; evil and wickedness may be accepted conversational fare at cocktail parties, but God is another matter*): "Yes."

GS: "Do you believe that God is good, and that every finite being, every creature, comes from God?"

IN: "Don't some creatures come from some others?"

GS (*earnestly*): "Creatures do come from others through natural processes of change, but it is the first or 'primary cause' who, in giving being to nature, gives to natural things their power to be 'secondary causes', that is, to effect change in other things already existing, though always in dependence on the primary cause. Nor can any creature account in a radical sense for any particular 'nature' itself as one of being's possibilities. The nature of every finite, positive reality is some kind of partial reflection of the infinite perfection of the primary cause which we call 'God'. Every actually existing creature moreover depends directly on God for its being—for its very existence or its 'to-be'. No mere creature, therefore, can be the 'whole' or 'unqualified' cause of any positive reality, but only a secondary, co-operating cause. Whereas a mere creature *can* be the 'whole' or 'unqualified' cause, if we want to put it this way, of a *negative* reality—that is, of a privation such as moral evil—by *failing* to be what it is made to be, by falling away from its own being, in a sense. Do you follow?"

IN (*after a few seconds*): "I think so. Maybe. I guess so."

GS (*relieved, smelling victory*): "So if wickedness itself were not a privation but some positive reality, then it would have to come from God, and that would contradict God's goodness, right?"

IN (*after a long pause*): "Maybe. I don't know. I see what you are saying, but I also see what I am seeing."

GS (*out of his element*): "What do you see?"

IN (*after another long pause, speaking slowly*): "I see the lack of ordering to a truly good end. I also see that the wicked one himself undergoes loss, just like his victim—maybe more so. But I also think I see that there is something that comes before this lack of order and this loss—you admitted it yourself. It seems to me that there is a wrongness itself that the wicked one wants. He doesn't just want the wrong thing; he wants something that is wrong. This wrongness that he wants isn't just a loss or a lack—that's ridiculous. You can't desire mere loss itself."

GS (*breaking in*): "That's right, you can't. And in fact..."

IN: "And it's interesting that you brought in religion. Didn't Jesus say that anyone who sins is a slave to sin?"

GS: "Well, yes, I brought God in as primary cause, so... yes, 'religion' in the more general sense of our relationship to the primary cause, but not necessarily any particular 'religion'..."

IN (*ignoring him*): "Didn't Jesus say that anyone who sins is a slave to sin?"

GS: "Yes."

IN: "How can a lack enslave?"

GS: "Well, the sinner is a slave to his or her own desire."

IN: "Desire for what?"

GS: "A relative good, like pleasure or power or wealth. The virtuous person would apply the standard of moral goodness to this relative good, whatever it happens to be, and decide against the inordinate pursuit of it—but the vicious person does not. Instead, he or she embraces it as the apparent good to be done here and now. That desire for a relative good—a desire that *lacks* appropriate order and measure, and to which the vicious person consents over and over—becomes more and more fixed as a matter of habit, and in that way the one who sins becomes a slave."

IN (*looking not at him but at a point in the space between them*): "No. I am pretty sure now that you are wrong. Evil—evil itself—isn't only privation. It is like a dream, a shadowy reality but a reality nonetheless, and evil. It is what the wicked want. Although—I think you are probably right about that 'habit' business—it is their own desire for it that makes them enslaved. It is not just a relative or apparent good—it is a counter-good, or an anti-good. To love it is to hate what is genuinely good. And it doesn't stay in their heads. It emerges and it spreads. Far or near, but it spreads. And the spreading of this shadowy reality creates little hells on earth."

GS (*glancing in the direction of the bar*): "Well, I guess we have to admit that wickedness is something of a mystery—the 'mystery of iniquity', as St. Paul called it! To be sure, what the wicked choose makes no sense—I think you've made that point very well. Would you like another drink?"

IN (*still gazing at the point between them*): "On the contrary, they choose it because of the sense it makes. (*meeting his eyes*) Yes, I would."

This dialogue is imaginary, certainly: most actual conversations at cocktail parties do not find themselves so soon in such deep waters! We have constructed this one to show how the phenomenon of moral evil affords a unique point of entry to a discussion of what "reality" ought to mean, for that is the underlying issue between the two interlocutors.

The divergence of perspectives surfaces in the wake of her tentative offering that "this wickedness itself is... real." His allowance for the "negative reality" of privation fails to impress her. In the end, he is left without a card to play, since "reality" for him signifies simply the being of the things of nature and their activities, including the free acts of moral beings. His vantage point is, in our modern parlance, "objective". From this vantage point, evil can be understood only in terms of deficiency, as a loss of form or of due perfection. To act virtuously is to act in accordance with the way things really are and the ends to which one's own being is ordered, and thereby to become fully real oneself—to attain the fullness of one's being. To act viciously is to undergo loss, to fall away from reality and the truth of one's being.

By contrast, her vantage point lacks clear definition. Her sense of the real revolves around meaning and (again, in our modern parlance) "subjectivity." At the same time, she seems able to incorporate his claims about nature more readily than he is able to incorporate her claims about meaning. His attention is fixed upon the realities of nature, the beings that are what they are independently of what we "subjectively" think about them. She understands what he says about those realities but does not think that the meaning of "reality" is thereby exhausted. If we sense that she is in some way correct, then by the end of the dialogue we have come to feel that what she sees—vaguely, but according to all its dimensions—he sees only in silhouette.

Where ought moral evil to be located? What is its proper context? The same context, no doubt, that is proper to moral goodness. It will be the context in which moral acts stand out and are appreciable in all their dimensions. Is this context simply the universe of nature, *ens naturae*, the being of nature as it exists independently of our cognition? One whose thought is fixed on the reality of nature may well wonder what other context is available. For apart from the being of nature, is there not only unreality? And unreality can hardly determine a context, can it?

We maintain that the proper context of moral evil and goodness is neither the realm of nature as such, nor some other realm discountable as "merely subjective and unreal", but rather the *objective world*, the world in which human beings actually live, the lifeworld in which cognized (objectified) aspects of the being of nature are woven together with pure objects in a single fabric of experience bearing public as well as private meanings.[2] The proper situating of

---

[2] John Deely developed the semiotic conception of the objective world (*Umwelt*, lifeworld) at length in many of his published works, from its foundations in sensation within animal perception, through the semiosis by which sensed environmental features are interpreted as positive, negative or neutral in relation to animal interests, through the transformation by human understanding of these objects of animal perception such that they are capable of being grasped as things existing in themselves independently of being perceived—a transformation that enables the formation of properly intellectual conceptions, including the very idea of "nature" itself as that which exists independently of our knowing it. See particularly the summary treatment in 2001: *Four Ages of Understanding: The First Postmodern Survey of Philosophy from Ancient Times to the Turn of the Twenty-First* Century, 6-10, and the more detailed development in 2002: *What Distinguishes Human Understanding?* chapters 3-6. The claim that human

moral evil in the objective world opens the way to a bridging of the chasm between our two interlocutors.[3]

> Our account of the nature of evil must include not only the metaphysical world of beings of nature but also the experiential world of beings of reason. An account of natural evils (such as blindness) can be given purely in terms of beings of nature, explaining the different ways that such beings are subject to privations (such as lack of sight). An account of moral evil, however, requires a broader vision of the world including beings of reason and the complex web of relationships to which these give rise.
>
> *Dodds, "Made of Flame and Air" [p.207].*

2. Objectivity Reconsidered

"'Reality' is also a word, a word which we must learn to use correctly." Niels Bohr directed this statement against the underestimation of the sign, the reduction of language to a pictorial delivery mechanism for the reality that is independent of language and lies beneath it. In fact, Bohr went on to say, "we are suspended in language in such a way that we cannot say what is up and what is down. 'Reality' is also a word, a word which we must learn to use correctly."[4]

---

understanding can come to know the being of nature in what is proper to it as existing in itself is the claim of the various forms of "realism", from the realism of the Latin scholastics to Deely's own semiotic realism, in contradistinction to the claim of various forms of "idealism" that the mind knows only what the mind itself makes: either "ideas" as pure mental products, or objects as synthesized by *a priori* structuring principles applied to an indeterminate sensible manifold in such a way that things in themselves remain unknowable, hidden forever behind the veil of "appearances".

[3] A somewhat comparable divergence of vantage points on the nature of evil can be observed in the conversation between John F. Crosby and Patrick Lee, the former writing from a phenomenological and the latter from a Thomistic perspective. See Crosby 2002: "Is All Evil Really Only Privation?"; Lee 2007: "Evil as Such Is a Privation: A Reply to John Crosby"; and Crosby 2007: "Doubts About the Privation Theory That Will Not Go Away: Response to Patrick Lee."

[4] French and Kennedy 1985: *Niels Bohr: A Centenary Volume*, 302.

Though Bohr's point can be conscripted in aid of an "idealist" stance, the question of the proper signification of the word "reality" need not imply taking issue with the claim of "realism" that human knowing can come to know the being of nature. The question concerns rather whether the being of nature is all that "reality" ought to signify.

2.1. The Objectification of Nature

Awareness of "reality" in the sense of that which exists independently of being perceived is a practical necessity for animal life in its many forms. If an animal's perception fails to deliver such awareness, the animal will suffer the consequences. A single misjudgment of perception can lead, for the hunting lion, to the loss of a meal; or, for a brachiating gibbon, to an untimely end on the forest floor. Though every object without exception is an object *construed*—that is, every object is the result (interpretant) of a prior signification that itself generates further interpretive results—such examples are evidence that, however the relation of knower and known is to be explained, cognition is a relation whose object-terminus is not, merely and without remainder in every case, cognition's own product.

Mistakes happen. If mistakes can teach, there is *something*, some otherness, that manifests itself against expectation to, say, the young lion learning to hunt. It is this dimension within experience of recurring resistance to expectations that awakens both humans and other animals to "reality" in the sense under discussion. In our language, we even refer to striking instances of it as "getting a dose of reality". For the young lion, such doses of "reality" result in the weaving of new patterns into its web of perceptual experience, a growth of meaning that makes of it in the end (barring catastrophe along the way) an expert hunter. For the human learner (and this is the difference that human understanding makes relative to animal perception) the ongoing encounter with "reality" occurs under the auspices of *the idea of reality*, of "that which is what it is," the paradigmatic type of which is that being, encountered through external sensation, that is able to resist expectations *because* (and this is precisely what human understanding grasps) "it is what it is" independently of our knowledge and desires.

An aspiration thus arises for the human animal that arises for no other animal on earth: the aspiration to know more and more of the being of nature in its natural constitution. Such knowledge is attained heuristically and recursively, as experience feeds the formation of hypotheses or trial conceptions that are tested in further experience, resulting in ever more adequate conceptions that lead gradually to deeper levels of understanding. Along the way, hypotheses that turn out to be false are (as hypotheses) functionally equivalent to hypotheses that turn out to be true. Guesses, however "educated", may be either good or bad; in either event, they teach.

As Charles Peirce pointed out, it is by way of hypotheses alone—by guesses false or true—that anything *new* is ever added to the "knowledge of reality" arrived at by human beings and communities of human inquirers.[5] Some hypotheses are good guesses that successfully (if only aspectually) render something of the constitution of the things of nature. Other hypotheses are not so good: in the long run (perhaps a very long run) they turn out to be renderings of what had been thought to exist in nature, but in fact does not. It is this "turns out to be" that is of interest, as the functional equivalence of true and false hypotheses brings to light the essential role played by *purely objective being* in human inquiry into the things of nature. To understand what is meant by "purely objective being", we need to grasp the difference between *objects* as such and the *things* that become objects insofar as they are known.

What is it that one conceives when one conceives a hypothesis that turns out to be false? If true and false hypotheses are *functionally equivalent* in the process of inquiry, what is it that they both *are,* so as to function equivalently? A minimal answer to this question is that they are both *objects*, where by "object" is meant *that which exists as known*, even if it turns out to exist in no other way. It is on

---

[5] From a letter to S. P. Langley (Peirce 1900: R 409, Letter "Peirce to Langley, c. May 20, 1900", retrieved from Commens.org): "Hypothesis is guessing, or if you please starting a question. A phenomenon is observed having something peculiar about it. Rumination leads me to see that *if* a certain state of things existed, of whose actual existence I know nothing, that phenomenon would certainly occur, or at any rate, would in all probability occur. I say, By George, I wonder if that is not the very state of the case! That is hypothesis. The justification of my attaching the slightest weight to such a mere guess is, that there are just these three modes of inference, and neither Deduction or Induction can furnish me with any new idea. Unless I can get to the bottom of things by hypothesis, I may as well give up trying to comprehend them. But not only that; but just as the general advantage of the inductive procedure admits of deductive proof, so induction in its turn shows that hypotheses have a very decent chance of turning out satisfactory, or at least answering well and being helpful for a long time."

account of this latter condition of "existing in no other way" that the false hypothesis ends up being called "false", but it is no less truly an *object* for all that, as well after its disconfirmation as before.

What then is a *purely objective being* or *pure object*? It is an object that exists *only* as an object—that is to say, its being as cognized or known is the only being that it has. The Latin scholastics called such an object a "being of reason" (*ens rationis*), a being that depends on the mind "as an object [depends] on the one knowing" (*ut objectum a cognoscente*).[6] These beings of reason, or mind-dependent beings, "are beings, certainly, because they are known in the way that being is known; but they are constructs or fictions [*ficta*, i.e., mentally formed], because no true being on the side of physical nature corresponds to them."[7] Nevertheless, such beings, though existing only as objects (existing only because they are known) possess an intrinsic intelligibility and consistency according to the being they have, despite the status of this being as mind-dependent or purely objective. Not merely the being of nature (*ens naturae*), but mind-dependent being as well, "is what it is"—if it were not, there would be no meaning and no progress represented by its "disconfirmation" in light of further experience.

The Aristotelian-Ptolemaic theory of the heavens—of those great spheres and their luminaries, mobile yet incorruptible, revolving about the earth—endured as established for many centuries before being exploded. That is to say, for many centuries, those spheres themselves, along with the conception of a corporeality both mobile and incorruptible, were objects *taken for* existing things of nature, which they were not. So taken, these objects amounted to a false hypothesis, but never throughout those centuries did that factual falsity hinder either the communication of these objects in discourse (long treatises were written) or their power of forming cultural awareness as to the very framework of the cosmos in which human beings took themselves to be living. This "discarded image" of the world, no less than the image we have of the world today which we take to be true(r), structured in profound ways the understanding, imagination and conduct of a civilization. As a theory of mind-

---

[6] Poinsot 1632b: *Tractatus de Signis: The Semiotic of John Poinsot* (*TDS*), 48/5-6.
[7] Poinsot 1632b: *TDS*, 49/5-8.

independent nature, it was merely false; as a mind-dependent socially-constituted reality, it was a form full of meaning and potency.[8]

It is unfortunate that our ordinary vocabulary, shaped as it is by the intellectual heritage of modern philosophy, makes it harder for us to discriminate, as we have been attempting to do, the being proper to the object as such. An "object" now commonly just means a thing, and "thing" means an entity existing (or at least capable of existing) independently of mind—a being of nature, possibly also shaped by human intelligence as an artifact. In keeping with this modern identification of objects with mind-independent things, the latter are commonly spoken of as "objectively real" and their totality as constituting "objective reality", where "objective" is used to signify precisely the mind-independence of the being in question. All that is not thus "objective" is commonly termed "subjective" by way of antithesis, often further qualified as "*merely* subjective"—as if a mind-dependent or constructed being invariably signified some idiosyncratic illusion or errant psychological state, a mental projection existing "only in one's head", and so forth.

Thus has the word "object" come to be severed from its original premodern rationale: an *ob-jectum* (Latin *ob + iacere,* "to throw") is not simply a "thing", but that which exists *in relation to* some power of a living being, particularly some power of cognition or desire. An *ob-ject* is that which is "thrown before" or "thrown in the face of" such a power. If an object of cognition is *also* a mind-independent thing, it is nevertheless an *object* as the *terminus of a cognitive relation*, from which it may follow that it is also the terminus of an affective relation (positive or negative). The hunting lion spots its prey—that is, the prey becomes object-terminus of a cognitive relation. Given the lion's hunger, that object-terminus becomes object-terminus also of a (positive) affective relation. The prey, when it becomes aware of the lion, is similarly established in a cognitive relation to the lion as object-terminus, and, if the danger is recognized, established also in a (negative) affective relation to the lion as threat, resulting in flight.

Scholastic realists such as Aquinas held that the things of nature in themselves (i.e., precisely in their mind-independent being or thinghood) can—in part, and

---

[8] For an overview of the older image of the cosmos and its literary impact in particular, see C. S. Lewis 1962: *The Discarded Image: An Introduction to Medieval and Renaissance Literature*.

via a fallible and laborious process of inquiry—become objects of human understanding. They also held that not every object is a thing of nature. A given object *may* be a thing of nature (understood aspectually) or it *may* be a mind-dependent being (*ens rationis*), and, in a given case and at a given time, the one for whom it is an object may not know which it is. Regardless of which it turns out to be, it has the existence proper to an object. The scholastics called this mode of existence "intentional" (*esse intentionale*), since an object, any object, exists as object precisely *for a knower* that "in-tends" or stretches toward it as an *ob-jectum*, as a thing thrown before awareness. If you are a realist who recognizes hypotheses about nature for what they are, namely guesses, then you recognize that your mind is constructing an objective pattern which may or may not be the pattern of a mind-independent thing.[9]

2.2. Shared Objects and Sign Relations

Why bother discriminating the being that is proper to objects as such? We have already discovered one good reason to do so: it helps to explain the possibility of errors regarding the being of nature in such a way as to do justice to the way the object—in the original meaning of *objectum*—functions in the process of human inquiry. Another good reason, also noted by the Latin scholastics, is that the conceptual structures by and in which we understand something of the being of nature are not in all cases direct renderings of nature's structures, but include ancillary structures added by the understanding itself in the course of inquiry. Of this kind are the various classificatory systems in which we articulate the intelligibility discovered in nature as our understanding moves from the vague initial grasp of various wholes to a more precise knowledge of what is contained in those wholes. Thus, we have the conceptions "molecule", "macromolecule", "nucleic acid", and "RNA"—objects that we take to be also things. The classificatory relations themselves, however, by which the species "RNA" is included in these several genera are—and are recognized within inquiry to be—logical (i.e., mind-dependent) relations rather than relations existing in nature independently of our understanding.

---

[9] We are not speaking here merely of theories in the practice of the specialized sciences, but of any inference from sense data, such as your belief that the person on the other side of the plaza with his back to you is in fact an acquaintance of yours.

In practice, this is where many "realists", including contemporary Thomists, stop in their account of the being proper to objects and the role of purely objective or mind-dependent beings in human knowing. For philosophers of this type—so like in this respect to the devoted practitioners of the "hard sciences"—the focus is overwhelmingly upon the being of nature and the tools of its investigation. In practice, this can bring about a tendency to regard *esse intentionale*, or the being proper to the object, as no more than a packaging and delivery mechanism for *ens naturae* as grasped by the understanding. The meaning of "reality" then collapses into an accepted synonym for the being of nature, and "realism" itself turns into a form of myopia that fails to see realities constituted by cognition for what they are.

To relieve and guard against such a myopia, the following exercise may help.

Consider a man who has fallen in love with a woman, and let us further stipulate that the woman is in love with him. Is this mutual love something real? If it is some kind of reality—something that "is what it is"—then what kind (or kinds) of being are involved in it? Can the reality of mutual love be accounted for on the terms of an identification of "reality" with the mind-independent being of nature? To be sure, the "state" of being in love, construed as the sum total of the relevant cognitive and affective states of the two lovers, is indeed a being of nature of a particular kind that is associated with the exercise of natural powers.[10] It is certain, moreover, that unless these two persons exist as beings of nature and exercise their natural powers in this way, they cannot be lovers. But in speaking only of cognitive and affective "states" we have done no more than further qualify the two persons in their distinctness. Love, however, is a "unitive force", as Aquinas would put it.[11] Love brings about a common life—a distinctive *milieu* that, being a reality precisely *between* the two, is over and above the two as individuals. In marrying, the two lovers commit themselves to the lifelong fostering of whatever this reality may be.

What kind of reality is this? We must move beyond the subjective (meaning the domain of existing subjects—that is, substances and their qualities) and locate this reality of love in the genus of the suprasubjective, that is, of relation. Now

---

[10] Whether we call these states "physical" or distinguish them as "psychological" makes no difference: neither denotation signifies mind-dependence in the sense of an *ens rationis* that depends on mind "as an *object* on the one knowing." We are speaking still of *ens naturae*, the being of nature.

[11] See 1271: *Summa theologiae, prima secundae* (*ST* Ia-IIae), q.28, a.1.

as every Thomist knows, any act of cognition or affection establishes its subject in a relation to an object. When this object is something "real" in the natural or mind-independent sense, this cognitive or affective relation is similarly "real", inasmuch as there is a dependence upon the naturally existing object affecting (or having affected) the knowing and loving subject and specifying or formally structuring the subject's acts of knowing and loving. Thus, when the man sees his beloved and is moved with affection at the sight of her, his cognition and affection are specified or formally structured by her in her mind-independent existence. This remains the case even when the woman disappears into another room and he lovingly remembers her—it is the selfsame naturally existing woman that continues to specify his acts of knowing and loving.[12] And of course the same analysis holds regarding her reciprocal acts of seeing and loving him, and the corresponding cognitive and affective relations.

Is this the end of the story? Not remotely. For though we have indicated how the psychological states of the two individuals are the foundation of cognitive and affective relations to the other—so far has *esse intentionale* made its appearance—we have arrived yet at a mutuality that is only a sum of such reciprocal "intentions", not at a common life or *milieu*. We have arrived yet at nothing that can be said to be shared. If the shared *milieu* of the spouses amounts to anything more than the furniture, the fireplace, and the fish in the fishbowl, what is it?

The missing reality is rooted in *communication* (literally, a "making common"), by which objects, always public (communicable) in principle, become public (communicated) in fact. By virtue of communication, that which is *one and the same* (this or that object) becomes shared by more than one. This outcome is brought about and sustained by a continual exchange of signs. A *sign* is that which is so related to an object that it is able to bring a third into a similar relation to that object. When this takes place, we have the "action of a sign", or *semiosis*.

---

[12] On the other hand, were we to speak of the woman herself as "seen and loved by him", i.e., of the opposed relations terminating in the man who sees and loves her, these would be mind-dependent relations of the kind the scholastics called "extrinsic denominations". That is, despite their terminus (the man) being a natural existent, the relations "seen" and "loved" themselves posit nothing "real" in the woman as the fundament of said relations (as the acts of seeing and loving are the natural fundaments of his relations to her), but are rather imputed to her as taken from something extrinsic. In other words, she is "thought of" as related to him in this way ("seen", "loved") because of the way in which he is "really" related to her.

For example, the woman's lover says to her, "I love you". The outcome of this semiosis is that she is brought into a renewed relation with what the utterance signifies.[13] This outcome is known as the sign's *interpretant*[14]: she is made aware of an object (his love for her). In fact, this semiosis will typically yield a series of interpretants: not only this awareness of his love, but a movement of reciprocal affection (affective interpretant) as well as some action (energetic interpretant) which might include a reciprocal sign-utterance ("I love you, too", a loving look, a caress).

If we consider the whole of what is communicated between spouses, all that they share—all the common understandings, goals, concerns, hopes and anxieties—we can discern the nature of this *milieu* or common life of love as *a web of shared objects linked by sign-relations*. It is not a collection but a web, since every object not only is what it is, but is a nexus of relations not only physical (we see that the table is between us) but mind-dependent (we see what we mean to and for each other). Because the web is not a mere network of things but a network of *objects* of experience, the relations constituting and sustaining the web are triadic, and not merely dyadic as are the relations of bodies in space and their dynamical interactions. That is, every conceiving of an object is the cognitive outcome or interpretant of a prior semiosis, and every object conceived becomes in its turn a sign generating a fresh series of interpretants—fresh awareness, fresh movement of affection, fresh action. What we are describing is nothing less than the stream of conscious life itself as an action of signs.[15]

---

[13] Not all signs are linguistic or cultural; some are natural signs, for instance the darkling clouds that are a sign of rain for the animal capable of interpreting it.

[14] The interpretant is a key notion in Peirce's semiotics. Peirce c.1897 (*CP*.2.228) is one of many texts that could be cited: "A sign, or representamen, is something which stands to somebody for something in some respect or capacity. It addresses somebody, that is, creates in the mind of that person an equivalent sign, or perhaps a more developed sign. That sign which it creates I call the interpretant of the first sign."

[15] Communication—the constituting and sustaining of this web—depends upon a form of causality distinct from the efficient causality of natural agents, and distinct as well from the intrinsic structuring causality that determines physical material to be this or that kind of natural substance. In their common life, spouses act upon each other, not principally as natural agents exercising efficient causality (though they do that too), but as utterers and receivers of signs—as co-weavers of the semiotic web. Efficient causality is presupposed: mouths must move if words are to be spoken, sounds must reach the

A shared object need not be a thing existing in the natural sense. "House rules" may govern actions in a home, but these rules are not things, they are objects. An object may be what does not exist now but existed formerly (the memory of the romance and adventures of youth), what does not exist now but might yet (the dream of a child's success), what does not exist and will never exist (children never born, plans destined to fail), or even what is impossible to exist (empty daydreams representing what is beyond the dreamers' power or place to bring into being). These objects are not things, or not merely things, but, according to a ratio that varies from one to the other, pure objects. Insofar as they are things, they exist or can exist, but they *signify* (one and all), not insofar as they are or may be things, but insofar as they are objects. Thus, to the extent that life is lived intentionally, it is objects and not things that rule.

In the web of married life, the spouses themselves become signs of a particular kind. In their common awareness, each one is *spouse* for the other—a kind of role or office, a relation irreducible to any physical or mind-independent relations, but a purely objective relation constituted and sustained by awareness. Inasmuch as this social role is public, it engenders interpretants in others besides these two. Offspring, in-laws, friends, and members of the larger community enter into this web of meaning which is, after all, a sort of objective "neighborhood" within the lifeworld of a particular human society.

The objective world of that society is a world of lovers, spouses, friends, neighbors, random strangers, parents, children, teachers, students, priests, politicians, peace officers, judges, nurses, cabbies and fry-cooks. It is a world ordered by rules and customs, laws and constitutions. It is a world saturated

---

eardrums of receivers, auditory nerves must undergo stimulation and in turn cause cortical areas to be stimulated, and so forth. Physical interaction is the necessary channel thanks to which a sign-vehicle is able to affect the senses and elicit the subjective structures of percepts—this dimension is required, but is only what Peirce called the "body" of the sign (see Peirce 1908: "A Neglected Argument for the Reality of God", *EP*.2: 435). What makes a sign essentially such is the power to generate an interpretant—that is, to mediate an object to a being that is capable of "catching on": "[E]very sign certainly conveys something of the nature of thought, if not from a mind, yet from some repository of ideas, or significant forms, and if not to a person, yet to something capable of somehow 'catching on'... that is, of receiving not merely a physical, nor even merely a psychical dose of energy, but a significant meaning." (Peirce c.1907: "Pragmatism", MS 318 in Robin 1967: *Annotated Catalogue of the Papers of Charles S. Peirce*, quoted in Deely 1994: *New Beginnings: Early Modern Philosophy and Postmodern Thought*, 190.)

with discourse—scientific, philosophical, literary, religious, political. It is a world of territory and artifact, state and nation, housing developments and heavy equipment, farms and financial districts, city parks and junkyards. It is also a world of meadows and wildflowers, forest streams and granite boulders, squirrels and beetles and kingfishers; of earth and sky, the sun and the other stars, galaxies and quasars and black holes.

This world, the objective world, is not a collection of things but a fabric of experience woven of natural as well as cultural strands, all alike objective or existing as known, and all alike public in principle. As we have seen, the cultural or mind-dependent strands contribute in varying ways to this fabric. Even when our attention seems focused on some "physical thing" such as a table, that thing—or rather, that object—will often on reflection turn out to be some kind of amalgam of nature and what is not mere nature, inasmuch as the object bears a cultural significance which is for us more formal and essential in the object than its physical constitution.[16] Often enough, objects in the human lifeworld have nothing in them of nature, but are pure objects. The Constitution of the United States, an object of supreme importance to many, is a being of reason (*ens rationis*)—indeed a great artifact of reason—a pure object with nothing in it of *ens naturae*.[17] It is the same with fictional creations of literary and cinematic arts that add their magic to the life of culture.

---

[16] Artifacts furnish one obvious example. A "table" with no physical constitution at all is a being of reason, and not much use; nevertheless, an existing and usable table is more (as an object) than its physical constitution. It is the mind-dependent functional relationship that is more formal and essential to "what a table is", for, after all, even a boulder could, in a pinch, be commandeered for use as a table. A somewhat different kind of amalgam is involved when we cross the Delaware River (a thing of nature) and remark, "Now we are in New Jersey". The civil boundary is real indeed, but it is something more than the river: it is the river clothed with a mind-dependent cultural significance, so that it is accurate to say that the river—so objectified within the lifeworld—*is* the boundary between two state jurisdictions. Social and cultural roles furnish another example, as when one says, "Look, there's the mayor!" These roles are relations constituted by cognition within the objective world, but, unlike mind-dependent relations of genus and species which obtain between universal conceptions of reason, social and cultural relations obtain between persons naturally existing.

[17] There is natural being in the written sign-vehicles of the Constitution, such as the august parchment that is housed in the National Archives. The destruction of such an historic vehicle, however, while tragic, would have no effect on the Constitution, which survives as long as any sign of it does (including conceptual sign-vehicles).

Such is the world in which we actually live. To be sure, the understanding or objectification of the being of nature is in our world a great value, to which some of us give the best part of our lives. Nevertheless, most of us are at most times occupied, not with the being of nature insofar as it is such, but with objects that turn out to be irreducible to that being even if they contain something of it, and frequently with pure objects that have nothing whatever in them of the being of nature. Indeed, the "world of nature" as we commonly conceive it, the world conceived as the object of natural science, is a kind of prescissive abstraction,[18] a projection onto one axis of the world in which we live. In light of this, what sense does it make to continue to take "reality" as a synonym for *ens naturae*, as is commonly done? If "reality" is meant as a sort of ontological compliment (which it generally is, and without distinguishing this meaning from that of mind-independent being)—that which "matters" or "makes a difference", then it must be said that purely objective being, the being constituted by cognition, has its own sort of reality, without which we cannot understand the life of families or neighborhoods or nations or even communities of scientific inquirers.[19] It is in

---

[18] Peirce c.1905: *The Branches of Geometry; Existential Graphs* (MS 96 in Robin 1967: *Annotated Catalogue*): "*Abstraction* names two wholly different operations. One of them consists in supposing some feature of the fact to be absent, or at least leaving it out of account. I call that *prescissive abstraction*."

[19] Even an excellent and penetrating text such as that of W. Norris Clarke (2001: *The One and Many: A Contemporary Thomistic Metaphysics*), while devoting more space than usual (29-31) to the purely objective, does not emerge fully from this alternately one-sided and ambiguous application of the term "reality". Clarke admits that the primary division of being is that between the being of nature and *ens rationis*, the former ("that which is present by its own intrinsic act of existence") receiving the understandable but nevertheless unhappy denomination "real being" (likely following the later Scholastic usage *ens reale*), and the latter receiving the equally unhappy denomination "mental being" ("that which is present *not* by its own act of existence, but only within an idea, i.e., as being-thought-about"). His examples of the latter include the past and future as such, dreams, abstractions, and mental constructs (including hypotheses for testing and plans for action). All these are said to be "present in real minds, but they are not themselves the 'really real', as Plato thought they had to be to ground eternal truths and values." Clarke would have done better at least to say that *entia rationis* are present *by* (rather than "in") real minds, so as not to leave the reader to the modern tendency to envision these beings under the heading of "private thoughts" rather than socially constituted objects public in principle. In any event, no sooner are these beings mentioned than they are devalued as "radically *secondary, dependent, parasitic on real being*, which is primary. Real beings (real minds) can generate ideas; ideas of themselves

this world (the world in which we actually live) that *moral acts* are posited and have their meaning, as specified by their objects. Being themselves signs that generate interpretants throughout the objective world as public, acts of this kind bind together (or rive apart) these human communities. To repeat, inasmuch as human life is lived intentionally, it is objects and not things that rule.[20]

---

cannot generate real beings." One could respond that a "real mind" cannot "of itself" generate an idea, either, but does so only as already inserted into a community of sign-users (other "real minds") and *shared objects*. Then, there is the matter of how we detect the difference between the two kinds of being (31): "What is real is what can act on its own... Real beings *make a difference* in the real world." Clarke means here to emphasize the capacity of *ens naturae* to resist expectations; what is left out of account is the formal causality of the object as structuring action and uniting those who communicate in knowledge and love. As we have said, there is no communication without efficient causality as *channel*, but communication involves a form of causality, distinct from both efficient and intrinsic formal causality, that is essential to the "action" of the sign as triadic event. Unfortunately, as soon as the subject of this "primary division of being" is left behind, mental being seems to fall between two stools (43): "Thus being signifies all that is, in everything that is, i.e., everything that is real in any way. Outside of this lies only 'nothing' or nothingness, non-being."

[20] Contemporary Thomists would do well to ponder the admonition of Deely (1971: *The Tradition via Heidegger: An Essay on the Meaning of Being in the Philosophy of Martin Heidegger*, 89): "Is there any need to point out that history, and with it, historical, cultural, social, and psychological determinisms are little more than strangers in the Thomistic house? Human solidarity, personality in culture, subconscious determinisms, creative intuition in art and poetry, the metaphysical character of motivation and meaning — all these are fundamental *data* of the human condition which find their primary basis in the mode of being human precisely not from the side of the *esse* of *existentia ut exercita* but from the side of the *esse* of *ens intentionale,* from the side, that is to say, of a *Daseinsanalyse*." Cf. also Benedict Ashley 2006: *The Way toward Wisdom*, who, while rejecting the transcendentalist reading of Aquinas, nevertheless writes (employing "objective" and "subjective" in the accepted modern sense), 49: "The achievement of modern thought has been to bring to attention the subjective aspects of human knowledge, which Aristotle and Aquinas certainly recognized, but to which, because of their concern to get right the objective elements of knowledge, they gave relatively little attention. While they placed problems in a dialectical context of opinion, they seldom touched on the way history and sociology color our view of the world, or on the way in which individual and social tendencies enter into its construction. The Transcendental Thomists have opened up such questions, and I am convinced that, if Thomism is to survive in our times, it must also deal with these issues." We would add that a basis within the Thomistic tradition for dealing with those issues is precisely what one finds in the semiotic of John Poinsot, as John Deely dedicated much of his scholarly life to demonstrating.

3. Evil from the Standpoint of Nature and Agency

3.1. Deprivation in Nature

There are excellent reasons for the position of our graduate student that any evil as such has the nature of privation. Thomas Aquinas gets to the heart of the matter in the opening question of his great work on evil:[21] every being, insofar as it is actual, is good. For what the notion of good (*bonum*) adds to being (*ens*) is nothing but a relation to appetite or desire. "The good is what all desire," as Aristotle put it, and what every being desires, or tends toward, is its own fullest actualization. Being tends toward its own fullness: this is the very meaning of action. Along the way, partial actualizations have the intelligible character of goodness and desirability insofar as they represent a greater fullness of being. It is true that diverse actualizations can be mutually exclusive in relation to the same subject: becoming a marine biologist generally excludes becoming a psychiatrist, since both are absorbing professions. If I follow the one path, I cannot follow the other. And yet, the good that I do not choose is still a *good* according to what it is in itself (*secundum se*) as fulfilling some potentiality of a human being, though not perhaps as suitable to me as to another, and I can appreciate it as the attainment of another who follows a different path.

Now evil (*malum*) signifies that which is directly opposed to good. Hence, if "good" signifies being under the aspect of fullness (including partial actualizations of being), then "evil" must needs signify that which is directly opposed to the fullness of being, and this is deprivation, or the loss of being. Further, if desire is universally directed to good as the fullness of being, then the loss of being is that which no being can desire or intend *secundum se*. One may endure the loss of one's leg to save one's life, but this is to intend one's loss, not *secundum se* insofar as it is loss, but insofar as this loss is unfortunately entailed in the benefit of avoiding still greater loss. For there is nothing in loss or deprivation *as such* to positively attract desire.

And yet, deprivation happens. The unique undesirability of privation as such, its direct opposition to the fullness that "every being desires", its incongruence with the very meaning of action—this is what justifies the identification of evil itself

---

[21] 1269-72: *Quaestiones disputatae de malo* (*De malo*), q.1, a.1. Parallel discussions are found in 1266: *Summa contra gentiles* (*SCG*) lib.3, c.3-9 and in 1266-68: *ST* Ia, qq.48-49.

(*ipsum malum*) with privation. The justification rests on a truth of metaphysics that seems unassailable; hence, the confidence of our graduate student.[22]

If privation is the one condition of existence that no being in the universe can tend toward, how does it occur? As our female interlocutor pointed out, unknowingly echoing Aquinas himself, any privation implies a depriving agency. Whenever we see a thing deprived of what it ought by nature to have, we seek a reason why.[23] As our graduate student pointed out, natural agencies are able to bring about deprivation simply by doing what they naturally do, which is oriented always toward actualization and not loss. Neither the lion in pursuit of its prey, nor the prey in fleeing the lion, are seekers of each other's death or starvation *per se*. Both are seekers of life, by means of inclinations that are as wholly natural as they are inevitably contrary: they are bound to clash whenever the lion is hungry and their paths cross. Or we might observe the clash between the natural activity of a toxic chemical or virus and the organismic processes it disrupts. Because natural activities are incessantly clashing in the material universe as a whole, such examples can be multiplied without end. Deprivation is ubiquitous in nature, but it is not necessary that the "depriving agents" be oriented toward anything other than their own actualization. Deprivation is thus brought about continually, but also "incidentally" (*per accidens*)—as an effect

---

[22] The example of the amputated leg illustrates that when we speak of loss or privation, we are not speaking of what we might call "opportunity costs" attached to life choices, e.g., the exclusion of life as a marine biologist by the decision to be a psychiatrist. One may at times be pained by this sort of "loss" and wonder what it would have been like to have done something else, but such consequences of our finitude are not privations as we are using the word (though this kind of rumination or daydream can furnish the occasion for moral evil, as we will see). Privation here signifies a loss in relation to the physical or moral integrity of a being or an action, as when an organism is born sterile or suffers a debilitating injury, or when a person becomes morally vicious. This is loss relative to nature or natural constitution as defining the meaning of "integrity", including the ordering to natural ends. If nature is not in this sense purposive, good and evil have no meaning apart from the gratification and frustration of chance impulses, themselves events without meaning. The purposiveness in nature is of course most evident in living things. A bird is born to fly, because it is ordered to natural ends for which flight is a path of actualization. A human being is born to be wise, just, brave, and self-controlled, because the excellence of virtue comprehends other excellences and leads to blessedness.

[23] 1269-72: *De malo* q.1. a.3: "Omne autem quod praeternaturaliter inest alicui oportet habere aliquam causam." — "Everything that comes about in a thing outside the condition of its nature must have some cause."

concomitant to some good aimed at *per se* by a natural agent. The impala manages to escape with its life—concomitantly, the lion is left hungrier than before. This incidental or *per accidens* cause is the only kind of cause such privations need.[24]

Some deprivations in nature are damaging enough that they render a being thenceforward deficient in its own agency, as when some infection or unfortunate encounter leaves an animal lame, psychologically impaired, or sterile. The now-deficient agent then gives rise to activities that lack normal integrity: a limping gait, rabid behavior, sexual unions that produce no offspring. In this way, something already deprived—the deficient agent—becomes the incidental cause of further privations. Note well that a deficient agent is still an *incidental* cause of privation and not a cause *per se*. For the ability to act at all depends upon the remnants of some natural power; the *deflection* of that power from its proper end and use is itself the expression of *no nature at all*, but rather the consequence of the damage sustained by this individual or its ancestors. And while various kinds of damage may propagate through long chains of deficient agents, privation in nature must finally be traced back, not to an evil principle of deprivation *per se* bringing about privation as its proper effect, but rather to the clashing of natural activities proceeding from the diverse natures of things.

In sum, evil (privation) in nature is brought about in two ways. Primarily, it is brought about by a clash of natural goods, that is, by natural and *non-deficient* agencies in pursuit of their own natural ends. Secondarily, it is brought about by the *deficient* agencies of beings already affected by evil. Thus, as Aquinas puts it, "while it does happen that evil is caused by some other evil (in the sense of a deficient good), we must finally arrive at the position that the *first* cause of evil is not evil, but good."[25]

3.2. Evil and the Voluntary

Now moral evil, says Aquinas, is a distinct case that shares some features with the evil found generally in nature, but not others, and this difference is due to

[24] I.e., it is the only kind of *efficient* cause such a privation needs. Privations also depend upon a subject or material cause.

[25] 1269-72: *De malo* q.1, a.3 (emphasis added): "Contingit autem et malum, quod est defectivum bonum, esse causam mali; sed tamen oportet devenire ad hoc quod *prima* causa mali non sit malum sed bonum."

the particular nature of the *voluntary*. For just as when the lion spots its prey there is a movement of animal appetite in respect of a perceived good, so also in voluntary action—including morally evil action—there is a positive movement of the will in respect of something apprehended as good in some respect (*secundum quid bonum*), as the prospect of sexual pleasure here and now may move a man to commit adultery. The difference in the movement of the will lies in its particular nature as a "self-mover"—an appetitive power able to determine freely its own response or lack of response to what is presented in apprehension. Aquinas writes:

> If the will were to receive the impression of something attractive and enjoyable with the same necessity that a natural body receives the impression of an agent, the case would be entirely the same as with natural things. But it is not so, because however much an exterior sensible attracts, it is in the power of the will to receive it or not to receive it. Thus, the cause of the evil that may stem from this thing's reception is not the enjoyable thing as mover, but rather the will itself.[26]

In other words, *the voluntary agent does not act simply by virtue of being acted upon*, as iron filings are attracted by a magnet, or as various animal appetites are stimulated by a smell or a touch (or even the sound of a bell, as with Pavlov's dogs). Rather the voluntary agent *determines itself* to will, and then to act, in respect of some apprehended good. Moral deprivation is not imposed on a voluntary agent from without.

When this self-determined willing and acting is *contrary* to the norm of morality, moral evil comes into existence. Here is the second difference of moral evil in comparison with natural evil: moral evil has to do with *deflection from a norm of which the voluntary agent is conscious*. This is the *norm of morality*, "the order of reason and of divine law" (*ordo rationis et legis divinae*) that properly measures the goodness of self-determined or free action. It is a norm that the rational being inevitably affirms in its most basic directives, for reason is connatural with this norm as the authentic measure of the very exercise of reason in the guiding of free actions. Thus, in being true to this norm, the

---

[26] 1269-72: *De malo* q.1, a.3: "Si ergo ita esset quod voluntas ex necessitate reciperet impressionem delectabilis allicientis, sicut ex necessitate corpus naturale recipit impressionem agentis, omnino idem esset in voluntariis et naturalibus. Non est autem sic, quia quantumcumque exterius sensibile alliciat, in potestate tamen voluntatis est recipere vel non recipere; unde mali quod accidit ex hoc quod recipit, non est causa ipsum delectabile movens, sed magis ipsa voluntas."

rational being is being true to its own nature, willing an end that is *due*—an end, in other words, that represents the excellence of its own way of being and acting.[27]

At the same time, the norm of morality is distinct from the agent's own (factual) volitions. In other words, it is not enough that I actually will *this*, for *this* to be simply or unqualifiedly good—good with the goodness proper to a free action. As obvious as this point may appear, it has an important consequence: in order to will and act well, it is required not only that I actually *will* whatever I will, but that I *will to apply* the norm of morality to whatever I will *as an appropriate measure* thereof. If, in a particular case, I will and act *contrary* to the norm of morality, it is evident that I am not thus applying the norm. In this way, my action contrary to the norm—that is, the morally evil action to which I consent—hinges on a *prior deficiency* in me, namely, my *non-application* of the norm of morality to the action as I conceived it prior to consent.

Now an apparent dilemma arises. For this evil to arise at all, the agent's attraction and adhesion to the apparent good clearly must be voluntary—that is, falling within the scope of the will's freedom to elicit or not to elicit a response to any particular good. Equally clearly, the prior deficiency of the *non-application* of the norm of morality to the prospective pursuit of this good must be voluntary—that is, falling within the scope of the will's freedom to elicit or not to elicit the willing of the norm's application. For if the agent is hindered from that application by something extrinsic to its own volition—if it is not free, in other words, actually to measure its own prospective action by the norm of morality—then the resulting evil is involuntary, moral responsibility vanishes, and the whole account of moral evil collapses.

Here then is the problem: if the agent freely omits or suspends the application of the norm of morality to a prospective choice, is this already a moral defect? For if it is, all we have done is to account for one moral evil by a prior moral evil that in turn demands to be accounted for. To avoid an infinite regress, explanation must stop at something that is *not* a moral evil, nor indeed an evil

---

[27] For example, the norm of morality commands that one shall not harm one's neighbor inasmuch as one's neighbor is another like oneself—that is, a person. This command is grounded in the intrinsic value of the person as such, a value that demands to be honored. The correct application of the norm depends, not only on awareness of the norm itself, but a correct judgment regarding the singular case: namely, that *this* individual is in fact a person.

of any sort, but a good. If the agent is to remain morally responsible, this good at which the explanation of moral evil stops must somehow be the good that *is* the voluntary agent as such. That is to say, the nature of such a being must somehow admit the possibility of a voluntary fault that undermines the goodness most proper to such a being. This terrible possibility may justly be called the "mystery of iniquity".

3.3. The Moment of Free Nihilation

It is mystery that presents more than one dimension. At present, we are looking along the dimension of the causality of agents as agents, the register of efficient causality. We are considering the evildoer as a deficient agent in nature, with the peculiarity that this deficient agent is the voluntary cause of its own deficiency, putting forth a deficient action by willing to do so. Let us see how Aquinas's illuminates this dimension of the mystery:[28]

> Whenever one thing is the due rule and measure of another, the good in that which is ruled and measured comes from its being ruled and conformed to that which is the rule and measure, whereas evil comes from not being so ruled and

---

[28] 1269-72: *De malo* q.1. a.3, emphasis added: "In omnibus enim quorum unum debet esse regula et mensura alterius, bonum in regulato et mensurato est ex hoc quod regulatur et conformatur regulae et mensurae; malum vero ex hoc quod est non regulari vel mensurari. Si ergo sit aliquis artifex qui debeat aliquod lignum recte incidere secundum aliquam regulam, si non directe incidat, quod est male incidere, haec mala incisio causabitur ex hoc defectu quod artifex erat sine regula et mensura. Similiter delectatio et quodlibet aliud in rebus humanis est mensurandum et regulandum secundum regulam rationis et legis divinae; unde *non uti* regula rationis et legis divinae praeintelligitur in voluntate ante inordinatam electionem. Huiusmodi autem quod est non uti regula praedicta, non oportet aliquam causam quaerere; quia *ad hoc sufficit ipsa libertas voluntatis, per quam potest agere vel non agere*; et hoc ipsum quod est non attendere actu ad talem regulam in se consideratam, non est malum nec culpa nec poena; quia anima non tenetur nec potest attendere ad huiusmodi regulam semper in actu; sed *ex hoc accipit primo rationem culpae, quod sine actuali consideratione regulae procedit ad huiusmodi electionem*; sicut artifex non peccat in eo quod non semper tenet mensuram, sed ex hoc quod non tenens mensuram procedit ad incidendum; et similiter culpa voluntatis non est in hoc quod actu non attendit ad regulam rationis vel legis divinae; sed ex hoc quod non habens regulam vel mensuram huiusmodi, procedit ad eligendum; et inde est quod Augustinus dicit in XII de Civitate Dei, quod *voluntas est causa peccati in quantum est deficiens*; sed illum defectum comparat silentio vel tenebris, quia scilicet *defectus ille est negatio sola*."

> measured. If, then, a carpenter were bound to cut a piece of wood straight according to a rule and did not cut it so—which is to cut badly—this bad cut will be caused by the [prior] defect that the carpenter was lacking the rule and measure.
>
> Similarly, sensual enjoyment and everything else in human affairs ought to be measured and ruled by the rule of reason and divine law. And so, *not to use* the rule of reason and divine law must be understood to be in the will before the disordered choice. It is not necessary to seek any cause for something of this sort, i.e., the non-use of the rule, because *for this the very freedom of the will, by which it either acts or does not act, suffices*. Now this actual non-attention to a rule is not an evil (either of fault or of penalty) considered in itself, because the soul is neither bound to, nor can it, always attend actually to a rule of this kind. Rather, the soul *first receives the character of [moral] fault from this: that, without the actual consideration of the rule, it proceeds to a choice of this kind*. For just as the carpenter commits fault, not by always failing to hold the measure, but by not holding it when he proceeds to cut, so similarly the fault of the will is not the lack of actual attention to the rule of reason or divine law; rather, [the fault] is that, not "holding" this kind of rule, it proceeds to choose. It is for this reason that Augustine says in the twelfth book of *De civitate Dei* that *the will is the cause of sin inasmuch as it is deficient*, but the defect he compares to silence or darkness—for *this defect [of free non-consideration] is that of negation only*.

Before considering the main thrust of this argument, we must take special notice of Aquinas's comparison of the non-application of the norm of morality with the non-use of a carpenter's square. Here in *De malo*, Aquinas makes it clear that the "actual consideration of the rule" that is omitted or suspended prior to consent to an evil action is not *any* kind of consideration of the norm of morality, nor indeed any kind of comparison of this norm with a prospective action, but the *particular* kind of consideration involved in the *actual use of the norm of morality as a practical measure*, in the same way as the carpenter *holds* the square and then *makes* a cut conformed to its edge.[29] Cognition is involved in comparing and guiding an action in accordance with the measure, but "use" is principally an act of the will motivated by the agent's desire to consent to no action that does not conform to the norm of morality, just as it is the will of the carpenter to make no cut that is not straight.

---

[29] See Aquinas 1271: *ST* Ia-IIae, q.16, a.1 on meaning of "using" a thing as the will applying that thing to an action.

Now to the main point of the argument. If an agent is to fail morally by consenting to morally evil action, there must be a moment *prior* to this consent in which the agent omits or suspends the application (in the sense just discussed) of the norm of morality to the preconceived action. As we have seen, this omission or suspension must itself be voluntary, if the evil action is to be voluntary. And indeed it is voluntary: it always falls within the scope of the will's freedom to apply or not to apply the norm of morality in this way. Now the *mere* omission or suspension of this act of application of the norm of morality to an action prior to consent is, Aquinas argues, a kind of "deficiency" (*defectus*) indeed, but *not yet* a moral evil or sin. It is only a *negation* (*negatio sola*)—a free non-action or absence of an act—but not a *privation*, since in fact it is not possible for the finite intellectual creature to be always actually "attending" to such a norm, but must rather continually will afresh the application of the norm in the course of life and the stream of conscious activity. It cannot be, then, that the free non-application of the norm can have *by itself* the character of moral evil. Rather, when a particular choice is imminent, this free nihilation (as Maritain called it) of the application of the norm sets the stage for moral fault, makes it a proximate possibility, and so becomes in retrospect the "prior deficiency" that gives rise to moral evil as stemming from a "deficient agent", whenever a voluntary agent, in the condition of this free nihilation, elicits consent to an evil action. Like the carpenter who cuts crookedly by not holding the square and then proceeding to cut, such an agent voluntarily commits sin by freely not "holding" the norm and then proceeding to choose.[30]

By this argument, Aquinas succeeds in illuminating something of the origin of moral evil as *freely defective action*, construed in a manner similar to deficient agency in the rest of nature. The cause of moral evil is not a good *per se*—not human will insofar as it is human will, which would impugn its Creator—but *a good together with a negation*, that is, a "good accompanied by the absence of some other good."[31] Since the inclination toward a *secundum quid bonum* as

---

[30] This insight was hailed by Jacques Maritain (1963: *Dieu et la permission du mal* [*God and the Permission of Evil*], 34) as "a metaphysical discovery of the first magnitude, absolutely fundamental, and without which no philosophy of evil is possible."

[31] See 1271: *ST* Ia-IIae, q.75, a.1, ad.3, which parallels the current discussion in much briefer terms: "Ad tertium dicendum quod, sicut dictum est, voluntas sine adhibitione regulae rationis vel legis divinae, est causa peccati. Hoc autem quod est non adhibere regulam rationis vel legis divinae, secundum se non habet rationem mali, nec poenae

well as the non-application of the norm of morality to this object are both voluntary, the evil action that arises from these two conditions is voluntary, including that very aspect of the evil action that is its moral fault.

Voluntary evil arises, then, not immediately, but by a two-stage process in the wake of the apprehension of a *secundum quid bonum*: a particular *non-act* (non-application of the norm of morality) followed by a particular *act* (of consent). Both the non-act and the act are *free*, lying within the scope of the will's freedom to elicit or not to elicit any particular volition,[32] and—most importantly—neither the non-act nor the act presupposes an agent *already morally deficient*. For the non-application (in and by itself) of the norm of morality prior to consent renders the agent "deficient" in a manner that reflects merely its finitude and the non-identity of the finite will with the norm of its own goodness.[33] The succession of the two moments—the free non-act followed by the free act—in the wake of an

---

nec culpae, antequam applicetur ad actum. Unde secundum hoc, peccati primi non est causa aliquod malum, sed bonum aliquod cum absentia alicuius alterius boni." — "The cause of sin is the will in the absence of employment of the rule of reason or divine law. Now in itself, this non-employment (*non adhibere*) of the rule of reason or divine law does not have the nature of evil, either of penalty or of fault, before it is applied to an act. And so for this reason the cause of the first sin is not something evil, but a good accompanied by the absence of some other good."

[32] If consent to evil followed *of necessity* from the condition of non-application of the norm, then the latter could not avoid having the nature of moral fault. In fact, the will remains always free to will a fresh application (or re-application) of the norm to the course of action under consideration. On the other hand, actual consent to evil does *presuppose* the prior free non-application, since an evil action is, by definition, an action unmeasured by the norm of morality.

[33] 1269-72: *De malo* q.1., a.3, ad 9: "Ad nonum dicendum, quod bonum ex hoc quod est creatum, aliquo modo potest deficere illo defectu ex quo malum voluntarium procedit: quia ex hoc ipso quod est creatum, sequitur quod ipsum sit subiectum alteri, sicut regulae et mensurae. Si autem ipsum esset sua regula et mensura, non posset sine regula ad opus procedere. Propter hoc Deus, qui est sua regula, peccare non potest; sicut nec artifex peccare posset in incisione ligni si sua manus regula esset incisionis." — "A good, from the fact that it is something created, is able to become deficient in this way (i.e., that deficiency from which voluntary evil proceeds), because from the very fact that it is created, it follows that it is subject to another as its rule and measure. Now if its rule and measure were its very self, it would not be able to proceed to act in the absence of the rule. It is on account of this that God, being His own rule, cannot sin, even as an artisan could not commit a fault in cutting wood, were his own hand the rule for cutting."

encounter with a *secundum quid bonum* is sufficient, it would seem, to account for the coming into existence of moral evil in the line of efficient causality.

Very good. But it is one thing to explain moral evil in this way as a (moral) deficiency following freely upon another (non-moral) deficiency. It is quite another thing to explain how evil is chosen as a matter of moral psychology, or better, moral psychosemiotics. Aquinas's account is important—a landmark, as Maritain says—but it is an account of moral evil, not in all its dimensions, but as projected onto the plane of *ens naturae* and efficient causality. To be sure, the being of the object appears in this account—for without a will there is no moral evil, and without an object there is neither any willing of a good, nor any voluntary suspension of willing the practical comparison of a good with another object, the norm of morality. What is omitted in the account, for it belongs to a different line of consideration, is the manner in which these objects are construed in particular cases within the objective world—the cognitive and affective interpretants engendered by these objects as signs, from which energetic interpretants (actions) then emerge.

For instance, granted that free nihilation of the application of the norm of morality belongs to moral evil as a necessary condition, does voluntary evil represent no more than the toleration of a loss—the loss of the excellence of conformity to the norm, a lack of order to a due end—for the sake of the gain represented by a *secundum quid bonum*, a "good in some respect"—say, a self-evident yet limited good such as wealth or pleasure or honor?

What, in fact, does it mean to will what is evil?

4. Moral Evil from the Standpoint of the Object

4.1. Two Ways of Predicating Evil

Significant indications are offered by Aquinas himself. In the earlier-referenced foundational discussion of *De malo* 1.1 on the nature of evil as privatively opposed to the good that every being is insofar as it is actual, the twelfth objector argues that evil must be something (*aliquid*) of a positive nature, since evil and good are the *constitutive differentiators* of vice and virtue, and whatever is such a differentiator is something that is both a unity and a being (*unum et ens*). This would suggest that moral evil is itself a form of some sort. Aquinas replies that evil is not such a differentiator, "*except in the domain of morals*, in which 'evil' means something positive, insofar as the very act of will is denominated evil from *what it wills*, although even this evil itself is not able to be willed except under the aspect of good."[34] Earlier, in his response to the fourth objector, Aquinas had agreed that the opposition of good and evil *in the domain of morals* is *not* a privative opposition between a form on the one hand and the simple lack of that form on the other, but is rather an opposition of contraries.

> This is because moral matters depend on the will, and the object of the will is good and evil. Now every act is named and receives its species from its object. In this way, then, the act of the will, insofar as it bears itself [positively] *to evil*, receives the intelligible structure and name of evil, and *this evil* is, in the proper sense, *contrary* to the good.[35]

The immediate import of these statements is that the malefactor, as our female interlocutor says, indeed does not merely *will wrongly*, as one might play a violin wrongly while intending to play well, but *wills what is wrong*. If I hurt someone inadvertently, my willed action is in that respect "beside" the norm of morality (*praeter rationem*), inasmuch it is deflected from what would have been morally right (that is, I should have omitted this action or done something different). Now if the inadvertence stemmed from neglect on my part, then I am blameworthy to some degree, but not to the degree I am blameworthy if I rather inflict pain and injury deliberately, out of cruelty. In that case, the action itself as proceeding from my will is not merely *praeter rationem* but *contra rationem*, not merely beside but *contrary* to the norm of morality. The same is true, though in a different mode, if I do wrong under the influence of a passion such as anger or lust. Moral evil is *transgression:* it does not merely fall away from the norm of moral goodness, it positively opposes it. It is set against it, even setting itself against it. My morally evil action is not merely deflected from the norm; it is

---

[34] 1269-72: *De malo* q.1, a.1, ad.12, emphasis added: "Ad duodecimum dicendum quod bonum et malum non sunt differentiae nisi in moralibus, in quibus malum positive aliquid dicitur, secundum quod ipse actus voluntatis denominatur malus a volito, licet et ipsum malum non possit esse volitum nisi sub ratione boni."

[35] 1269-72: *De malo* q.1, a.1, ad.4, emphasis added: "Ad quartum dicendum quod ideo in moralibus magis quam in naturalibus malum contrarium bono dicitur, quia moralia ex voluntate dependent, voluntatis autem objectum est bonum et malum. Omnis autem actus denominatur et speciem recipit ab objecto. Sic igitur actus voluntatis, in quantum fertur *in malum*, recipit rationem et nomen mali; et *hoc malum* contrariatur proprie bono."

deflected because *in some manner I will it to be so*. That is to say, in willing this action, *I will this being-opposed* to the norm of morality.[36] Not merely killing, but murder, is what the murderer wills. It is this willed positive opposition that constitutively differentiates evil from good in the domain of morals.

> The moral act itself is fundamentally a being of reason. Aquinas says that whether an act is good or bad depends on its object. The object "is not the matter of which (a thing is made), but the matter about which (something is done)." The nature of this object has been a matter of considerable dispute. What is clear is that the object involves not just the thing that happened (a trigger was pulled and someone died), but the understanding and will of the doer (who may, for instance, intend the act as either self-defense or murder). Aquinas teaches that, in choosing to do evil, one desires the good to which the evil is attached more than the good of which the evil is the privation (as one may desire the perceived good of being free of a blackmailer to which the act of murder is attached more than the good of justice of which murder is the privation. When evil is desired in this way, the act must be viewed not as essentially good and

---

[36] In interpreting Aquinas's discussions of deficient agency in moral evil (as in *De malo* q.1, a.3 and parallel passages), it is important to avoid the misunderstanding that would construe "voluntary non-consideration" or "voluntary inattention" to the norm of morality as mere forgetfulness of the norm, or the absence of any actual awareness of the norm whatever during the interval prior to evil choice. This explains our previous emphasis upon Aquinas's comparison of "non-consideration" to the carpenter's use of the square in our discussion of *De malo* q.1, a.3 above. What is essential in this matter is what we have emphasized by our preference for the expression, "voluntary *non-application*": the free omission or suspension of the *use* of the norm of morality *as the guiding norm* for the action to be put forth. What *other* forms of "consideration" the norm of morality may receive from the agent in this interval depends on the mode of transgression as stemming from an occasion of emotional arousal (sins from passion or weakness), or from factors intrinsic to the will and the considerations of reason—sinning from "malice" or "determined evilness" (*ex certa malitia*), which is characterized by a consideration of the norm of morality different from its practical use as a norm, the attitude of "contempt."

incidentally evil (as involving some privation), but as essentially evil...

Dodds, "Made of Flame and Air" [p.208-09].

We may thus distinguish between two distinct ways in which evil is predicated. Following Gregory Reichberg, we refer to them as the *ontological predication* and the *moral predication* of evil.[37] Taken simply and without qualification as to domain—that is, taken as it is in opposition to good in the sense in which the good is interchangeable with being-as-actual (*bonum quod convertitur cum ente*)—evil is *nothing but* privative non-being. It represents the loss of being. It is applicable to all natures, and thus applicable in a special way to free actions (and their agents) that suffer loss of the specific actuality or excellence they ought to have. This is evil predicated ontologically. This is the point of view of the discussion of voluntary evil as deficient agency in *De malo* 1.3 and the discussion of the previous section.

In the moral domain of vice and virtue, evil is predicated differently. In this domain, evil and good are specific differentiators of voluntary actions, inasmuch as they qualify the *objects* of these actions in light of their relation to the norm of morality, namely, whether these objects (and hence the actions of which they are the objects) *accord* with the norm of morality or *oppose* it. This is largely the point of view of the treatment of morals in the massive second part of the *Summa theologiae*, questions 8-16 of *De malo* on the capital sins, and other similar discussions.[38]

---

[37] Reichberg 2002: "Beyond Privation: Moral Evil in Aquinas's *De malo*". This article contains the best exposition we have found of moral evil as privation that also includes a clear discussion the limits of this notion.

[38] Reichberg (2002: "Beyond Privation", 776) suggests that the two modes of predicating evil, as they are employed in moral matters, can be seen as an instance of an analogy of attribution, with moral loss or privation (ontological mode of predication) as the primary referent, and the willing of the evil end which positively excludes the due end (moral mode of predication) as the secondary referent. From this standpoint, the primary or *unconditioned* meaning of evil remains simply privation, even in the domain of morals. The secondary or *conditioned* meaning of evil is distinct, but contains a reference to the primary meaning: to will an evil end is to *refuse one's own true good,* including the

The two modes of predicating evil are, of course, not equivocal, but connected. Freely opposing the norm of morality *always*, and *by its very nature*, incurs the loss of being:[39]

> First, on the part of the act itself, insofar as it is deprived of its due excellence, and second, on the part of the agent who, having freely posited a disordered act, is himself deprived of valuable internal goods, natural and supernatural. The loss of psychic harmony, the obfuscation of moral consciousness, and the penchant for accrued wrongdoing are among the natural effects of sin, and from the privation of divine grace there results the loss of supernatural goods such as faith, hope, charity, and the share in the divine beatitude which they confer. The malefactor thereby harms himself most grievously by his misdeeds. Indeed, he harms himself in a way that he could never harm others (or them him) since it is in the invisible root of selfhood—the soul—that he suffers this damage.

Augustine even went so far as to call sin "nothing", a non-being (*peccatum est nichil*). Aquinas interprets:[40]

> A sin is 'nothing' in the manner in which human beings become 'nothing' when they sin: not that they become nothing itself, but that insofar as they sin, they are deprived of a certain good, and privation itself is a non-being in a subject. Similarly, a sin is an action deprived of due order, and according to that privation it is said to be 'nothing'.

The loss suffered by the agent is not the evil of sin as such, but the inevitable *consequence* of it. Sin itself is "an action deprived of due order". But here is where the matter becomes interesting. There is privation in the evil action indeed, but the evil action *as such* is *more* than an action that lacks a certain rectitude. It is an action with a certain kind of object, an *evil end*. What is an evil end? An evil end is an *un-due* end—that is, an end whose pursuit *positively*

---

excellence that ought to belong to one's actions, and *thus* to endure its loss as a consequence of choosing an end incompatible with that good.

[39] Reichberg 2002: "Beyond Privation", 759.

[40] 1269-72*: De malo* q.2, a.1, obj 4: "Eo enim modo peccatum nichil est, quo nichil fiunt homines cum peccant: non quidem ita quod sint ipsum nichil, sed quia inquantum peccant, privantur quodam bono, et ipsa privation est non ens in subjecto; et similiter peccatum est actus privatus ordine debito, et secundum ipsam privationem dicitur nichil."

excludes action in accordance with the norm of morality.[41] By virtue of its evil end, the evil action is positively opposed to the norm of morality, and it is *because* of this positive opposition to the norm that *both* forms of deprivation are incurred: the loss of rectitude in the action itself put forth, and the loss of being incurred by the agent.

4.2. Moral Evil as "Mixed" Privation

In *De malo* 2.9, Aquinas rejects the definition given by some Stoics (whom he does not name) of evil action as nothing but an action lacking moral rectitude. For instance, adultery is a sin, according to them, not because intercourse with the person is evil in itself (*secundum se malum*), but because it is beside the rule of reason (*praeter rectitudinem rationis*). Their analysis thus cleanly separates the positive intentional character of an action from its morally deficient character, with the latter held to consist in the pure privation of rectitude. Since the very same pure privation would belong to any sin whatever, one consequence of this clean analytical separation is the conclusion that all sins are equal, which is the very point at issue in *De malo* 2.9. A second consequence pointed out by Aquinas is that every evil action would become a sin of omission: for what the Stoic definition fails to capture is precisely the element of *transgression*—voluntary opposition to the norm of morality.[42] While even sins of omission are in fact susceptible of degrees according to extrinsic factors such

---

[41] The moral specification of acts from their ends comprehends also acts that are willed as means to further ends, whether the further ends be evil or not. To use one of Aquinas's examples (borrowed from Aristotle), the man who steals in order to commit adultery is *both* an adulterer *and* a thief, though he is *more* an adulterer than a thief, inasmuch as it was only the prospect of adultery that made it seem good to him also to steal. See 1271: *ST* Ia-IIae, q.18, a.6.

[42] See Reichberg 2002: "Beyond Privation", 756-758. In particular (757): "A wrongful deed has the character of privation insofar as it lacks a due ordination to the agent's rightful end; it is something more than privation insofar as it is an act posited in opposition to the moral rule. Significantly, Thomas expressly indicates that of these two elements, transgressing the rule [of morality] is more essential to the intelligibility (*ratio*) of moral evil than the corresponding failure to achieve the end. The former undergirds the latter." Reichberg cites *De malo* q.2, a.1 on the nature of fault in general (in nature, art, or morals): "[M]agis est de ratione peccati preterire regulam actionis quam etiam deficere ab actionis fine." — "It is more of the nature of fault to disregard the rule of an action than even to fail to achieve the end of the action."

as the dignity of the precept violated, it is above all from the varying modes of transgression that degrees of gravity accrue to sin. Not all sins are equal.

In rejecting the Stoic analysis, Aquinas is led to distinguish between two kinds of privation. One kind is pure privation (*privatio pura*) in which nothing is left of the form taken away, as death leaves nothing of life. The other kind is non-pure or mixed privation (*privatio non pura)* in which something is left—something positive (*aliquid*), as sickness does not remove the entire equilibrium constituting the health of an organism, but leaves something of that balance remaining:[43]

> With the first kind [i.e. pure privations], the cause or manner in which something is deprived is irrelevant as regards possible differences of degree, because the removal is entire, and whatever we then say in a positive way does not fall within the intelligible sense of this privation. For the man who dies from one wound is not less dead than the man who dies from two or three... But with the second kind [i.e., mixed privations], the removal is not entire, and whatever is said then in a positive way does fall within the intelligible sense of that which is said in a privative way. And for this reason, these latter [privations] are susceptible of degree according to the difference of that which is said positively, just as sickness is said to be greater according as the cause taking away health be greater or more multiple.

Whereas sins of omission involve a pure privation insofar as they are omissions,[44]

---

[43] 1269-72: *De malo* q.2, a.9: "Quia ergo in primis privationibus totum privatur, et id quod positive dicitur non est de ratione privationis, non differt in talibus privationibus quacumque ex causa vel quocumque modo aliquis privetur, ut propter hoc dicatur magis vel minus privatus; non enim mortuus est minus qui uno vulnere percussus interiit, quam qui duobus vel tribus; .... In secundis autem privationibus non totum privatur; et quod positive dicitur, est de ratione eius, quod dicitur privative; et ideo talia recipiunt magis et minus secundum differentiam eius quod dicitur positive: sicut aegritudo dicitur maior si fuerit causa tollens sanitatem aut maior aut multiplicior."

[44] 1269-72: *De malo* q.2, a.9: "Peccatum vero transgressionis consistit in deformitate alicuius actus, quae quidem deformitas non tollit totum ordinem rationis, sed aliquid eius: puta, si aliquis comedat quando non debet, et remanet quod comedat ubi debet vel propter quod debet. Nec potest actu remanente totaliter rationis proportio tolli; unde dicit philosophus in IV *Ethicorum*, quod si malum sit integrum, importabile fit, et se ipsum destruit. Sicut ergo non omnis deformitas corporis est aequalis, sed quaedam est alia maior, secundum quod privantur plura ad decorem pertinentia vel aliquid principalius; ita non omnis deformitas vel inordinatio actus est aequalis, sed quaedam est alia maior. Unde nec omnia peccata sunt paria."

> the fault of transgression consists in the deformity of some action, which deformity indeed does not take away the whole order of reason but something of it. For example, if it is at the wrong time that someone eats, it remains the case that he eats in the place and for the reason that he ought. Nor while the [evil] action persists can the whole proportion of reason by entirely taken away from it, as the Philosopher says in the fourth book of *Ethics*, that were evil entire (*integrum*), it would become insupportable and destroy itself.

Aquinas's point here is that it belongs to the very nature of transgression that there can be no clean separation between the positive intention of the will and its defective character, for it is the positive willing of some object—in Aquinas's example, to eat *now*—that is actually *transgressive* and bears the morally evil character. Moreover, this positive intending of the object is conceptually prior to the lack of rectitude that affects the action in consequence.[45]

---

[45] From Michel Labourdette's lecture course on the morality of human acts (1958-59: *Cours de théologie morale,* "Les actes humains", 135, emphasis added): "Qu'est-ce qui fait une moralité objective mauvaise? — Ce n'est pas seulement l'absence d'une conformité positive à la règle de la raison: on aurait simplement un objet moralement indifférent; c'est un rapport de répugnance, une opposition de contrariété au bien que la raison demanderait. L'acte humain qui se porte à un tel objet l'atteint précisément comme opposé à la raison, opposé en toute sa positivité; c'est cela qui le spécifie. *Il s'ensuit,* bien sûr, dans l'acte la privation de la conformité a la raison qu'il devrait avoir; il n'a plus son intégrité humaine. Par là, il *s'oppose privativement* a l'acte moralement bon; mais c'est parce qu'il lui est *déjà positivement opposé* d'une opposition de contrariété à raison de l'objet qui le spécifie. Dans la moralité mauvaise, spécifiquement opposée à la moralité bonne, il y a donc deux choses: (a) la spécification de l'acte par un objet contraire à l'exigence de la raison; (b) et, *par suite* la privation de la rectitude qui ferait son intégrité humaine. C'est par cette privation que l'acte mauvais entre dans la grande catégorie du mal au sens transcendantal; mais ce n'est pas cette privation comme telle qui spécifie l'acte mauvais; ce qui le spécifie, c'est l'objet positivement contraire à la raison, sur lequel cette privation se fonde. Cela est déjà d'ordre moral et d'une moralité déjà justement dite mauvaise parce qu'elle implique immédiatement la privation conséquente de rectitude." — "What makes the object [of a human action] morally evil? It is not solely the absence of a positive conformity to the rule of reason, for then one would have simply an object morally indifferent. It is a relation of repugnance, an opposition of contrariety to the good that reason would demand. The human action which bears itself toward such an object attains it precisely as opposed to reason, opposed in all its positivity; it is this [opposition] which specifies it. *There follows* in the action, of course, the privation of the conformity to reason which it ought to have: the action is deprived of human integrity, and it is on that account *privatively opposed* to the morally good act; but this is because it is *already positively opposed* to it with an

Now "to eat" is the expression of a natural appetite, and food for a living organism is a good that needs no explanation. When food is readily available (as it is not, for too much of humankind), it is the sort of good that one simply *takes* (even if it is with effort, as in a hunt) or leaves. The same may be said of various pleasures, including the sexual kind. Such goods are self-evident and ready to hand, and it is perhaps understandable that goods of this kind furnish the matter for elementary examples of moral transgression, even as it is stressed that, for moral agents that have the "use of reason" and access to the requisite knowledge, transgression involves not merely a voluntary turning-toward (*conversio*) a relative good, but a voluntary turning-away-from (*aversio*) the norm of morality.[46]

---

opposition of contrariety by reason of the object which specifies it. In the morally evil as specifically opposed to the morally good [action], there are thus two factors: (a) the specification of the action by an object contrary to the requirement of reason, and (b) *by consequence* the privation of that rectitude which would constitute its human integrity. It is by this privation that the evil action enters into the great category of evil in the transcendental sense, but it is not this privation as such which specifies the evil action. What specifies it, is the object positively contrary to reason, upon which this privation is founded. This is already of the moral order and of a moral character already rightly called evil insofar as it immediately implies the consequent privation of rectitude."

[46] Consider the relative goods that figure in this discussion of Aquinas in i.1259/65: *SCG*, lib.3 c.9: "Quod igitur in moralibus sortitur speciem a fine qui est secundum rationem, dicitur secundum speciem suam bonum: quod vero sortitur speciem a fine contrario fini rationis, dicitur secundum speciem suam malum. Finis autem ille, etsi tollat finem rationis, est tamen aliquod bonum: sicut delectabile secundum sensum, vel aliquid huiusmodi. Unde et in aliquibus animalibus sunt bona; et homini etiam cum sunt secundum rationem moderata; et contingit quod est malum uni, esse bonum alteri. Et ideo nec malum, secundum quod est differentia specifica in genere moralium, importat aliquid quod sit secundum essentiam suam malum: sed aliquid quod secundum se est bonum, malum autem homini, inquantum privat ordinem rationis, quod est hominis bonum." — "In moral matters, that which is specified by an end that is in accord with reason is called good specifically; and that which is specified by an end contrary to the rational end is termed evil specifically. Yet that contrary end, even though it runs counter to the rational end, is nevertheless some sort of good: for instance, something that delights on the sense level, or anything like that. These are goods for certain animals, and even for man, when they are moderated by reason. It happens as well that what is evil for one being is good for another. So, evil, as a specific difference in the genus of moral matters, does not imply something that is evil in its own essence, but

4.3. Moral Evil as Interpretant

On the other hand, constant recourse to examples of this self-evident kind can encourage the habit of thinking that transgression is always a matter of selective attention, or singular fixation upon something self-evidently "good in a particular way"—upon pleasure or bodily health or status—in such a way as to freely neglect consideration of the true "good according to reason" represented by conformity with the norm of morality. In transgressions that stem from a failure to arrest the progression of sensual or emotional arousal, this may be the case. But it is not always the case.[47] Any man who commits adultery is in an obvious sense motivated by arousal, but some particular man might have been quite ready to do this even before encountering some particular woman. When such a man commits adultery, he does not act out of passion or weakness (*ex passione vel infirmitate*), but rather out of a sense of purpose—out of an evil conviction that has now found an opportunity for greater realization (*ex industria, ex certa malitia*).

The difference between acting out of weakness and acting out of a sense of purpose lies in *the objective context within which the moral object signifies*. In the case of the man who has an affair out of a sense of purpose, it is the prior constitution of the objective world (that part of it that is public, as well as that part of it that is *de facto* private to him) that determines him to have the affair, far more than—and in a more formal way than—the particular occasion determines him. For him, who does evil *ex industria*, it is not a question of the

---

something that is good in itself, though evil for man, inasmuch as it takes away the order of reason which is the good for man." The concern of this passage is the same as that in *De malo* q.1, a.1, namely, to show that evil itself is not *aliquid*, something "having an essence" in nature that the malefactor seeks, even though evil is, according to a different mode of predication, a specific differentiator of human acts.

[47] Some authors seem to overinterpret Aquinas's theory of voluntary non-consideration in psychological terms as a lack of "thoroughness" in deliberation, or a partial consideration of an action that focuses only on self-evident benefits (e.g., the material benefits of theft), followed by consent to an action from this "freely chosen myopic perspective." See Dewan 1992: "St. Thomas and the First Cause of Moral Evil", 1228–29, and also Sherwin 2005: *By Knowledge and By Love: Charity and Knowledge in the Moral Theology of St. Thomas Aquinas*, 104, who follows Dewan's lead. While one can agree that moral evil must be "myopic" in some way or other (*sub specie aeternitatis*), general psychological characterizations of this sort tend to obscure the phenomenon of contempt that rejects application of the norm of morality in favor of a norm that the agent consciously prefers.

norm of morality slipping from view or becoming weightless on account of emotional arousal. It is a question rather of the opposition between the norm of morality and a *counter-norm* that the agent takes as a superior measure of what is to be done. This is *contempt* for the norm of morality, a deliberate devaluation that can reach the extreme of conscious hatred for the norm of morality itself and for the goodness that accords with it, and even the practical effort, within an agent's scope of influence, to bring that goodness to ruin.

The *sense* in an agent's contempt for the norm of morality stems from the patterns of signification that obtain in the objective world. This sense, in other words, is the interpretant of some action of a sign. The objective world is also where the expressions of this contempt—further interpretants including wicked actions (energetic interpretants) themselves—*live* in the whole of their being. These expressions do not live merely in the natural cosmos subsisting independently of awareness. Finally, it is in the objective world where we can find the key to the "positivity" of moral evil. For discoverable in the webs of signification sustaining particular moral evils are pure objects functioning within the objective world as *counter-norms* opposed to the norm of morality—that is how they are taken, that is how they signify.[48] In our view, Aquinas's notion of moral evil as a mixed privation comprehends, even as it also conceals, the reality of such pure objects. And here we discover the link between the questions of the nature of moral evil and the meaning of "reality".

For our graduate student and those of a similar habit of mind, that which is "real" in a positive sense is that which exercises (or can exercise) the being proper to nature, *ens naturae*, precisely insofar as it does (or can) exercise it. Since every being in nature desires its own fullness, mind-independent being thus comes to be thought of as the repository of all that is appetible in the manner of an end, and an "evil end" comes to be reduced to the intention of some particular good whose appetibility is grounded in the givenness of nature and its possibilities, *albeit creatively taken up by human intelligence.*

It is that final clause that contains the clue to something more. "Reality", for human intelligence, is not merely the being of nature it has managed to grasp; but the being that it creates. It happens that the creativity of human intelligence

[48] We explore this genus of pure object in a monograph in preparation, which advances our previous work (Kanzelberger 2011: *The Mystical Daydream: Fictive Being and the Motive of Evil*) in the direction of a psychosemiotics of moral evil.

can engender a positivity that oversteps the understood possibilities of nature, including moral possibilities.

Jacques Maritain once censured a "Cyclopean Thomism" that sought to illuminate every matter exclusively from the perspective of the line of being (*ens naturae*) without due consideration of the line of non-being. It is in the line of non-being, he wrote, that the sinner has the first initiative: absent this acknowledgment, the divine innocence itself is impugned.[49] The non-being Maritain had in mind was privative non-being and the darkness of voluntary non-consideration, the absence of an act. But if "being" is equated with the being of nature, then it must be said that there is another kind of "non-being", namely, the pure object—*ens rationis*, mind-dependent being posited in the practical order—the creative fantasy, the castle in the air, or what we have called a mystical daydream. It is true, as Aquinas says, that "every sin is founded upon a natural appetite." Among these natural human appetites lies a most primordial desire, the desire to create.

5. The Moral Causality of Signs

5.1. Moral Evil as Semiotic Disorder

Let us return to the example of adultery and consider the cases of two men. For both, the marital covenant along with its duties are objects in the semiotic web. Each man understands that these objects are not his inventions, but intersubjective realities and specifications of the norm of morality that are relevant to such a matter as an extramarital affair, relative to which pursuit these objects represent a constraint. This understanding is "practical" inasmuch it concerns a matter of action, but the standing of this course of action relative to the norm of morality may be "considered" in a theoretical way only, or it may be "considered" in the manner of a fully practical—that is, a directive—cognition that guides deliberation and the subsequent actions in the way that the use of the square guides a carpenter's action of cutting. While the two forms of "consideration" may yield similar judgments regarding the moral standing of a course of action, it is the latter form of consideration alone whose omission or suspension is posited by the theory of defective voluntary agency as a necessary moment prior to evil choice.

---

[49] See Maritain 1963 [1966]: *God and the Permission of Evil*, 30-31.

First Case. Consider the series of interpretants in the case of a man whose marriage is unhappy, but whose "consideration" of the norm of morality is that of full practical application, inasmuch as he intends to act virtuously. First, there is the practical judgment concerning the standing of a course of action in relation to the norm of morality; then, a feeling of aversion and fear of moral danger (affective interpretants); finally, the declining of an invitation to dinner for two with an attractive female colleague in an exotic yet charming locale while traveling on business (energetic interpretant).

That is one possible action of signs. The *ground* or rationale of this particular semiosis lies in collateral conditions: the connaturality of the man's rational nature with the norm of morality, his cognitive and affective habits, his consciousness of the vow he took, and—most central to this exercise of his freedom—the free identification of the good of his married state[50] with his own good. The man's freedom is expressed in the critical control he exercises over his own semiosis: for he would always be free to shift his construal of objects to one that engenders a very different series of interpretants, and there is no object save one that he desires with a necessity of nature.

That sole object desired by a necessity of nature is "his own good" taken in formally and simply—"his own good" in an unqualified and therefore complete sense. This is "happiness", the objective correlate of the metaphysical truth that the rational being, like every being, seeks its own fullness. It belongs to a rational nature to be able to think expressly in terms of its own fullness, and to will it as the "ultimate end." As the ultimate end, happiness functions as the principle of principles in matters of action, the norm of all norms. As Aquinas writes: "That in which one reposes as in an ultimate end is the master of one's affections, for from it one takes the rules for one's entire life."[51] The man feels the attractions of dinner and the woman, their significance for some kind of fullness in life, but he masters these attractions on account of his vision of what is simply good for him. He has freely identified **his own good** with a good that transcends these goods and his own ego. The norm of morality as he relates it to his situation is nothing but the representation of such a transcending good as freely identified with his own good. This free identification is why these "relative goods" *are* relative, not merely in truth, but *to him*. The action he puts forth, or the

---

[50] Not in the abstract, but concretely: that is, union with *this* woman, forsaking all others.
[51] 1271: *ST* Ia-IIae, q.5, a.1, s.c.: "[I]llud in quo quiescit aliquis sicut in ultimo fine, hominis affectui dominatur, quia ex eo totius vitae suae regulas accipit."

restraining of an action, bears this precise meaning—a meaning which makes of his action (whose exterior and natural aspect is but the "body" of this sign) a good that is unrepeatable under heaven.

In putting forth this action, this man has acted as a creator: a good has come to be that could only come to be through his freedom. His moral struggle consisted precisely in this: that he, immersed in these conditions of existence—a less than happy marriage, an attractive colleague with an open smile meant for him on her face, the beginnings of a daydream of a new and unburdened future...—fulfills himself as creator instead by a transcending of himself as a lover of God and his family as other selves.

Second case. Now consider the man who begins an affair out of a sense of purpose. He has convinced himself that what is simply good for him (his happiness) is at odds with the norm of morality. To be sure, as Aquinas says, even the evil that consists in the transgression of this norm is not able to be willed except under the aspect of a good. In other words, the decision to transgress is not merely a question of "what a thing is", but of "how it is taken". With regard to "what it is," the norm of morality constrains by virtue of a relation to his action that is not subject to the man's will. With regard to "how it is taken", his consideration of the norm of morality engenders a series of interpretants by which he relates to it in a practical way as corruptive of a good that is specified by his own vision of happiness, in which he reposes as in an ultimate end. Taken in this way, the norm of morality has the aspect of an evil and is hateful to him (affective interpretant), even as it is lovable when taken otherwise.[52] The transgression of this norm therefore represents the removal of an obstacle to what he takes as simply good for him. The outcome of his deliberation is that he acts in contempt of the norm of morality (energetic interpretant) in light of a preferential judgment which is not merely a judgment in favor of the particularity of a certain pleasure or other self-evident good that is ready to hand and merely taken "out of context", but a judgment representing the application of a counter-norm as superior to the norm of morality.

---

[52] Cf. Aquinas, i.1256-59: *De veritate* q.22, a.1, ad.7: "Eiusdem autem rationis est in appetendo et fugiendo, aliquid esse bonum et corruptivum mali, vel esse malum et corruptivum boni" — "In matters of seeking and avoiding, it pertains to the same rationale for something to be good and to be corruptive of evil, or to be evil and to be corruptive of good."

The disorder in such a man, says Aquinas, is that, from the point of view of the order of reason and virtue, he "loves more a lesser good"[53] and judges it preferable to what is greater. This is the practical error that Aquinas says is inseparable from a perverted appetite.[54] For moral goodness, "acting for a due end," belongs to the intrinsic excellence of free actions. There can be no fullness of being for the rational creature, no genuinely complete good, in the absence of moral goodness. Thus, this man is a fool, like Esau who sold his birthright for a mess of pottage. But this fool is wise in his own eyes. He will strike a moral pose. He will say that he has a right to this. He may even utter a sentence such as, "I have my own truth," which is meant quite literally: "truth" for him is the meaning with which all things are imbued as they fall under the norm of norms, his construal of the ultimate end from which his choice here and now acquires the character of a pseudo-*debitum*.

It is no wonder that the temptation arises to explain moral evil away as a form of ignorance. To be sure, there is always some form of "not knowing" in evil action. Aquinas himself is clear, however, that this man who acts from evil conviction (*ex certa malitia*) knows that what he does is evil (against the norm of morality)—not just generally, but in this particular case. What he does not "know" is that *this evil is not to be accepted for the sake of attaining the good he wants*.[55] In other words, his "ignorance" consists in the "not knowing" embodied in the very practical judgment he makes.

This practical judgment, though it lacks moral rectitude, does not lack a rational character, for if it did it would not be a practical judgment at all, and evil would have annihilated itself.[56] The man makes a comparison between two proposed

---

[53] 1271: *ST* Ia-IIae, q.78, a.1.

[54] 1269-72: *De malo* q.16, a.6, ad.11: "'[A]ppetitus perversus semper est cum aliqua falsitate practicae cognitionis." See the comments in Reichberg 2002: "Beyond Privation", 779-780.

[55] 1271: *ST* Ia-IIae, q.78, a.1, ad.1: "Ad primum ergo dicendum quod ignorantia quandoque quidem excludit scientiam qua aliquis simpliciter scit hoc esse malum quod agitur, et tunc dicitur ex ignorantia peccare. Quandoque autem excludit scientiam qua homo scit hoc nunc esse malum, sicut cum ex passione peccatur. Quandoque autem excludit scientiam qua aliquis scit hoc malum non sustinendum esse propter consecutionem illius boni, scit tamen simpliciter hoc esse malum, et sic dicitur ignorare qui ex certa malitia peccat."

[56] Here our analysis makes its point of contact with Aquinas's notion of mixed privation, as discussed above.

deprivations, and in its light he chooses to sustain the deprivation following from moral transgression, not for its own sake as deprivation (which is impossible), but for the sake of avoiding another deprivation—the deprivation of what he loves more.

We infer, then, that, in his private semiosis at least, such a man has fashioned in objectivity a context in which the lesser good may be, and is, taken as greater. Purposeful evil is not a matter of ignoring the moral context of courses of action, but a semiotic disorder involving a particular kind of fictive construction or pure object that functions collaterally as the ground for patterns of interpretation guiding practical life: a particular vision of life, an imagined future.[57] It is within that invented context that such a man convinces himself concerning what is necessary for fulfillment and thus what is "due" to him simply. As for the norm of morality, it is not at all absent from this context—it is even an object of a certain form of preoccupation for him—but it is reticulated into this context in ways that depend upon the stages of descent into evil, from self-deceptive rationalization in the beginning, to the unfortunate possibility of outright hatred of moral goodness in the end.[58]

The error of the malefactor is a practical error. That is, it does not affect human reason precisely as a mirror of nature, as if the malefactor were engaged for the moment in a bit of "theoretical nonsense." The malefactor is not necessarily in error that way. This kind of error affects human reason as creative.

5.2. The Creative Dimension of Reason

The creative dimension of reason brings us back to a consideration of the order of mind-dependent being (*ens rationis*). To gain further purchase on it, we need to review some of the categories of mind-dependent being (a true menagerie) that pervade the objective world. Here are a few broad ones:

---

[57] Aquinas alludes to such a construction in i.1256-59: *Quaestiones disputatae de veritate* q.22, a.6, where he explains the indetermination of the will in respect of good and evil in terms of actions "as orderable to a certain pretended image of happiness" (*ut ordinabilem in beatitudinem, velut quamdam imaginem eius*). See our discussion of this passage in Kanzelberger 2011: *The Mystical Daydream*, 170-77.

[58] It is beyond the scope of our argument here to outline that downward course. See Kanzelberger 2011: *The Mystical Daydream*, 183-200.

1) *Negations of* ens naturae *grasped on the pattern of being*. The simplest kind of example of a mind-dependent being is reason's conception of a negation or privation obtaining in the order of mind-independent being (*ens naturae*). For example, blindness is conceived as if it were a sort of quality of the blind animal, though on the side of nature blindness is nothing but the (privative) negation of something positive, namely, the power of sight in an animal. Thus, the *pattern or model* on which blindness is conceived is something positive (a quality). Nevertheless, *what* is conceived by this means, the object properly speaking, is (as the conceiver well knows) not something positive at all, but a negation in the order of *ens naturae* as pertaining to animals. This *non-being* (*non ens*) in the order of nature, which is not knowable in itself because it is not in itself a being (*ens*), is *rendered knowable* by the intellect on the pattern of a quality, and so becomes a certain kind of "being of reason" (*ens rationis*, mind-dependent being).[59]

2) *Mind-dependent relations in the order of second intentions.* These mind-dependent relations relate objects to objects insofar as they are objects—that is, insofar as they exist already in cognition (which is what "second intention" signifies). These relations are involved in scientific classification and the study of logic. For example, "animal" is a *genus* (that is, relatable to inferior genera and species) only insofar as it is already an object (existing in cognition).

3) *Mind-dependent relations in the order of first intentions.* These mind-dependent relations relate, not objects as such, but mind-independent beings in nature. That is, the subject of the relation is an existing (mind-independent) thing, but the relation itself is purely objective or mind-dependent. One kind of example is an extrinsic denomination such as "known" or "seen", which relates a thing to the one who knows or perceives it. A more interesting and important kind of example, already mentioned, is the social and cultural roles in the objective world of a given human community. For instance, a particular woman has the role of a municipal judge in the city of Pasadena. The role belongs to the existing woman herself, not to a conception of her. The role (that is, the relation) itself, however, depends upon the common awareness that cognitively

---

[59] As Aquinas remarks in connection with the notion of truth as applied to non-being (1266-68: *ST* Ia, q.16, a.3, ad.2): "Ad secundum dicendum quod non ens non habet in se unde cognoscatur, sed cognoscitur inquantum intellectus facit illud cognoscibile. Unde verum fundatur in ente, inquantum non ens est quoddam ens rationis, apprehensum scilicet a ratione." — "Non-being does not have anything in itself whereby it can be known, but it is known insofar as the intellect makes it knowable. Hence, truth is [still, in this case] founded upon being, inasmuch as non-being is a certain kind of 'being of reason', apprehended, namely, by reason."

constitutes her in it. It would mean nothing for her to "be a judge" if no one agreed to recognize her as such.

4) *Beings constructed as patterns of mind-dependent relations*. This is a most irregular category, embracing outright fictional characters (Mister Darcy, Peter Rabbit), hypotheses about nature that are thought to be true but turn out to be false (the heavens of Ptolemy), purely objective practical artifacts (civil laws, treaties), mythical "secondary worlds" (Middle Earth), wish-motivated "as if" or "what if" or "if only" scenarios (daydreams), and other constructs.

Every mind-dependent being of whatever sort is a *being* inasmuch as it is an *object* known in the way that being is known; but it is a *mind-dependent* being inasmuch as it is an objective construct to which no (positive) being corresponds on the side of nature. In the case of the first category given above, *what* is conceived "on the pattern of being" is *in* nature, but it is a negation or privation in nature. Because this "non-being" is not knowable as such (insofar as it is non-being), reason must overcome this deficit of being and *render* this non-being knowable by conceiving it on the pattern of some being of the natural categories (for example, a quality). Nevertheless, *what* it knows by this rendering "on the pattern of a being" is a (mind-independent) negation or privation.

The succeeding categories are different. They do not merely reflect a necessary means for conceiving structures of nature and their negations, but they represent *realities that are positive, even as they are purely objective* (that is mind-dependent). We draw attention to the last category: patterns of mind-dependent relations that constitute fictive beings, whether or not their fictive status is recognized by the one who conceives them. We have already noted the formative power of false beliefs about nature. The formative power of any fictive being stems from the *positivity of relation in the order of mind-dependent being, just as relation is positive in the order of mind-independent being,*[60] and is exercised by means of the action of signs, the engendering of interpretants.

---

[60] A relation, any relation, is always what it (positively) is. It is that kind of relation, and no other. The "category" of relation itself, however, belongs *neither* to the order of nature *nor* to the order of mind-dependent being, but straddles the two orders. Indeed, one and the same relation may migrate from one order to the other depending on circumstances. A simple example: you have a conception of the layout of furniture in your parents' home: a pattern of physical relations that are also objective inasmuch as

As with the conceiving of negations, fictive constructions overcome a deficit of being.[61] But here the construction reflects not the mere attempt to understand nature as given, but a desire to *create*. The toolshed in the backyard does not exist, but it ought to. My status as a well-known statesman does not exist, but it ought to. My marriage does not make me happy, but it ought to. Sherlock Holmes does not exist, but he ought to. Hobbits and Elves do not exist, but they ought to.

> Kirk explains that a moral act involves both a free movement of the will and a consideration of the norm of morality which entails both "the order of reason and of divine law (*ordo rationis et legis divinae*)". This norm is not just some arbitrary code of morality, but a standard that is connatural to the human being since "in being true to this norm, the rational being is being true to its own nature, willing an end that is due—an end, in other words, that represents the excellence of its own way of being and acting".
>
> The question is, if this norm is connatural to the human being, how or why would a human ever act against it? This brings us back to our capacity for story-telling. This ability

---

you know that pattern. At Christmas one year, you visit and discover that that layout no longer exists, thanks to the wholesale moving around and replacement of items. The pattern of objective relations remained undisturbed when the physical changes took place, even as they became *purely* objective and no longer physical relations. This "singularity" pertaining to relations as "having a positive structure or 'essence' that is indifferent to the difference between what exists independently of and what exists dependently upon thought" (Deely 2007: *Intentionality and Semiotics: A Story of Mutual Fecundation*, 124) is pivotal for a semiotically coherent realism, and is explored by Deely in many works. See, for example, 2007: *Intentionality and Semiotics*, 119-25; and 2009: *Purely Objective Reality*, 22-37.

[61] Fictive constructions are classified as *negationes* in the Latin tradition alongside negations of *ens naturae* grasped on the pattern of being, despite their being essentially (as to what the mind puts forth) patterns of objective relations. The reason such a pattern of relations is called a "negation" is that it serves to *model* what in fact it is *not*: for example, a fiction such as a mountain of gold or a dragon is a pattern of objective relations *modeling* a substance which in fact it is not. See Deely's discussion of this point in 2002: *What Distinguishes Human Understanding?* 85-109, which comments on texts such as Poinsot 1632b: *TDS*, 96/7-28.

can be a good thing, as Kirk notes in his wonderful review of Tolkien's account of fairy tales. The positive aspect of story-telling is also exemplified in the musical, *The Man of La Mancha,* when the priest character expresses a very favorable view of Don Quixote's story-telling delusions in seeing a wretched kitchen wench as a great lady whom he names "Dulcinea": "There is no Dulcinea. She's made of flame and air. And yet how lovely life would seem, if every man could weave a dream to keep him from despair. To each his Dulcinea, though she's only flame and air."

Dodds, "Made of Flame and Air" [p.209].

Fictive being enters into the conceiving of every object in the order of practical reason. There is a fictive or purely objective element contained in the intention of any end: the overcoming of the deficit of being represented by the end's futurity[62]—in order that the toolshed, as the being-to-be-realized, may be envisioned as such and that it may motivate. Even in such a prosaic example, we can begin to see that the meaning of "reality," as it pertains to the problem of how one is to live and dispose of one's freedom, embraces not merely "the world" as it appears to me already given, but also that world which I would wish to bring into being through my free action. An end—any end at all—begins as a kind of dream of practical reason.[63]

---

[62] Aquinas 1271: *ST* Ia-IIae, q.8., a.1, ad.3: "Ad tertium dicendum quod illud quod non est ens in rerum natura, accipitur ut ens in ratione, unde negationes et privationes dicuntur entia rationis. Per quem etiam modum futura, prout apprehenduntur, sunt entia. Inquantum igitur sunt huiusmodi entia, apprehenduntur sub ratione boni, et sic voluntas in ea tendit." — "That which is not being in the sense of the things of nature is taken as being in the reason, and thus negations and privations are said to be beings of reason. So also, future things, insofar as they are apprehended, are beings, and inasmuch as they are beings, they are apprehended under the aspect of good, and in that way the will tends to them."

[63] When an intended end is something "realizable" in physical terms, it is not the mere conception of a "possible being", but that of a future existent whose "realization" hinges upon my actions. A possible being is mind-independent in its possibility (which is inscribed in the nature of things), but the end in intention is mind-dependent in its aspect

As our consideration ranges over the wide realm of fictive being, we confront the question of how the *desirability* of an end correlates with its *possibility* (in itself, or for a particular individual). While it is clear there need be no strict proportion between desirability and possibility, does *impossibility* necessarily extinguish desire? Or are desirability and possibility finally independent variables?

In the creation of a fictive being such as Sherlock Holmes—and all the more in the creation of dragons or Elves—desire outstrips the givenness of nature and even nature's possibilities. This literary magic puts before our apprehension beings we come to know quite as well as we know many naturally existing individuals of whom we know only what we have heard or read.[64] The magic derives from the positivity of relations, a positivity that is indifferent to the mind-independent or mind-dependent status of the relation's terms. This positivity-*cum*-indifference of relation is, metaphysically speaking, a fact: it is the ground of the possibility of human intellectual creation. Its moral correlate is the primordial human desire, God-like in character, to create and to take delight in what is created.

In his landmark essay, "On Fairy-Stories", J. R. R. Tolkien explored the human art of creative fantasy, the creation of a "secondary world", which takes the form of a narrative inasmuch as we desire to *live* in it. In a secondary world, the constraints of natural possibility and impossibility—"natural" within what we may call the primary world—are loosened, in order that, for example, the dragon might be. "I desired dragons with a profound desire." As he grew up, fairy-stories, Tolkien discovered, "were not concerned with possibility, but with desirability. If they awakened *desire*, satisfying it while often whetting it unbearably, they succeeded."[65]

Some might object that this is but a lofty approach to what is in the end mere entertainment, an elaborate pretense, a jest. We do not "really believe" in such

---

of an *ens realizandum* (something to be made to exist) that overcomes the deficit of being represented by its futurity.

[64] As we have considered the functional equivalence of the patterns of relations that build up true versus false hypotheses about nature, we should consider also the functional equivalence of the patterns of relations that constitute ideas of fictional characters on the one hand, and ideas of existing persons (formed say, by reading biographies) on the other.

[65] J. R. R. Tolkien 1947 [1966]: "On Fairy-Stories", 40.

things. To which Tolkien might respond: if the primary world is not a laughing matter, why should a secondary world be a laughing matter? If divine creation is not a jest, why should "sub-creation" be a jest? The motive of creative fantasy is that the secondary world should *be*—that it should *be*, indeed, in its very unlikeness to the primary world, an unlikeness that bespeaks "freedom from the domination of observed fact."[66] As "sub-creation," fantasy is the human art that Tolkien regarded as "most nearly pure..., and so (when achieved) the most potent,"[67] which sounds rather serious indeed. As for the matter of whether we "believe in it", the fact is that we do believe in it, to the extent that the art of sub-creation has succeeded. Corresponding to the secondary world is not the oft-mentioned "suspension of disbelief" (if anything, a signal of poor art), but rather "secondary belief", a form of belief that corresponds to the way the secondary world *is*.[68]

5.3. Daydreams and Dark Magic

Now let us consider a daydream. I am a concert pianist, playing the Tchaikovsky piano concerto brilliantly before appreciative classical audiences. I can imagine my way through the whole score, fingers delicate when they need to be delicate, flying when they need to fly. At the final chord of the third movement, thunderous applause. In the primary world, many years ago, I had thought to study music, but became an insurance underwriter instead. In this secondary world, I am a concert pianist. Banal? Perhaps, but not as banal as life as an insurance underwriter seems to me.

Desire always tends in some way toward actual existence, in the primary world sense of "actual." I would not even dream this daydream but as a means to perfect myself "actually" by this satisfaction, banal as it is. Desire tends toward actual existence, but, for lack of "natural possibility" (for it is far too late to become a concert pianist), it must rest in this case in the good of an "as if". Desire tends toward actual existence, but lack of natural possibility does not compel the laying aside of desire, which may continue to adhere to an object "as

---

[66] Ibid, 47.
[67] Ibid.
[68] Ibid, 36-37.

if it were possible." "As if it were possible"... and it is, in the secondary world of the daydream.

We would desire the true power of enchantment, said Tolkien—a power that would enable us (the creators and the receivers of art) to enter a secondary world "to the satisfaction of [our] senses", as "partners in making and delight."[69] This would be the true Elvish magic, but this we do not possess. As it is, we must fall back on a lesser magic involving "another view of adjectives," a magic that can

> make heavy things light and able to fly, turn grey lead into yellow gold, and the still rock into a swift water... [W]e may cause woods to spring with silver leaves and rams to wear fleeces of gold, and put hot fire into the belly of a cold worm. But in such "fantasy", as it is called, new form is made; Faërie begins; Man becomes a sub-creator.[70]

The danger in the magic of sub-creation is that of self-idolatry, of coming to worship oneself in one's own works.[71] Further, inasmuch as every object (pure object or not) is public in principle, one may use the magic of discourse—not merely literary discourse, but other fictions woven into the discourse of ordinary practical life—to seduce and dominate others.

Or, perhaps, the failure to face the moral demands of one's state in life may sink one into a listlessness in which one attaches oneself to a different sort of daydream, preferring to embrace *this*, rather than the moral task lying before one. So, the man in the unhappy marriage carries on an imaginative life with someone else, an elaborate mythology replete with vivid compensations. In his ordinary domestic setting, he moves about like a sleepwalker, even as his mind and heart live in a secondary world.

A daydream becomes *mystical* when the "deficit of being" that is overcome by the fictive capacity is that very *futility* that moral demands would impose upon

---

[69] Ibid, 52-53.

[70] Ibid, 22-23.

[71] Ibid, 55: "Men have conceived not only of elves, but they have imagined gods, and worshipped them, even worshipped those most deformed by their authors' own evil. But they have made false gods out of other materials: their notions, their banners, their monies; even their sciences and their social and economic theories have demanded human sacrifice. *Abusus non tollit usum.* Fantasy remains a human right: we make in our measure and in our derivative mode, because we are made: and not only made, but made in the image and likeness of a Maker."

the daydream. The mystical daydream triumphs over moral constraints, as creative fantasy triumphs over natural constraints, through the positing of new forms of relativity that amount to a reimagining of the moral universe, in which the daydream is no longer a "relative good" (*secundum quid bonum*) but that which is *simply good*. The demands represented by the norm of morality become the demands of an adversary, the enemy of what is simply good. So, the man who chooses the affair: "This is my right. I will shed this old life of mine—the fragments of it must fall as they will—and emerge into the sunshine. The one who would blame me is the blameworthy one."

Even as the non-application of the norm of morality is a necessary condition of moral evil from the standpoint of agency in nature, the distinctive fiction of the mystical daydream is a necessary condition of moral evil from the standpoint of the being of objects, some of which are mind-independent being "objectified", and others pure objects. Every object is an object construed, engendered as an interpretant within the objective world, and every object becomes, in its turn, a sign within that world.

Moral evil is dark magic. It weaves a web that bewitches its author, and draws others into its web.

In a particular house on a particular street, there lives a man who is offended by whatever contradicts his will. He was born clever, his wife ingenuous. His discourse in her regard is nothing but reproach. He makes use of his "marital rights" (as he would put it) from time to time. Apart from that, he never lays a hand on her, either in violence or in tenderness. But she is continually violated. She is convinced that she is a poor wife, that she deserves every single one of his reproaches. In the end, she accepts that, being fundamentally inadequate, she is bound to fail him but, for all that, no less bound to keep trying. And in the end, he becomes cruel. His reproaches become ever more searching and ingenious, and an undercurrent of pleasure with himself begins to flow beneath the aggravations of the moment.

When he wounds her, it is most vital that she understand exactly what he wants her to understand: the precise mode of her failure, how particularly undeserving she is of consideration in this case, how remote she still is from the level of "what any man has a right to expect." The heart of this evil, its vital reality, is the reality of signification.

From the standpoint of *ens naturae*, both his being and hers undergo loss. The locus of evil, however, is not mere nature, but the objective world. His dominion over her—the dominion in which he particularly exults—is a dominion of one who weaves webs of meaning, a dominion over chains of interpretants. The exercise of this dark power is an exercise, not of efficient causality which is only the body and the channel, but of the causality of signs.

THE END

References Historically Layered

AQUINAS, Thomas (1225—1274).

i.1256-59. *Opera omnia iussu Leonis XIII P. M. edita, t.22: Quaestiones disputatae de veritate* (Rome: Editori di San Tommaso, 1970-76).

i.1259/65. *Liber de veritate catholicae fidei contra errores infidelium seu Summa contra Gentiles* (*SCG*). Edited by P. Marc, C. Pera, P. Caramello (Turin-Rome: Marietti, 1961).

1266-68. *Opera omnia iussu impensaque Leonis XIII P. M. edita, t 5: Pars prima Summae theologiae* (*ST* Ia). (Rome: Ex Typographia Polyglotta S. C. de Propaganda Fide, 1888-89).

1269-72. *Opera omnia iussu Leonis XIII P. M. edita, t.23: Quaestiones disputatae de malo*. Rome-Paris: Commissio Leonina-J. Vrin, 1982. English translation by Richard Regan, edited with an introduction by Brian Davies (New York: Oxford University Press, 2003).

1271. *Opera omnia iussu impensaque Leonis XIII P. M. edita, t.6-7: Prima secundae Summae theologiae* (*ST* Ia-IIae). (Rome: Ex Typographia Polyglotta S. C. de Propaganda Fide, 1891-92).

ASHLEY, Benedict (3 May 1915—2013 February 23).

2006. *The Way toward Wisdom* (South Bend, Indiana: University of Notre Dame Press).

CLARKE, W. Norris (1 June 1915—2008 June 10).

2001. *The One and Many: A Contemporary Thomistic Metaphysics* (Notre Dame, Indiana: University of Notre Dame Press).

CROSBY, John F.

2002. "Is All Evil Really Only Privation?" *Proceedings of the ACPA*, vol.75: 197-209.

2007. "Doubts About the Privation Theory That Will Not Go Away: Response to Patrick Lee", *American Catholic Philosophical Quarterly*, 81.3: 498-505.

DEELY, John N. (26 April 1942—2017 January 7).

1971. *The Tradition via Heidegger. An Essay on the Meaning of Being in the Philosophy of Martin Heidegger* (The Hague: Martinus Nijhoff).

1994. *New Beginnings: Early Modern Philosophy and Postmodern Thought* (Toronto: University of Toronto Press).

2001. *Four Ages of Understanding: The First Postmodern Survey of Philosophy from Ancient Times to the Turn of the Twenty-First Century* (Toronto, Canada: University of Toronto Press).

2002. *What Distinguishes Human Understanding?* (South Bend, Indiana: St. Augustine's Press).

2007. *Intentionality and Semiotics: A Story of Mutual Fecundation* (Scranton, Pennsylvania: University of Scranton Press).

2009. *Purely Objective Reality* (Berlin: Mouton De Gruyter).

DEWAN, Lawrence (22 March 1932—2015 February 12).

1992. "St. Thomas and the First Cause of Moral Evil." *Moral and Political Philosophies in the Middle Ages: Proceedings of the Ninth International Congress of Medieval Philosophy*, Volume III. (Société pour l'Étude de la Philosophie Médiévale: Legas): 1223–30.

FRENCH, Anthony Philip, and KENNEDY, P. J., editors.

1985. *Niels Bohr: A Centenary Volume* (Cambridge, Massachusetts: Harvard University Press).

KANZELBERGER, Kirk George.

2011. *The Mystical Daydream: Fictive Being and the Motive of Evil* (unpublished doctoral dissertation) (Bronx, New York: Fordham University, 2011).

LABOURDETTE, Marie-Michel (26 June 1908—1990 October 26).

1958-59. *Cours de théologie morale* (unpublished typescript of lecture course). (Toulouse, France).

LEE, Patrick.

2007. "Evil as Such Is a Privation: A Reply to John Crosby." *American Catholic Philosophical Quarterly*, 81.3: 469-488.

LEWIS, Clive Staples (29 November 1898—1963 November 22).

1962. *The Discarded Image: An Introduction to Medieval and Renaissance Literature* (Cambridge: Cambridge University Press. Author's preface dated 1962; appeared in print posthumously, 1964).

MARITAIN, Jacques (18 November 1882—1973 April 28).

1963. *Dieu et la permission du mal* (Paris: Desclée de Brouwer). English translation by Joseph W. Evans, *God and the Permission of Evil* (Milwaukee: The Bruce Publishing Co., 1966).

PEIRCE, Charles Sanders (10 September 1839—1914 April 19).

Note: The abbreviation CP stands for *Collected Papers of Charles Sanders Peirce*. Vols. 1-6 edited by Charles Hartshorne and Paul Weiss; vols. 7-8 edited by A. W. Burks. (Cambridge: Belknap Press of Harvard University Press, 1958-1966). Citations refer to volume and paragraph number, separated by a period, e.g., 2.228. The abbreviation EP refers to the two-volume set of the Peirce Edition Project, *The Essential Peirce*, where EP volume 1 covers 1867-93 and EP volume

2 covers 1893-1913 (Bloomington, IN: Indiana University Press, 1992 and 1998). Citations refer to volume and page number(s), separated by a period.

c.1897. "Ground, Object, and Interpretant", in *CP*.2.227-229.

1900. Letter, "Peirce to Langley, c. May 20, 1900", in *Historical Perspectives on Peirce's Logic of Science: A History of Science,* 2 vols. edited by Carolyn Eisele. (Berline, New York, Amsterdam: Mouton De Gruyter, 1985). Vol.2: 876-879.

1908. "A Neglected Argument for the Reality of God" in *EP*.2: 434-50.

POINSOT, John (1589—1644).

1631. *Artis Logicae Prima Pars*, vol. 1, in *Cursus Philosophicus Thomisticus*, ed. B. Reiser in 3 vols. (New York: Georg Olms Verlag, 2008): 1-247.

1632a. *Artis Logicae Secunda Pars*, vol. 1, in *Cursus Philosophicus Thomisticus*, ed. B. Reiser in 3 vols. (New York: Georg Olms Verlag, 2008): 249-839.

1632b. *Tractatus de Signis: The Semiotic of John Poinsot* (*TDS*), extracted from *Artis Logicae Prima et Secunda Pars* of 1631-1632 (see entries above) and interpretively arranged by John N. Deely in consultation with Ralph Austin Powell. 1st ed.: Berkeley: University of California Press, 1985. References to this Latin-English bilingual edition are given by page number, followed by a slash, followed by the line number(s) of the referenced passage.

1633. *Naturalis Philosophiae Prima Pars*, vol. 2, in *Cursus Philosophicus Thomisticus*, ed. B. Reiser in 3 vols. (New York: Georg Olms Verlag, 2008): 1-529.

1635. *Naturalis Philosophiae Quarta Pars*, vol. 3, in *Cursus Philosophicus Thomisticus*, ed. B. Reiser in 3 vols. (New York: Georg Olms Verlag, 2008): 1-425.

REICHBERG, Gregory.

2002. "Beyond Privation: Moral Evil in Thomas Aquinas's *De malo*." *Review of Metaphysics* 55.3:731–64.

ROBIN, Richard S.

1967. *Annotated Catalogue of the Papers of Charles S. Peirce* (Worcester, Massachusetts: The University of Massachusetts Press).

SHERWIN, Michael.

2005. *By Knowledge and By Love: Charity and Knowledge in the Moral Theology of St. Thomas Aquinas* (Washington, D.C.: Catholic University of America Press).

TOLKIEN, John Ronald Reuel (3 January 1892—1973 September 2).

1947. "On Fairy-Stories." Originally published in *Essays Presented to Charles Williams* (Oxford: Oxford University Press). Republished in *The Tolkien Reader* (New York: Ballantine Books, 1966): 3-84.

Made of Flame and Air

A Comment on Kirk Kanzelberger[1]

Michael J. Dodds, O.P.
Dominican School of Philosophy and Theology
Berkeley, CA

Abstract: I comment on certain aspects of Kirk Kanzelberger's article, "Reality and the Meaning of Evil", especially the distinction between "beings of nature" and "beings of reason" in the account of evil. For this, I employ the analogy of C. S. Lewis's "Meditation in a Toolshed." I also consider the nature of the object of the moral act as a being of reason. I conclude with some reflections on Kirk's notion of the "mystical daydream."

Kirk Kanzelberger begins his article, "Reality and the Meaning of Evil," with a bit of fiction. This seems appropriate since, in the course of his reflections, he will show how our ability to create stories for ourselves plays a crucial part in our capacity for evil. Here, I'll comment on some of his arguments, by no means doing justice to their depth and insight, but highlighting certain aspects of them.

Kirk's opening story is about an encounter at a cocktail party between an avid, neo-Thomist graduate student and his friendly conversation partner. Our tendency, on hearing any story, is to identify ourselves with one of the characters. In Kirk's story, I found myself identifying with both characters.

Over many years of teaching philosophy, I've often explained (as Kirk's graduate student does) that evil consists not in something positive but in a lack of being or actuality that should be present. Like Kirk's student, I've been quite pleased at how this explanation shows that God, the First Cause of all being, is not the cause of evil. I've suggested that Thomas Aquinas uses a kind of "metaphysical scalpel" to dissect the evil act, showing God to be the ultimate cause of the act

---

[1] Correspondence to editors@realityjournal.org.

insofar as it has being, but not insofar as it is lacking in being. It is precisely insofar as it is lacking in being, however, that the action is evil.[2]

Much as I agreed with Kirk's graduate student, however, I was also drawn by the arguments of the other character, who says: "Evil—evil itself—isn't only privation. It is like a dream, a shadowy reality but a reality nonetheless, and evil. It is what the wicked want... And it doesn't stay in their heads. It emerges and it spreads."[3] Evil doesn't feel like, and isn't experienced as, just a lack of being. It feels like something more. Somehow the metaphysical account is not the full story, and Kirk's article fills us in on what's missing.

To find that, though, as Kirk explains, we have to take another look at the world we're living in. It's not just the metaphysical world of "beings of nature" but also the semiotic world of "beings of reason," the "lifeworld" of our language, thoughts and experience. This world is also real and, in comparison with it, the metaphysical world is something of an abstraction since it leaves so much out. As Kirk points out, when the world is taken simply as a collection of beings of nature, "[t]he meaning of 'reality' then collapses into an accepted synonym for the being of nature, and 'realism' itself turns into a form of myopia that fails to see realities constituted by cognition for what they are".[4]

---

[2] See Michael J. Dodds 2012: *Unlocking Divine Action: Contemporary Science and Thomas Aquinas*: 240-41: "The effect of the deficient secondary cause is reduced to the first nondeficient cause as regards what it has of being and perfection, but not as regards what it has of defect; just as whatever there is of motion in the act of limping is caused by the motive power, whereas what there is of obliqueness in it does not come from the motive power, but from the curvature of the leg. And, likewise, whatever there is of being and action in a bad action, is reduced to God as the cause; whereas whatever defect is in it is not caused by God, but by the deficient secondary cause" (St. Thomas Aquinas, 1266-68: *ST* Ia, q.49, a.2, ad.2. For this reason, as Edward Schillebeeckx explains, it is not God but human beings who are the "first cause" of moral evil: "[H]ere we have finitude, as it were, as 'the first cause.' As soon as there are creatures, there is the possibility (not the necessity) of a negative and original initiative of finitude, if I can put it that way... For Thomas, it is a senseless philosophical undertaking to look for a particular cause, a ground or motive for evil and suffering in God; these do not necessarily follow from our finitude, but they do draw their fundamental possibility from there". Schillebeeckx 1980: *Christ: The Experience of Jesus as Lord*: 728-29).

[3] Kanzelberger 2019: "Reality and the Meaning of Evil", *Reality: a journal for philosophical discourse* 1.1 (2020): 151.

[4] Kanzelberger 2019: "Reality and the Meaning of Evil", 159.

In his article, "Meditation in a Toolshed," C. S. Lewis alludes to something like this distinction between "beings of nature" and "beings of reason".[5] He makes a distinction between "looking at" an experience from the outside and "looking along" it by entering into it. He imagines himself in a darkened toolshed where a small beam of light shines through a chink in the roof. When he "looks at" the beam, he sees a bright patch with a few dust motes floating in it. When he shifts his position to let the beam strikes him directly in the eye, he "looks along" it, and suddenly sees through the chink in the roof to the bright blue sky and white clouds beyond it. Similarly, if one stands outside of any experience and "looks at" it, one sees something quite different than if one enters into the experience and "looks along" it. If one simply "looks at" the experience of falling in love, for instance, one may be able to see and measure brain activity and gland secretions, but one will miss the true depth of the experience which can be found only by entering into it and "looking along" it. Lewis concludes that, in order to discover reality in its fullness, we must look not only "at" experiences (as empirical science tends to do), but also "along" them (to encompass the depth of reality that goes beyond the empirical).

I think that limiting oneself to "looking at" is something like limiting one's account of reality to include only "beings of nature" and leaving out the rich world of experience to be found in "beings of reason." When that world is included, the "beings of nature" are recognized as "objects" of experience, part of the broader "objective world" of human life. As Kirk explains: "This world, the objective world, is not a collection of things but a fabric of experience woven of natural as well as cultural strands, all alike objective or existing as known, and all alike public in principle".[6]

Our account of the nature of evil must include not only the metaphysical world of beings of nature but also the experiential world of beings of reason. An account of natural evils (such as blindness) can be given purely in terms of beings of nature, explaining the different ways that such beings are subject to privations (such as lack of sight). An account of moral evil, however, requires a broader vision of the world including beings of reason and the complex web of relationships to which these give rise.

---

[5] C. S. Lewis 1945: "Meditation in a Toolshed," in *God in the Dock: Essays on Theology and Ethics*: 212-15.

[6] Kanzelberger 2019: "Reality and the Meaning of Evil", 163.

> This world, the objective world, is not a collection of things but a fabric of experience woven of natural as well as cultural strands, all alike objective or existing as known, and all alike public in principle. As we have seen, the cultural or mind-dependent strands contribute in varying ways to this fabric. Even when our attention seems focused on some "physical thing" such as a table, that thing—or rather, that object—will often on reflection turn out to be some kind of amalgam of nature and what is not mere nature, inasmuch as the object bears a cultural significance which is for us more formal and essential in the object than its physical constitution. Often enough, objects in the human lifeworld have nothing in them of nature, but are pure objects.
>
> *Kanzelberger, "Reality and the Meaning of Evil" [p.163].*

The moral act itself is fundamentally a being of reason. Aquinas says that whether an act is good or bad depends on its object.[7] The object "is not the matter of which (a thing is made), but the matter about which (something is done)."[8] The nature of this object has been a matter of considerable dispute.[9] What is clear is that the object involves not just the thing that happened (a trigger was pulled and someone died), but the understanding and will of the doer (who may, for instance, intend the act as either self-defense or murder). Aquinas teaches that, in choosing to do evil, one desires the good to which the evil is

[7] 1271: *ST* Ia-IIae, q.18, a.2, c.

[8] 1271: *ST* Ia-IIae, q.18, a.2, ad.2.

[9] See, for instance, John Abraham Makdisi 2017: "The Object of the Moral Act: Understanding St. Thomas Aquinas through the Work of Steven Long and Martin Rhonheimer." Dissertation. The Catholic University of America, <https://islandora.wrlc.org/islandora/object/cuislandora%3A64685/datastream/PDF/view> (accessed February 15, 2020); Martin Rhonheimer 2011: "The Moral Object of Human Acts and the Role of Reason according to Aquinas: A Restatement and Defense of my View," *The Josephinum Journal of Theology*, 18.2: 454-506; John Finnis 1991: "Object and Intention in Moral Judgments according to Aquinas," *The Thomist* 55.1: 1-27; Lawrence Dewan 2008: "St. Thomas, Rhonheimer, and the Object of the Human Act," *Nova et Vetera* 6.1: 63-112.

attached more than the good of which the evil is the privation: as one may desire the perceived good of being free of a blackmailer, to which the act of murder is attached, more than the good of justice of which murder is the privation.[10] When evil is desired in this way, the act must be viewed not as essentially good and incidentally evil (as involving some privation), but as essentially evil (just as the conversation partner in Kirk's opening story intuitively recognized): "The action done is a deficient good, which is good in a certain respect, but simply evil."[11]

Kirk explains that a moral act involves both a free movement of the will and a consideration of the norm of morality which entails both "the order of reason and of divine law (*ordo rationis et legis divinae*)".[12] This norm is not just some arbitrary code of morality, but a standard that is connatural to the human being since "in being true to this norm, the rational being is being true to its own nature, willing an end that is due—an end, in other words, that represents the excellence of its own way of being and acting".[13]

The question is, if this norm is connatural to the human being, how or why would a human ever act against it? This brings us back to our capacity for story-telling. This ability can be a good thing, as Kirk notes in his wonderful review of Tolkien's account of fairy tales. The positive aspect of story-telling is also exemplified in the musical, *The Man of La Mancha,* when the priest character expresses a very favorable view of Don Quixote's story-telling delusions in seeing a wretched kitchen wench as a great lady whom he names "Dulcinea": "There is no Dulcinea. She's made of flame and air. And yet how lovely life would seem, if every man could weave a dream to keep him from despair. To each his Dulcinea, though she's only flame and air."[14]

---

[10] 1266-68: *ST* Ia, q.19, a.9, c.: "Never therefore would evil be sought after, not even accidentally, unless the good that accompanies the evil were more desired than the good of which the evil is the privation".

[11] 1271: *ST* Ia-IIae, q.18, a.1, ad.1.

[12] Kanzelberger 2019: "Reality and the Meaning of Evil", 169.

[13] Ibid, 169-70.

[14] See https://lyricsplayground.com/alpha/songs/t/toeachhisdulcinea.html (accessed 14 February 2020). The lyrics seem to resonate with Cervantes' own poetry: "¡Oh vanas esperanzas de la gente! / ¡Cómo pasáis con prometer descanso, / Y al fin paráis en sombra, en humo, en sueño" (Miguel de Cervantes 1605-1615: *El Ingenioso Hidalgo Don Quijote De La Mancha*, in the English translation by J.M. Cohen, *The Adventures of Don*

Often enough, however, we freely and consciously manufacture the wrong sort of story for ourselves—a story that deludes us into thinking that the good which is really connatural to us (and in which alone we can find true happiness) is evil. As Kirk explains:[15]

> A daydream becomes *mystical* when the "deficit of being" that is overcome by the fictive capacity is that very *futility* that moral demands would impose upon the daydream. The mystical daydream triumphs over moral constraints, as creative fantasy triumphs over natural constraints, through the positing of new forms of relativity that amount to a reimagining of the moral universe, in which the daydream is no longer a "relative good" (*secundum quid bonum*) but that which is simply good. The demands represented by the norm of morality become the demands of an adversary, the enemy of what is simply good.

Kirk is to be commended for his article, not only for showing us the speculative importance of recognizing the "lifeworld" of ideas and signs, but also for alerting us to the practical importance of seeing how easily we may slip into our own mystical daydream.

Quixote, 460: "How vain are all the hopes of humankind! / How sweet their promises of quiet seem, / And yet they end in shadow, smoke, and dream".

[15] Kanzelberger 2019: "Reality and the Meaning of Evil", 197-98.

References Historically Layered

AQUINAS, Thomas (1225—1274).

1266-68. *Summa theologiae, prima pars* (*ST* Ia). Reference to the English translation by the Dominican Fathers (New York: Benziger Brothers, 1946).

1271. *Summa theologiae, prima secundae pars* (*ST* Ia-IIae).

CERVANTES SAAVEDRA, Miguel de (29 September 1547—1616 April 22).

1605-1615. *El Ingenioso Hidalgo Don Quijote de la Mancha* (Madrid: Espasa-Calpe, S.A., 1984). English translation by J.M. Cohen, *The Adventures of Don Quixote* (Middlesex, England: Penguin Books, 1975).

DEWAN, Lawrence OP (22 March 1932—2015 February 12).

2008. "St. Thomas, Rhonheimer, and the Object of the Human Act", *Nova et Vetera* 6.1: 63-112.

DODDS, Michael J. OP.

2012. *Unlocking Divine Action: Contemporary Science and Thomas Aquinas* (Washington D.C.: The Catholic University of America Press).

FINNIS, John (28 July 1940—).

1991. "Object and Intention in Moral Judgments according to Aquinas", *The Thomist* 55.1: 1-27.

KANZELBERGER, Kirk.

2019. "Reality and the Meaning of Evil" in *Reality: a journal for philosophical discourse*, 1.1 (2020): 146-204.

LEWIS, Clive Staples (29 November 1898—1963 November 22).

1945. "Meditation in a Toolshed", originally published in the *Coventry Evening Telegraph*. Reference is to the edition published in *God in the Dock: Essays on Theology and Ethics*, edited by Walter Hooper (Grand Rapids, MI: Walter B. Eerdmans Publishing Co., 1970): 212-15.

MAKDISI, John Abraham.

2017. *The Object of the Moral Act: Understanding St. Thomas Aquinas through the Work of Steven Long and Martin Rhonheimer*. Dissertation. The Catholic University of America <https://islandora.wrlc.org/islandora/object/cuislandora%3A64685/datastream/PDF/view>. Retrieved 15 February 2020.

RHONHEIMER, Martin (1950—).

2011. "The Moral Object of Human Acts and the Role of Reason according to Aquinas: A Restatement and Defense of My View", *The Josephinum Journal of Theology*, 18.2: 454-506.

SCHILLEBEECKX, Edward (12 November 1914—2009 December 23).

1983. *Christ: The Experience of Jesus as Lord* (New York: Crossroad).

Political Science and Realism

A Retaking of Political Science for the Post-Modern Age[1]

Francisco E. Plaza, PhD Candidate
University of St. Thomas, Houston, TX
Editor, REALITY

This article contrasts the pursuit of political science from a classically realist perspective versus a modernist one. We suggest that with the developments in modern philosophy and science, political science has stopped examining the common good itself, instead pursuing what is called a "value-free" analysis based on materialism, or a utopian ideal based on subjectivism. Neither path, however, arrives at the true good itself, as both approaches begin from a flawed set of metaphysical principles divorced from reality. Our proposal is that for political science to properly seek what is the actual common good, it must begin with a solid metaphysical foundation of true realism. To accomplish this, we shall look first to the foundation of political science with Aristotle, then, we shall examine what changed with the arrival of modernity. Finally, we will rely upon contemporary critics of political philosophy (Leo Strauss, Eric Voegelin, and Jacques Maritain specifically) to account for the problems with political science in its current form, and consider how these problems may be addressed through a return to classical realism within political philosophy.

---

[1] Correspondence to plaza@realityjournal.org.

Table of Contents

I. Introduction: Intersection between Realism & Political Science

In the wake of positivism and post-modernism[2], political science in the academy today has ceased by-and-large to offer any real prescription for the common good, content instead with providing mathematical models to quantify the material reality of different political regimes. Here, the universal has been abandoned and replaced only with knowledge of the particular.[3] This is the opposite of what the classical philosopher (such as Plato or Aristotle) would consider "science." For the ancient or medieval philosopher, science had to deal with universals in order to have a sense of permanence.

Beginning with Parmenides and Heraclitus, the Greeks understood the realm of particulars to be one of constant change. If one were to try to create a science based solely upon particulars, this science would also undergo constant change. What one claims to know one day could become false the next day, then perhaps

---

[2] Here we use "post-modern" in its commonly accepted form, referring generally to a contemporary philosophical disposition that takes modern idealism and subjectivism to its logical conclusion, denying truth in any metaphysical sense in favor of subjective "truths" that vary according to the observer. In reality, there is nothing "post-modern" about this, given that it merely continues the trajectory established by modern thought that preceded it. To call it "post-modern" would suggest that it successfully moves beyond modern thought, when in fact the opposite is true. For this reason, we would argue that what is typically labeled as "post-modern" would be better understood as "hyper-modern," whereas the thought of thinkers such as Jacques Maritain or Eric Voegelin would be "post-modern" in a genuine sense, given that they actually do move beyond modernity.

[3] We refer here to one of the oldest divisions in philosophy: universals versus particulars. By universals, we refer to generalities such as "justice" or "the good," whereas particulars would be individual instances of these generalities. A pleasant meal, for example, can be taken as a particular instance of the good. The universal, however, would be whatever general principles follow that make a pleasant meal a true instance of the good (or more simply, whatever makes it "pleasant" rather than "unpleasant" in a meaningful sense). The basic division between classical realism and modern idealism (or nominalism overall) is that the classical realist treats universals as something metaphysically real in some manner, whereas the idealist (or nominalist) thinks of universals as only an artificial creation of the mind. The consequence for these views is that the realist can uphold that there are truths which exist about a universal such as "justice" that are independent from human opinion, whereas the idealist would have to say the opposite, namely, that there is no such thing as "justice" outside of arbitrary human opinion.

true the next week as the particulars change. On the contrary, science must seek what is true in a fixed way.[4] This allows for the basic distinction between opinion and knowledge. Let us suppose, for instance, we wanted to study aesthetics, and more specifically, what would cause a painting to be beautiful. If we could not look beyond the particulars, all we would do is point to individual paintings and say, "I like this one." If we wished to claim, on the other hand, that we knew why a particular painting is beautiful, we would have to speak to beauty itself as a universal, that is, the nature of beauty itself. Perhaps beauty requires a kind of symmetry. If this is the case, we recognize symmetry in the universal sense and note how it is present in a particular painting such that it makes it beautiful. In the case of political science, we would look beyond particular cities and seek instead what is universally just or unjust.

Historically, political science began as a search for the common good, which meant specifically to figure out what the final end of a society is, and how the government must be structured as means to reach that purpose. However, a tension grew between theory and practice, as even the best blueprint for the state was not enough to guarantee success in the real world. In attempting to address this problem, political science split in two directions: the abandonment of political theory altogether in favor of immediate action, and the refounding of political science based upon modern thought. In our own time, the former became the foundation for what is now thought of as "political realism" (i.e., *realpolitik*), whereas the latter became known as political idealism. With these changes, classical political theory (from the Greeks to the medievals) was left behind.

Outside of the academy, in the domain of politics itself, modern debates are largely dominated by those falling into either the pragmatic, *realpolitik* camp or the political idealist camp. From the standpoint of the classical realist, however, neither alternative is acceptable. In this article, we seek to analyze the shortcomings with the aforementioned two modern approaches to political science, and propose instead what actual realism (based on the classical tradition) would offer to political science. The simplest explanation is that classical realism allows for a true *via media* between theory and practice. A

---

[4] Aristotle c.335/4BC: *Nicomachean Ethics*, VI.6, 1140b30-35: "Scientific knowledge is judgment about things that are universal and necessary, and the conclusions of demonstrations, and all scientific knowledge, follow from first principles (for scientific knowing involves apprehension of a rational ground)".

realist framework means that while the political good is sought in the universal, it is done so with an appreciation for reality as it stands independently from our perception. In other words, the political "ideal" from the realist standpoint is not merely an idea (i.e., an *ens rationis*, a being of reason); it is an account of the good that must consider things as they are, rather than how we would like them to be.

> Plaza's critique of modernity is offered with respect to a unique shift in the history of thought, one which is ultimately concerned with the intellectual *content* characteristic of the modern age. As mentioned above, numerous cases have been made that such an approach is almost entirely neglected in contemporary political science. And while this is certainly the case, recovering a kind of realism in political science, or in politics more generally, necessitates something of a more nuanced *account* of modern democracy.
>
> *Jones, "Classical Realism in a Democratic Context" [p.254].*

Against the classical realist, what modern political realism and idealism have in common is that they begin by reducing reality to the material alone. The primary difference between them is that the political realist does not believe in any further good beyond the present material condition nor any possible alternative than to deal with what we are given, while the political idealist believes in our ability to replace our current material condition with a better one. Both, however, will measure success purely in terms of immediate results on the basis of a strictly empirical metric. This differs drastically from the classical realist tradition (from the Greeks to the Medievals) that began with an understanding of reality beyond just the material order, as noted prior.

Every political scientist will claim to be "realistic" given that they are engaging precisely with a practical science rather than a speculative one. Nevertheless, from a classically realist standpoint, neither modern approach is realistic in the proper sense given that they begin from either an incomplete view of reality or a fundamentally distorted one. To demonstrate this point, we shall conclude by looking to the thought of Eric Voegelin and Jacques Maritain, both of whom critiqued modern political science in all of its contemporary forms, while proposing a new political science in harmony with a true philosophy of being. We will also include the thought of Leo Strauss, as he dealt with this broader issue, treating especially its historical development.

Voegelin criticized the modern's rejection of the transcendent order, characterizing it largely as an ideological revolt against God, in which man himself has striven to take the place of the divine. Here, Voegelin thought primarily of the political idealists, whom he considered more as Gnostics than actual philosophers. He explained throughout his work that it was Gnosticism, rather than science in any real sense, that lies at the core of the modern project. The Gnostic stubbornly believes that he has the "secret answer" to reality. This cannot be countered as simply an alternate philosophical viewpoint. Thus, the modern political idealist (operating as a Gnostic) can only offer ideology that runs contrary to being itself.

Like Voegelin, Maritain also critiqued the modern idealists, explaining that what they offered was merely an *ens rationis* that was no longer rooted in reality. Instead, Maritain proposed what he called the "concrete historical ideal," which immediately established a contrast between his "ideal" political state and that of a modern ideologue like Marx. Moreover, unlike *realpolitik*, Maritain did not deal with the current state of affairs purely in a "pragmatic" sense, focusing only on immediate, material consequences. On the contrary, Maritain began with an integral view of the human person in reality, both in his objectivity and subjectivity, marking out the direction we must work toward for the sake of the good in universal terms, but also as a real potential in the here and now. This "ideal" good does not require (as with Marx) a change in nature; rather, it arises from a consideration of nature as it stands. In this manner, Maritain was able to combine his metaphysical realism as a Thomist with a corresponding political philosophy for the present time. This creates a third position between the so-called political realist and idealist, as Maritain's classically realist approach seeks the political good in universal terms while still maintaining a concern for the particulars in history.

It is important to note, finally, that this critique against modern political science is not limited to Voegelin or Maritain. Several other thinkers, and in particular, many Catholic philosophers, have worked along these same lines.[5] Most notably, perhaps, is the work of John Paul II and Benedict XVI, each of whom dealt directly with the political problems of Western civilization in the present moment (with secular liberalism on the one hand and totalitarian ideologies on the other) along with their modern philosophical root. Prior to this, however, Voegelin and Maritain were especially influential in the twentieth century, and continue to serve not only as important points of departure on this subject, but also as guides to a new way forward. Further, while their perspective on political science is based on a classical model, it should not be mistaken as a mere retreat to the past. Rather, both offer a truly "post-modern" resolution that responds to the modern world without discarding the perennial truths of classical realism.

2. The Classical Understanding of Science and Politics

Prior to the modern age, Aristotle had set the standard for defining and structuring what we take to be as "science" in the first place. Generally speaking, while modern science (following the lead of modern philosophers beginning with Rene Descartes and Francis Bacon) is limited to the mathematically quantifiable and the empirical (taken in a purely materialistic sense), Aristotelian science was defined more broadly as a knowledge of causes attained through demonstration. As Aristotle stated in the *Posterior Analytics*: "We consider that we have unqualified knowledge of anything (as contrasted with the accidental knowledge of the sophist) when we believe that we know (i) **that the cause from which the fact results is the cause of that fact**, and (ii) **that the fact cannot be otherwise**."[6] Clearly, Aristotle stressed that the cause must, in truth, be the actual cause for the fact in question. This is an ontological point, and indeed, for our knowledge itself to be actual in this regard, it must really be the case that such a cause pertains to such a fact, as opposed to another. But for both Plato and Aristotle, reality is not confined to just the sensible material realm. For the modern empiricist, knowledge (and therefore, science) begins and ends with empirical observation. In the Aristotelian understanding, while knowledge may begin from empirical observation, it is not confined to it, just as nature is not limited in this way either.

---

[5] For example: Yves Simon, Christopher Dawson, Rémi Brague, Fr. James Schall, David Walsh, John and Russell Hittinger, et al.

[6] Aristotle c.348-7aBC: *Posterior Analytics*, I.2, 71b9-12. Emphasis added.

While science itself is an epistemic state (more specifically, the knowledge of what causes a certain effect in reality), what makes actual scientific knowledge true depends upon the reality of the things themselves being discussed. Our language is somewhat redundant on this point (i.e., speaking of "true" or "actual" knowledge), as the classical understanding of "knowledge" incorporates truth *per se*. In other words, one cannot have "fake knowledge." We can only know what is true, or rather, what is real. For us as moderns, however, we may be accustomed to an underlying subjectivist bias on this point, thinking of "knowledge" as simply what we take to be as fact, focusing more upon the knower rather than the thing known. We would posit, however, that this is really the only framework which would make any sense. If we cannot know reality, no true science (or even knowledge for that matter) would be possible. All we could "know" is how different individuals perceive different phenomena.

In order to pursue political science in the classical sense, it is necessary to rethink our paradigm for science to begin with, and to do this, we must revisit the Aristotelian foundation. The primary locus for Aristotle's philosophy of science in particular is his *Posterior Analytics*. Within this work, Aristotle established the fundamental structure of a science, as well as the nature of scientific demonstration. Now, while it has been generally recognized throughout the philosophical tradition that Aristotle had his own scientific outlook of philosophy as a whole, the details for what this would mean for each science within philosophy (for example, metaphysics, ethics, politics, etc.) are not a trivial matter for one to uncover. Moreover, this task may be simpler or more complex depending upon which particular philosophical discipline is chosen for the analysis. Within an Aristotelian context, it is an easier task to demonstrate the scientific nature of the speculative sciences, such as natural philosophy, as they each clearly deal with universals within their respective scopes. The practical sciences (ethics, economics, politics), however, appear to deal with the more contingent matters of human life rather than universals in nature. While politics certainly admits room for contingency, it must be guided by universals for it to retain any legitimate character of truth whatsoever.

An Aristotelian science is ordered into three parts: its subject matter, its principles, and its conclusions.[7] The subject matter of a science is, generally

---

[7] Ibid, I.10, 76b12-15: "Every demonstrative science is concerned with three things: the **subjects** which it posits (i.e., the genus whose essential attributes it studies), the so-

speaking, what the science itself is about; it resolves the basic question of what a particular science studies, or what it is meant to answer. For example, Aristotle states that the subject matter of metaphysics is "being as being,"[8] while the subject matter of biology is living being (or say, being as living). With regard to the principles of a science, this can be understood in a twofold manner: common (an "axiom") and proper (a "thesis").[9] Axioms are "that which must be grasped if any knowledge is to be acquired."[10] These principles are common to all sciences, and are fundamental to every science. The principle of non-contradiction (that something cannot be true and false simultaneously), for instance, is a common axiom. It is necessarily assumed by every science, and one could not even begin a demonstration without it; to deny it would be absurd. As all demonstrations must presuppose such an axiom to begin with, however, there cannot be a scientific demonstration of a common axiom. One cannot assume what he is trying to prove. A proper principle on the other hand is one which belongs properly to a particular science.[11] For example, Euclid's postulates serve as proper principles in geometry, such as the principle that a straight-line segment can be drawn joining any two points. Like axioms, however, they are immediate, indemonstrable, first, and necessary within their respective science. Finally, as stated prior, a science is also composed of its conclusions (or its "attributes") which are essentially the answers to our original scientific inquiries, arrived at through demonstration following from the principles of the science taken as premises. Again, taking geometry as the example, we can conclude through demonstration that the sum of the interior angles in a triangle equal to 180 degrees.

At the beginning of *Nicomachean Ethics*, he provides a basic outline for how to structure the science of politics, as well as ethics as a part of political science. Aristotle's first move in this regard was to lay down a definition of the good as "that at which all things aim" in reference to human action.[12] Moreover,

called **common axioms** upon which the demonstration is ultimately based, and thirdly the **attributes** whose several meanings it assumes". [Emphasis added]

[8] Aristotle c.348-7cBC: *Metaphysics*, IV.1, 1003a20-25.

[9] Aristotle c.348-7aBC: *Posterior Analytics*, I.2, 72a15-25.

[10] Ibid, I.2, 72a19.

[11] Ibid, I.2, 72a15: "an immediate indemonstrable first principle of syllogism the grasp of which is not necessary for the acquisition of certain kinds of knowledge..."

[12] Aristotle c.335/4bBC: *Nicomachean Ethics*, I.1, 1094a1-2.

Aristotle continued this thought by giving a *reductio ad impossibile* argument for the chief good among human ends, stating:[13]

> If, then, there is some end of the things we do, which we desire for its own sake (everything else being desired for the sake of this), and if we do not choose everything for the sake of something else (for at that rate the process would go on to infinity, so that our desire would be empty and vain), clearly this must be the good and the chief good.

Now, it is clear from this that Aristotle was intending to establish the starting principles of his inquiry, so the fact that he was operating under certain assumptions should not confuse us in this regard. Following Aristotle's initial consideration of the chief human good, he immediately proposed the following: "Will not the knowledge of it, then, have a great influence on life? ... If so, we must try, in outline at least to determine what it is, and of which of the sciences or capacities it is the object."[14] Here, Aristotle provided the primary consideration for the science, namely, the human good. Having done so, Aristotle then had to identify a science which would follow from that particular subject matter. This science in question, Aristotle argued, has to be politics, because political science determines the good for man in the collective, that is, in the state.[15] More importantly, Aristotle identified politics as being the "master art" of the human good because it sought it in a more universal manner; that is, political science seeks the good of the state as opposed to a single man: "For even if the end is the same for a single man and for a state, that of the state seems at all events something greater and more complete whether to attain or to preserve; though it is worthwhile to attain the end merely for one man, it is finer and more godlike to attain it for a nation or for city-states."[16] Thus, we may distinguish ethics and politics in a hierarchical manner, rather than thinking of them as two completely different sciences.

Indeed, ethics lies underneath politics, as ethics studies the human good in the case of the individual, whereas politics will study the same in a higher, more universal sense. Aristotle echoed these statements in the *Politics* as follows: "... the state is by nature clearly prior to the family and to the individual, since the

---

[13] Ibid, I.2, 1094a17-21.
[14] Ibid, I.2, 1094a21-26.
[15] Ibid, I.2, 1094a26-1094b7.
[16] Ibid, I.2, 1094b6-10.

whole is of necessity prior to the part..."[17] Moreover, Aristotle confirmed this link between the individual good and that of the state (that is, the concern of ethics and politics, respectively) in stating that they are the same, thereby affirming in a simultaneous fashion the place of ethics within the higher science of politics.[18]

While we have been speaking of politics as a science dealing with universals, clearly it does not seem to possess the same character as a science like arithmetic. This is a basic objection from the modern mind against all of the disciplines within the humanities, namely, that they cannot offer "concrete" answers. Even though we would argue that philosophy can and does provide truth, we can readily concede that philosophical truths by their nature are not as simple to grasp as basic arithmetic, and this is especially true with practical philosophy. Aristotle cautioned us regarding an unavoidable lack of precision within political science as such:[19]

> Our discussion will be adequate if it has as much clearness as the subject-matter admits of, for precision is not to be sought for alike in all discussions, any more than in all the products of the crafts. Now fine and just actions, which political science investigates, admit of much variety and fluctuation of opinion, so that they may be thought to exist only by convention, and not by nature. ... We must be content, then, in speaking of such subjects and with such premises to indicate the truth roughly and in outline, and in speaking about things which are only for the most part true and with premises of the same kind to reach conclusions that are no better.

This ought to give one some pause; after all, science is defined by its judgment over what is universal and necessary.[20] Aristotle, however, appeared to state here that this would not be possible for political science as it will deal with what is true in general. For a modern reader, to say that something is true "in general" might suggest that we are dealing with a contingent matter that is sometimes true or false. This is not what Aristotle had in mind. The natural point here is that while political science and ethics provide necessary truths regarding the good, it is not so precise as to suggest one definite course of action for the individual or the polis, whereby each individual human person and each human city must exist in the same way, down to every particular detail (which would

---

[17] Aristotle c.335/4aBC: *Politics*, I.2, 1253a20.

[18] Ibid, VII.15, 1334a11.

[19] Aristotle c.335/4bBC: *Nicomachean Ethics*, I.2, 1094b12-23.

[20] Ibid, VI.6, 1140b31.

obviously be impossible). In this way, even though Aristotle still conceived of ethics and politics as a science, there is still a clear distinction between these and a science such as mathematics or geometry. Aristotle resolved this by distinguishing between practical and speculative sciences.

The basic distinction between the two is that practical science is pursued for the sake of action, while a speculative science is done for the sake of contemplation. While Plato united these two forms of science under the banner of wisdom, Aristotle made a distinction between practical and theoretical wisdom. According to Aristotle, moral virtue is concerned with choice, but choice comes out of a deliberate desire, thus, he concluded that if a choice is to be morally good, it must be done under the right reason and desire.[21] The practical intellect, then, is precisely this form of reasoning within moral virtue (that is, the right deliberation before making a choice) which must exist alongside right desire, as opposed to the contemplative, which is only concerned with truth or falsity in and of itself.[22] Ultimately, the purpose of practical wisdom is to make the right choice at a particular point in time. Aristotle called this the "ultimate particular," and stated that this is what separates practical wisdom from the contemplative, since it is concerned with what must be done right now.[23]

With regard to the process of practical wisdom, Aristotle described what is now commonly referred to as the practical syllogism.[24] The first premise of a practical syllogism is universal (e.g., "it is wrong to steal," "it is good to study philosophy," etc.), the second premise would be a particular (e.g., "this action would be stealing," "reading this book is part of studying philosophy," etc.), and finally, the conclusion would be the action (or refraining from a particular action in the case of deliberation over a wrong choice) which results from the particular deliberation (e.g., not stealing, reading the book, etc.).[25] Aristotle also clarified this process in his *De Anima*:[26]

> Since the one premise or judgment is universal and the other deals with the particular (for the first tells us that such and such a kind of man should do such and such a kind of act, and the second that *this* is an act of the kind meant, and

---

[21] Ibid, VI.2, 1139a21-25.
[22] Ibid, VI.2 1139a25-30.
[23] Ibid, VI.8, 1142a24-25.
[24] Broadie 1968: "The Practical Syllogism", *Analysis*, 29.1, 26-28.
[25] Aristotle c.335/4BC: *Nicomachean Ethics*, VII.3, 1147a25-b4.
[26] Aristotle c.330BC: *De Anima* ,III.11, 434a15-21.

I a person of the type intended), it is the latter opinion that really originates movement, not the universal; or rather it is both, but the one does so while it remains in a state more like rest, while the other partakes in movement.

Thus, what political science offers with respect to the universal would be in the first premise of the practical syllogism; however, since the purpose of practical wisdom overall is to conclude with action, political theory itself cannot provide us with necessary knowledge at each step. In the case of ethics (within political science), for instance, we can examine universals with regard to actual virtue or moral goodness in the case of the individual (e.g., that stealing is wrong, or that murder is wrong), but the individual still carries the task of relating these universals to a particular circumstances, which can only be done through prudence (that is, practical wisdom).[27] To be clear, the general truths given through the science of ethics and politics are indeed necessary truths; there is a right answer, so to speak, in any moral question. However, given that the particulars of life vary from person to person, it is a matter of practical wisdom, rather than purely contemplative wisdom, to determine how the necessary, universal truths of ethics and politics align with their particular actions. This is said within reason, of course. While each individual must decide for himself in a sense, the end point (i.e., the good) is still the same. We must make this qualification because of the obvious point that no two lives or two cities are exactly the same, but we must also caution the modern reader not to exaggerate this point, so as to suggest that what is "adultery" for one person is perfectly acceptable for another. A quick illustration of this point could be with the virtue of moderation. Given the physical differences between people, the amount of alcohol necessary for inebriation is completely different between say, a 100-pound woman vs. a 200-pound man. As human beings, both are meant to exercise moderation, but given their physical differences, a moderate amount of alcohol for the 200-pound man will most likely be an excessive amount for the 100-pound woman. These are the types of particulars we are referring to, but

[27] Gerson 1994: "Why Ethics is Political Science for Aristotle", *Proceedings of the ACPA*, vol.68, 94: "Since all science is of the universal, if there is such a thing as practical science it is rooted in the universal. What makes a practical science practical is that the universal truths in which it is rooted are truths relevant to practice just as a productive science is productive insofar as its universal truths are truths relevant to production. Therefore, the universality of all science does not in itself interfere with the particularity of practical science. ... Practical science would be, so to speak, science plus practice".

notice that in spite of these, the universal truth about the good remains: one must have moderation.

The whole point of studying ethics is to aid us in establishing the true nature of happiness. Likewise, political science must do the same for the community, that is, establishing the best good for the community. As a practical science, however, this study is not meant to terminate in the mere contemplation of such truths, but in action. The study of ethics itself will not make one virtuous, but if pursued correctly, it will help in this regard nonetheless by examining the universal truths regarding the real nature of happiness and the good human life. By considering all the virtues in this regard, the science of ethics offers a variety of particular virtues and norms which build up the virtuous life itself. We can say the same for political science. Political theory itself will not provide for us the best state on the ground, but it will help us to understand what to aim for and what to avoid. If we understand ethics and politics as sciences in the classical sense, it allows us to realize that there are indeed general necessary truths to uncover when considering the good human life as such. This means that there is in actuality a universal answer to the nature of a good human life in the broad sense, but it is still up to the individual to prudentially align his or her own particular circumstances of life to the universal itself. So, for example, while the political scientist knows that the exercise of the intellect is a virtuous perfection of every human being, qua rational, he cannot say precisely how every individual should obtain this perfection: perhaps as scientist, or a professor of the humanities, or perhaps in regular dialogue with one's friends and family after work. These particular manifestations must be determined by individual persons through prudence.

3. The Split in Political Science at the Beginning of Modernity

The modern departure from classical political science came arguably with the philosophy of Thomas Hobbes and Niccolò Machiavelli, each providing his own distinct path which remains today. Machiavelli was first, spawning a new form of political realism (albeit, a pseudo-realism), one he claimed was not of his own imagination, but a simple description of the particulars as they stand on the ground.[28] Machiavellianism, as it is called today, is not really a philosophy in the

[28] Maritain 1968: *Integral Humanism*, 294.

traditional sense. If anything, it primarily signifies the lack of one. It is not that Machiavelli denied the existence of virtue or justice necessarily, he just did not care to consider them one way or the other. Machiavelli famously declared that he was advising the ruler to be vicious when necessary because that is what brought actual results in the world (an echo of Thrasymachus' argument in Plato's *Republic*), whereas one who tried to be virtuous at all times would end up in ruins.[29] The only thing that matters is what he perceived to be concrete results, which boil down to military strength, economic wealth, and political stability. This cynical approach to politics became known as "political realism" (*realpolitik*) in the modern world because its adherents claim that they are the only ones honest enough to deal with the game of politics as it is truly played on the ground, far from the mind of the man in the ivory tower. There is no room for discussion on this matter, as the political realist does not care for contemplation, he is only a man of action. *Realpolitik* is not a science, nor does it pretend to be either. Machiavelli only spoke to politics as an admittedly perverse *techne* at best, a craft of manipulation and power, nothing more.

> In theory, much of modern science has rejected the Aristotelian doctrine that the aim of science is to discover the form or nature of what things are. Modern science has exchanged knowledge of nature with the ability to manipulate it for the sake of greater power and dominance. This is precisely the stated goal of Francis Bacon's *New Organon,* whereby knowledge is reduced to engineering and coercion. In the same way, this is how Pope Francis portrays modern science, conceived in the Cartesian vision of "a technique of possession, mastery and transformation." For

---

[29] Machiavelli 1532: *The Prince*, XV: "Many writers have imagined republics and principalities that have never been seen nor known to exist in reality. For there is such a distance between how one lives and how one ought to live, that anyone who abandons what is done for what ought to be done achieves his downfall rather than his preservation. A man who wishes to profess goodness at all times will come to ruin among so many who are not good. Therefore, it is necessary for a prince who wishes to maintain himself to learn how not to be good, and to use this knowledge or not to use it according to necessity."

Pope Francis, without seeing nature as "form," it eventually succumbs to domination and procedural control.

Jones, "Classical Realism in a Democratic Context" [p.253].

Hobbes also fancied himself to be a realist of sorts, but unlike Machiavelli, he did care to engage in some form of political science. Even though Hobbes had a similar perspective on politics as Machiavelli, he did still believe he could couch his ideas in seemingly universal terms (even as an outright nominalist). In this manner, Hobbes created a new form of political idealism, creating a path for others to follow (like Marx) even as they differ with Hobbes' own prescriptions overall. As Strauss explained, "Hobbes regarded himself as the founder of political philosophy or political science," knowing that this claim is originally linked to Socrates.[30] Ironically though, Strauss noted that Hobbes was actually indebted to the tradition he set out to reject.[31] First, Hobbes had to accept that political philosophy or science was possible to begin with.[32] Again, this is where we see the split from *realpolitik.*

While he claimed to be more grounded than his predecessors, Hobbes only acknowledged the "idealistic" form of political philosophy (that is, the search for the best regime), ignoring the anti-idealistic tradition of political thought in history.[33] In so doing, Strauss argued, Hobbes implicitly accepted the idealistic formulation of political philosophy as being political philosophy itself.[34] Where Hobbes parted ways with classical political philosophy, however, was in his rejection of defining man as a political or social animal by nature.[35] Hobbes saw man as apolitical, and like an Epicurean, equated the good with the pleasant.[36]

---

[30] Strauss 1953: *Natural Right and History*, 166.
[31] Ibid.
[32] Ibid, 167.
[33] Ibid, 168.
[34] Ibid.
[35] Ibid, 169.
[36] Hobbes 1651: *Leviathan*, XV: "And the science of them is the true and only moral philosophy. For moral philosophy is nothing else but the science of what is good and evil in the conversation and society of mankind. Good and evil are names that signify our appetites and aversions, which in different tempers, customs, and doctrines of men are different: and diverse men differ not only in their judgement on the senses of what is

The twist for Hobbes was to utilize man's apolitical nature in a political manner, and in so doing, Hobbes became the founder of what Strauss called "political hedonism."[37]

Just as Aristotle and Plato derived their respective ethical and political philosophy from their natural philosophy (particularly with regard to human nature, of course), so too was this the case for Hobbes. If we wish to understand what led Hobbes away from the tradition before him (as with all other modern philosophers), we must consider his natural philosophy.[38] Hobbes was a materialist at heart, which ultimately led him toward a very mechanical view of nature. The consequence for Hobbes in this regard was to adopt the idea that human beings are meant to be masters of nature itself, to have power over nature through science (just as Bacon and Descartes).[39] Also, as materialism then feeds into skepticism, Hobbes separated human wisdom from the reality of the universe.[40] Wisdom then, for Hobbes, was a matter of "free construct."[41] If we combine these different claims, we end up with the following: the universe is unintelligible; control of nature does not require an understanding of nature itself; there are no knowable limits to man's conquest of nature.[42] Now, to explain the first point, one way in which materialism can morph into skepticism comes back to what we established prior in terms of universals and particulars. If one is a materialist (i.e., holding that only matter is real), nominalism (i.e., the denial of universals) follows naturally. The prima facie difficulty for the realist is the manner in which universals exist, since clearly there is no material object in the world which could encapsulate a universal such as "justice." Still, while it may be easier for the nominalist to surpass this difficulty (that is, by simply denying the reality of universals altogether), a more challenging problem arises. If universals have no reality of their own in some way, then true knowledge is impossible, as all we know are the changing particulars in matter. Skepticism

---

pleasant and unpleasant to the taste, smell, hearing, touch, and sight; but also of what is conformable or disagreeable to reason in the actions of common life." See also Strauss 1953: *Natural Right and History*, 169.

[37] Strauss 1953: *Natural Right and History*, 169.

[38] Ibid.

[39]Ibid, 174.

[40] Ibid, 170-171.

[41] Ibid, 175.

[42] Ibid, 175.

(i.e., denying the possibility of true knowledge) is an easy way out of this dilemma even if the result is unsatisfactory.

Finally, another paradox with Hobbes was that, according to his own system, the human good must be regarded as the highest good, and thus, the highest science must be that of politics.[43] In spite of Hobbes' rejection of idealistic political philosophy, Hobbes' own expectations for political philosophy were more grandiose than those of the classical tradition he was rebelling against (for Aristotle, metaphysics is the highest science). Yet, Hobbes' thought also consisted primarily of simplifications, particularly with respect to virtue and political society. As with the Machiavellian *realpolitik* movement, Hobbes reduced all of human virtue to a kind of political utility, that is, usefulness to the state.[44] Where Machiavelli only reserved this dispensation for the ruler, however, Hobbes was not afraid to state this reduction of virtue in a universal fashion, covering both citizen and ruler alike. Moreover, both Hobbes and Machiavelli dramatically lowered the expectations for justice in political society, abandoning the common good in favor of an overall state of peace. Ultimately, the goal of a political society for Hobbes was purely to satisfy the passion for self-preservation within each individual.[45]

This initial split in political thought has led to a false dichotomy that persists today. One could either give up on political science entirely, or if one still cared to do it, he would have to do so in a similar manner to Hobbes, resting upon the modern reformulation of science. Where Hobbes succeeded was in taking a route similar to Descartes, proposing a new scientific method entirely that would serve as the foundation to the rest of his thought. Both Hobbes and Machiavelli rejected the classical form of political science; while Machiavelli replaced

---

[43] Ibid, 177.

[44] Ibid, 178.

[45] Ibid, 201: "There is a remarkable parallelism and an even more remarkable discrepancy between Hobbes' theoretical philosophy and his practical philosophy. In both parts of his philosophy, he teaches that reason is impotent and that it is omnipotent, or that reason is omnipotent because it is impotent. Reason is impotent because reason or humanity have no cosmic support: the universe is unintelligible, and nature "dissociates" men. But the very fact that the universe is unintelligible permits reason to rest satisfied with its free constructs, to establish through its constructs an Archimedean basis of operations, and to anticipate an unlimited progress in its conquest of nature. Reason is impotent against passion, but it can become omnipotent if it co-operates with the strongest passion [**self-preservation**] or if it puts itself into the service of the strongest passion".

political science with pure action, Hobbes redefined science at its root and constructed a new form of political science at the exclusion of what came prior. This new form of science, unlike all that which came before, would have the same precision as mathematics. Finally, like mathematics, it promised to be "value free" in the sense that its conclusions are not colored by any pre-existing bias. Whether we speak of a liberal pragmatist or outright totalitarian ideologue today, if they claim to be scientific in their approach, it is still on these Hobbesian terms even if their conclusions go in different directions.

4. Maritain on the Progression of Modernity from Inception to Present

While the split between Machiavelli and Hobbes brought about a new direction in political philosophy, it was a change precipitated by a greater movement in Western culture and philosophy beyond ethics and politics. The transition from medieval to modern culture can be traced especially with the rise of humanism. Originally, humanism was founded upon theocentric principles in keeping with the broader medieval perspective, but this morphed overtime to an anthropocentric or secular form of humanism that not only exalts man's inherent greatness but places him at the center of reality.

The Middle Ages started to dissolve once man began to feel the pressures of being under so great an order as God's.[46] Man seemingly became nothing considered alongside God, and so the struggle emerged for how man could come to grips with this sobering reality. After all, when we consider ourselves from our own vantage point, our life is our central focus. From our perspective, we are at the center of the universe. Nevertheless, we are all too aware that each of us individually form an infinitesimally small piece of the universe. Maritain described this phenomenon as man's "horror of being nothing."[47] This medieval despair led man to desire being despised, lest one forget his place within the hierarchy of being.[48] Yet, this anguish was not meant to last. The shift toward

---

[46] Maritain 1968: *Integral Humanism*, 161.
[47] Ibid.
[48] Ibid.

humanism was meant to be a rehabilitation of sorts; an attempt at rescuing man from his nothingness.[49]

Now, this rehabilitation of man in the modern era did not undergo a singular expression. Maritain argued that we can differentiate two main paths of modernity through what he called the problem of grace and freedom. First, Maritain pointed to the Protestant movement, which emphasized divine grace at the expense of human freedom.[50] On the other hand, there is the rationalist camp in modernity which professed human freedom without grace.[51]

The Protestant movement affirmed man's nothingness, carrying pessimism to its logical extreme. Under this view, man is seen as being "essentially corrupted," yet in reality, man advanced this on his own.[52] It is not God who reveals man's nothingness; it is man who uncovers it, mistaking his own voice for God's.[53] For the Protestant, man's corruption has stripped him of his freedom, whereby all that is left is grace.[54] What originally became man's source of despair is now his crutch. With freedom gone, man is no longer responsible. Thus, in the grand scheme of man's salvation, it is God who does all of the work.

Inverting the Protestant order, the rationalist chose instead to deny divine grace for the sake of exalting human freedom. Here, it is man alone who triumphs. Under this account, man's final end is to dominate nature, and to become a quasi-god within creation. This became the predominant path for modernism as we know it. As a result of such an exaltation, the rationalist view established two ultimate ends, one being supernatural, and the other natural.[55] Again, the medieval world held that there was only one ultimate end, namely, the supernatural. The moderns overall, however, began by trying to promote both, simultaneously seeking perfect happiness both on Earth and in Heaven. As Maritain explained, this move led to the "theology of natural goodness" by Jean-Jacques Rousseau, whereby man is essentially good (a direct reversal of the Protestant schema).[56] Evil, then, comes from without.

---

[49] Ibid.
[50] Ibid, 164-65.
[51] Ibid.
[52] Ibid, 162.
[53] Ibid.
[54] Ibid.
[55] Ibid, 166.
[56] Ibid.

In the history of philosophy, the beginnings of modernism are placed between the sixteenth and seventeenth centuries with thinkers like Francis Bacon and Rene Descartes. By this point, we can see clearly what Maritain identified to be the first of three distinct moments in the progression of modernism. This first moment, labeled as the "classical" moment by Maritain, saw man seeking to advance culture in isolation, casting tradition aside in favor of human reason's absolute power.[57] Yet, in spite of man's attempt to abandon his roots in this moment, he was able to retain, nevertheless, the Christian ideals inherited from the preceding age. The second moment occurred in the eighteenth and nineteenth centuries, in which modern man came face-to-face with his opposition toward God's order.[58] This is the "bourgeois" moment, characterized by its "rationalist optimism."[59] Finally, in the third moment (from the twentieth century onward), man comes back to despair, no longer able to bear the machinations of the world according to his own creation. Now, man wages war upon himself, seeking instead to create a new man from the rubble.[60] This is, according to Maritain, the "revolutionary" movement.

Criticizing these three moments, Maritain began by arguing that the first erred in reversing the order of ends.[61] Here, culture's supreme end was itself, and God was merely the means to its possession, in that God gave man the power to reign.[62] The second movement carried this problem forward to an extreme, no longer accepting the limitations of nature, seeking instead to have nature conform to man, rather than the reverse.[63] God was no longer a means to the natural end, but simply an idea along the way.[64] Lastly, the third movement bows to the demands of technology in a desperate attempt to lord over the material realm.[65] Man is forced to encounter the harsh reality of nature, submitting himself to inhumanity in a stubborn denial of what is in front of him,

---

[57] Ibid, 171.
[58] Ibid.
[59] Ibid.
[60] Ibid.
[61] Ibid.
[62] Ibid, 172.
[63] Ibid.
[64] Ibid.
[65] Ibid.

so as to continue the ongoing struggle for ultimate dominance. Here, God is an obstacle; "God dies," enabling man to take His place.[66]

The allure of modernism stemmed ultimately from its offer of an "earthly beatitude," a violent retaking of the Garden of Eden where man avenges his original fall by exiling God from the paradise instead.[67] Blinded by this temptation, man simply lost his soul in the process, "turning the universe upside down in his effort to find himself again."[68] These unfulfillable promises of the enlightenment led to the rising of the bourgeois, which saw man settle with mediocrity, confusing a vacuous sense of temporal comfort for true happiness as such. With the passing of time, however, history itself bore testimony to this failure as an "irrationalist tidal wave" inevitably began to sweep modernity in a violent reaction to the extremes of an optimistic, yet utterly despotic, rationalism.[69]

Maritain credited Marx, Nietzsche, and Freud for unmasking the bourgeois man, "but not without disfiguring man himself in the process."[70] Moreover, the irrationalist thread as expressed through Nietzsche, Kierkegaard, Barth, and Chestov, while "noble" in their attack of rationalism, nevertheless strayed from the proper path, culminating in a "counter-humanist" movement that simply brought us back to the beast.[71] "In the end," Maritain explained, "Nietzsche gives way to Mr. Rosenberg."[72] Maritain pointed out that what was ultimately missing from Nietzsche's revolt against mediocrity is that man only has two roads before him: "the road to Calvary and the road to the slaughterhouse."[73]

---

[66] Ibid.

[67] Maritain 1946: *The Twilight of Civilization,* 6.

[68] Ibid.

[69] Ibid, 7.

[70] Ibid, 6.

[71] Ibid, 7-8.

[72] Ibid, 8. The reference appears to be to Alfred Rosenberg, one of the main authors of Nazi ideology who claimed Nietzsche as a direct inspiration. Apart from helping to build Nazi racial theory, Rosenberg also promoted "Positive Christianity", which was founded not upon the Apostle's Creed, or in Jesus Christ as the Son of God, but in Adolf Hitler as the herald of a new revelation. Positive Christianity denied the Semitic origins of Christianity, replacing the Bible with *Mein Kampf*, and the cross of Christ with the crooked cross.

[73] Ibid, 9.

As the modern man attempts to work out his salvation "by himself alone," he moves only in the temporal realm as though God did not exist.[74] For the modern project to succeed, God cannot exist, and all of humanity must coalesce into one body seeking to dominate history. Against this, a new humanism ought to rise, sanctifying the temporal through grace and virtue.[75] This form of humanism will be called "integral" in that it takes into account all of reality, both supernatural and natural.[76] It sets "no *a priori* limits to the descent of the divine into man," "no conflict between the vertical movement toward eternal life ... and the horizontal movement" which finds its expression in genuine human culture.[77] While this horizontal movement may have temporal aims, it "nevertheless prepares the way, within human history, for the Kingdom of God" beyond history.[78]

Concerning the concrete instantiation of the modern crisis, Maritain identified the phenomenon of totalitarianism, both as Communism and Nazism/Fascism, as the incarnations of the modern project. While both forms of totalitarian systems arrive at the same destruction, they differ nonetheless in their metaphysical principles.[79] For its own part, Marxism professes an atheism that "makes a social idol its god" as an effort to fill the void.[80] Nazism and Fascism, on the other hand, make "God Himself an idol," denying actual truth and transcendence in favor of a "pseudo-theism," a "demon of the blood" "attached to the glory of the people."[81] Both of these movements were made possible through the preceding dialectic of modernism noted prior, and seen within that context, it is clear that these are but the logical conclusions of a new political theory based upon the underpinnings of modern thought rebelling against the past. It is for this reason that the totalitarian regimes themselves are not the only problem at hand. They are a symptom, not a cause.

---

[74] Ibid, 10-11.
[75] Ibid, 12-13.
[76] Ibid, 13.
[77] Ibid, 13.
[78] Ibid, 14.
[79] Ibid, 18.
[80] Ibid, 18.
[81] Ibid, 18 and 21.

5. True Political Realism: A Genuinely Post-Modern Return to Reality

Like Maritain, Voegelin also recognized the modern's rejection of the transcendent order, characterizing it largely as a Gnostic revolt against God, in which man himself has striven to take the place of the divine. For Voegelin, Gnosticism lies at the core of the modern project, and given the stubborn Gnostic belief that they have the "secret answer" to reality, this cannot be countered as simply an alternate philosophical viewpoint. Rather than philosophy, the modern Gnostic only offers ideology, one which is hostile to truth and reality itself from the start. For this reason, no dialogue can be possible, because the Gnostic has ensured this from the beginning. While there are immediate parallels here with Maritain's own critique of modernity the difference between him and Voegelin is that his answer is not to reject modernity entirely and substitute it with something completely different. Maritain remained hopeful (as was Pope John Paul II) that certain strands of modern thought can be reoriented toward the good, and that even practically, it is indeed possible for a just order to arise even within the contemporary historical sky.

5.1. Eric Voegelin and the New Science of Politics

Totalitarianism is a political phenomenon of the twentieth century which continues to haunt modern civilization. As stated prior, totalitarian movements are an outgrowth of modern political idealism, and as such ideas persist, so too does the threat of a new totalitarian state wherever the culture of political idealism takes hold. Totalitarian regimes are not merely autocratic; totalitarianism grants unlimited control and power to a ruler, and its entire *raison d'etre* is to transform man and society into a perfect unit. A normal autocratic regime, on the other hand, is primarily concerned with external control alone.

The classical tyrant or despot heading an autocratic regime is a selfish ruler who cares only for his own individual good against that of the community. While the tyrant seeks what he perceives as the good for himself, the populace serves as simply a means to this end. Thus, the tyrant only cares for himself; there is no concern for the common good, save perhaps for the purposes of rhetoric as a means to control the masses. The totalitarian leader, on the other hand, assumes the role of God, seeking not only his own good, but what he perceives to be the good overall. What makes the totalitarian ruler a creature of modernity is that it presumes an idealist framework, in which the leader alone determines what truth is entirely. Where traditionally government was limited by a "higher law" to which all men are subject, the totalitarian regime rejects the view that the foundation of truth lies beyond the ruler and maintains that the ruler is perfectly justified to mold humanity as he sees fit by any means necessary. The totalitarian leader will boldly assert that he alone declares what is law, and what is truth.

One of the first issues that Voegelin addressed in his introduction to *Science, Politics, and Gnosticism* is the inability of modern political science to fully comprehend the totalitarian phenomenon as it ravaged Europe: "Europe had no conceptual tools with which to grasp the horror that was upon her .... The confused state of science and the consequent impossibility of adequately understanding political phenomena lasted until well into the period of World War II."[82] This was necessarily the case given the contemporary shift toward "value-free" inquiry, which Voegelin called a "degradation of political science to a handmaid of the powers that be," arguing that "a restoration of political science to its principles implies that the restorative work is necessary because the consciousness of principles is lost."[83] For this reason, he begins *Science, Politics, and Gnosticism* by reestablishing political science in the classical sense. The "new" political science then, refounded upon classical realism, is actually the one of old.

"Political science, *politike episteme*, was founded by Plato and Aristotle,"[84] began Voegelin. Their goal was to discover the "right order of soul and society" and to create a corresponding political structure.[85] There were differing opinions (*doxa*) in Greek philosophy at the time regarding this matter, so the question became how to determine which one is truly best. Political science arose from this very question as the methodology to determine the answer.[86] The subject matter of political science, then, involved such questions as: "What is happiness? How should man live in order to be happy? What is virtue? What,

[82] Voegelin 1968: *Science, Politics, and Gnosticism*, 5.
[83] Voegelin 1952: *The New Science of Politics*, 3—4.
[84] Voegelin 1968: *Science, Politics, and Gnosticism*, 15.
[85] Ibid.
[86] Ibid.

especially, is the virtue of justice? How large a territory and population are best for a society? What kind of education is best? What professions, and what form of government?"[87] Again, the point of such an examination was not to advance mere opinion, but to "advance beyond opinion to truth through the use of scientific analysis."[88]

True scientific analysis must rest upon the assumption that "truth about the order of being ... is objectively ascertainable."[89] This is the core of classical realism and was the obvious starting point for all human inquiry prior to the modern break. With the introduction of idealism, what was once an unstated and necessary component for human knowledge (i.e., the belief that human beings are capable of knowing what is real), was now cast into doubt and treated as an alternative philosophical perspective, another "-ism." Against this, the classical realist (or simply the philosopher in the traditional sense), having accepted the possibility that the order of being is knowable to him, is led further to the realization that "the levels of being discernible within the world are surmounted by a transcendent source of being and its order."[90] This realization was brought about by the movements of man's soul toward the divine being "experienced as transcendent."[91] Wisdom (*sophia*) is rooted in the divine being, and the experience of love (*philia*) toward this as the "origin of being" is how "man became philosopher."[92] Voegelin concluded that: "Only when the order of being as a whole, unto its origin in transcendent being, comes into view, can the analysis be undertaken with any hope of success; for only then can current opinions about right order be examined as to their agreement with the order of being."[93] In other words, what enables man to pursue science at all is an openness to the order of being as independent from one's own cognition, and moreover, an openness to the transcendent as its first principle. Coming back to the problem of totalitarianism, the rationale for these movements is borne out of precisely the opposite of this spirit.

As modernity has progressed, Voegelin argued that what we have been left are not political philosophers, but Gnostics. It is important for us to discuss the

---

[87] Ibid, 16.
[88] Ibid.
[89] Ibid.
[90] Ibid, 18.
[91] Ibid.
[92] Ibid.
[93] Ibid.

difference between true political science and political Gnosticism to see exactly what the consequences are of pursuing political science without a basis in realism. Voegelin traced this difference back to the Greeks, recalling the distinction between the philosophers and the sophists: "When Phaedrus asks what one should call such a man, Socrates, following Heraclitus, replies that the term *sophos*, one who knows, would be excessive: this attribute may be applied to God alone; but one might well call him *philosophos*. Thus, 'actual knowledge' is reserved to God; finite man can only be the 'lover of knowledge,' not himself the one who knows."[94] Here, the Gnostic would think himself to be "the one who knows," standing against the humility of the philosopher following the Socratic dictum, "know that you know nothing." Yet, this Gnostic hubris is easily noted in modernist thinkers, particularly with political philosophers like Hobbes and Marx. If anything, it would be more challenging to think of a modern political philosopher that did not possess this disposition. Indeed, while the classical philosopher is open to discovery, the modern Gnostic who carries on the name of the philosopher has disguised will to power as science. As Voegelin pointed out: "philosophy springs from the love of being; it is man's loving endeavor to perceive the order of being and attune himself to it. Gnosis desires dominion over being; in order to seize control of being the Gnostic constructs his system."[95]

The Gnostic system is all-encompassing and flawlessly comprehensive; it seeks only to replace the actual order of being. A Gnostic promises absolute knowledge of the whole, but with a special caveat: what the Gnostic comes to "know" about all of reality is a matter of special, individual revelation. Gnosticism is not science in any real sense (although it claims itself to be the only real science). Instead, it stumbles upon a bevy of "secret knowledge" which conveniently allows for every loose end to fall into place within its intellectual system. As the Gnostic claims dominion over the entirety of being, no mysteries remain. The "transcendent" becomes that which is unknown to the uninitiated, but known fully to the Gnostic.

Yet, for all of Gnosticism's claim to discovery and intellectual advancement, it also completely rejects the pursuit of science beyond itself. After all, no further inquiry is necessary. Again, for the Gnostic, traditional scientific demonstration will not provide him with the answers. The special revelation possessed by the

---

[94] Ibid, 41.
[95] Ibid.

Gnostic is simply handed down and accepted without question. However, if one were to try and analyze a Gnostic system, it would inevitably crumble under any scrutiny. The Gnostic excuses this failing by asserting that it only demonstrates the folly of human science outside of itself. Since a Gnostic movement cannot withstand questioning, then no questions can be allowed at all: the Gnostic prophecy must be accepted as it stands. Here, Voegelin recalled the example of Rudolf Hess who, when asked why he did not refuse to partake in mass executions at Auschwitz, replied: "At that time I did not indulge in deliberation: I had received the order, and I had to carry it out .... I do not believe that even one of the thousands of SS leaders could have permitted such a thought to occur to him."[96]

If one were to reject the Gnostic prophesy, the Gnostic portrays this denial as a qualitative failing on their part. Rather than abandon his pursuit, the Gnostic will simply attack the questioner.[97] The Gnostic mindset in this regard is simply that if one does not see eye to eye with him, then it can only be because the skeptic is wicked in some way. This can easily be seen in the West today as modern minds are further polarized. The underlying tension is between those who find themselves celebrating the modern turn, pushing further into that direction, and those who sense that modernity has taken a wrong turn. Of course, there is a difference between the mass adherents of an ideology (Lenin's "useful idiots") and its thought leaders. For Voegelin, these thinkers (like Marx) are merely intellectual swindlers.[98]

This intellectual swindle on the part of the Gnostic could be restated as an act of self-deception, one that is animated by an underlying will to power that disguises itself as an intellectual move.[99] Such an impetus within man beckons him toward absolute mastery. It results in a complete rebellion against the transcendent itself, as the subject feels imprisoned within the order of being.[100] Even though man is nowhere near the top of this hierarchy, he wishes to be. In examining the depths of the will to power, Nietzsche states: "To rule, and to be no longer a servant of a god: this means was left behind to ennoble man."[101] Through this will to power, then, the Gnostic man attempts to make himself God ruling over

---

[96] Ibid, 26-27.
[97] Ibid.
[98] Ibid, 28.
[99] Ibid.
[100] Ibid, 30.
[101] Ibid.

all of existence. This profound self-deception becomes the dogma of a political mass movement which hails the Gnostic thinkers as "prophets."[102] These mass movements in turn take on the character of a religion, but it is only a kind of ersatz religion with man at the head, rather than God. To identify oneself as a Marxist, then, becomes akin to identifying oneself as a Christian or Jew.

> Echoing Vermeule, we could add that a movement such as identity politics is not merely a new form of religion. This contention would usurp its own self-understanding. As a religion, identity politics is not only a set of doctrines, but is patently *liturgical.* The pseudo-liturgical activity of identity politics reveals its connection to the new condition of modern man. Its worship is made visible in public denunciations of illiberalism, racism, xenophobia, hatred, privilege, nourished by its nominal *telos* where humanity become witness to the final overcoming of all forms of discrimination and oppression. The vitality and tenacity of identity politics becomes intelligible by seeing it within this deracinated liturgical context. In this way, liturgy truly is the "source and summit" of identity politics.
>
> *Jones, "Classical Realism in a Democratic Context" [**p.257**].*

5.2. Jacques Maritain and the "Concrete Historical Ideal"

Being more concerned with the root philosophy as its source, Voegelin offered more of a prescription for philosophy itself rather than its application in practice. That is to say, Voegelin focused on the problems of modern thought and argued for a better philosophy inspired more by what the moderns left behind. Maritain did this as well, but he also endeavored to speak about the regimes of his day, taking care to give a proposal for what Western governments ought to aim for in the current time. He did this in a way, however, that remained faithful to his realist principles without succumbing to either modern extreme (either that of *realpolitik* or political Gnosticism). Maritain called this a "concrete historical ideal," and while the particular ideal itself is not our focus here, what we wish to

---

[102] Ibid, 33.

call attention to is the nature of this "ideal" in the abstract, as it demonstrates how a contemporary political science should operate when engaged as a classical realist.

The concrete historical ideal for Maritain is distinguished explicitly from a modern utopian ideal (which can properly be called "idealist"), as it is only "ideal" in a qualified sense, grounded upon a realist conception of metaphysics.[103] First, Maritain proclaimed, the concrete historical ideal is not an *ens rationis*.[104] Unlike the utopian ideal, the concrete historical ideal cannot be a pure construct of the mind *against* nature, whereby in the utopian ideal, reality is *submerged* under the *ens rationis*. That is to say, the utopian Gnostic fashions for himself an ideal wholly separate from nature, stemming purely from his own will of how he, in particular, *wishes* for the world to be. Again, this is the Nietzschean will to power we discussed earlier noted by Voegelin. The utopian ideal is founded upon knowing what the world *is not*, and wishing to *transform* the world according to this ideal which is purely a construct of the mind.[105] This transformation can only be accomplished by force, as the utopian seeks to change reality itself to suit his ideal. Reality must conform to the idea for the utopian, not the inverse. The concrete historical ideal, on the other hand, must be established according to what the world *truly is*.

Maritain's concrete historical ideal can only be understood from the vantage point of realism, and can only exist as an outgrowth of it. It is not a transformation of being, rather, it is an understanding of it as it exists on its terms. For this reason, Maritain explained, the concrete historical ideal must be fashioned under a *historical sky* (the current state of the world, here and now).[106] Unlike the utopian, the concrete historical ideal does not describe the end of history. The utopian, given his Gnostic disposition, seeks to "immanentize the eschaton," (as Voegelin famously put it throughout his *New Science of Politics*) to bring the end of history by force, understood as the perfection of man brought about through the ideal itself. With a concrete historical ideal, however, we admit of a certain flexibility, taking into full account man's imperfections, knowing that while we may have a long-range goal in sight, the concrete

---

[103] Maritain 1968: *Integral Humanism*, 236.
[104] Ibid, 233.
[105] Ibid, 234.
[106] Ibid.

historical ideal is a constant *movement toward*; it is not a state of rest on earth, as the utopian dream would wish for.

Now, let us consider briefly Maritain's conception of integral humanism itself, as this complete understanding of the human person is the foundation for his political thought. The notion of "integral humanism" refers to Maritain's proposed "new" humanism, a post-modern humanism that recovers what the moderns had left behind.[107] This has political ramifications, of course, seeing as one's political philosophy stems from their philosophy of the human person. We discussed this above, for example, with the changes made by Hobbes. Let us begin by understanding the terms. First, "integral" refers to the fact that we are considering the human person in a complete manner, both in terms of his objectivity as a metaphysical being, a "rational animal" so to speak, and as one who possesses a unique and unrepeatable dynamism of subjectivity, a universe unto himself, that is, man as a *person*. While the medieval humanist emphasized the objectised aspect of the person (that is, man as substance; a part within the whole of the universe), the moderns focused on man's subjectivity without his ontological basis. In the medieval conception, Maritain explained, we understood man in a theocentric light. This is the proper way, as God is truly at the center of reality. Maritain, however, is not simply returning to this medieval conception; what Maritain attaches onto it is, as a result of the modern turn, a new appreciation for man's subjectivity. This is why his integral humanism can rightly be described as being *personalist*.[108] However, we must also stress that over and above the modern approach, we move away from placing man at the center of reality (the anthropocentric move) and recognize that in spite of our own worth as persons, we still exist within a greater order of being which, as Voegelin argued, is subject to and caused by a transcendent order. This is why the realist element is so important in Maritain's concrete historical ideal for the politician; because while we recognize the good of political action, and indeed, the autonomy (in Maritain's words) of the intermediate ends on this earth, we also understand that our ultimate end lies beyond this world to God Himself.[109]

With this properly theocentric conception of the human person in modernity, the politician operating under a concrete historical ideal no longer faces the pressure of human praxis having to conquer the ultimate void. It is not, in fact,

---

[107] Ibid, 208.
[108] Ibid, 237.
[109] Ibid, 226-27 and 288.

our responsibility to create the ultimate end and meaning here on earth through labor or will as Marx and Nietzsche would say. There is indeed a true good to be driven at, yes, but it stands to us more as the "city in speech" by Plato (as illustrated through his *Republic*) than it would as the final state of communism by Marx. We recognize the concrete historical ideal as a model for our own political action in striving toward the good, but we simultaneously note that supreme goodness will not be achieved in this life. Maritain's vision here encapsulates the words of St. Thomas Aquinas: *quantum potest tantum aude*, to do as much as one can, as much as one is able. Moreover, Maritain described our continual striving with regard to the concrete historical ideal as continuously fashioning a "rough draft" of the good. This is in keeping with the Socratic dictum of the philosopher, "know that you know nothing," in the sense that no instantiation of the concrete historical ideal promises to be the final word.

In his own time, Maritain conceived of the concrete historical ideal as a Christian democracy with certain features dictated by the present historical sky. So far, we have alluded to some of these such as the understanding of both man and God at their proper place in reality. Obviously, this prevents us from making the move of anthropocentric humanism in seeking the utopian ideal: we do not seek to usurp God's throne. Our goal is not to remake the world unto our own image; we do not stand before God as Prometheus. What Maritain argued is that in being brought back to a proper notion of integral humanism (as grounded on the thought of St. Thomas Aquinas), we also must come back to the gospel. Now, even though Maritain promoted democracy (in its modern form as a mixed regime), he (like Aristotle before him) acknowledged that democracy was not the only possible form, just the best one available for the time. Regardless, whatever may come, it must be a refraction from the truth of the Gospel which stands as truth itself.[110] Finally, Maritain argued that the features of this political regime would be that it is: pluralist, personalist, and Christian at its core.[111]

It must be pluralist in order to stand against the temptation of those who seek the *sacrum imperium* (adherents of *caesaropapism*, in which the ruler is also the top religious authority); Maritain's concern was that the Christian faith cannot be forced, and the dignity of each human person demands that everyone be given the chance to assent to the truth freely.[112] Only then could it be a true

---

[110] Ibid, 288.
[111] Ibid, 279.
[112] Ibid, 243.

form of charity toward God. This goes hand in hand with the principle of personalism, recognizing the intrinsic dignity of each human person. Moreover, Maritain described the pluralist state of modern societies to be a reality of the historical sky, such that it cannot be swept aside. Nevertheless, a Christian democracy is obviously Christian inspired, meaning that while we may have a diverse body politic, we must nevertheless be in general agreement regarding the reality of the good. If there is disagreement on these matters of first principle, no unity is possible.

> The deeply religious character of modern politics allows us to affirm Plaza's reliance upon Voegelin and Maritain as rather illuminating. To overcome the disorientating forces stemming from an excessive emphasis upon particulars, or an abstract utopian lens, something more than reason will be needed. To put it differently, the battle against Enlightenment rationalism, what Benedict XVI called the "pathologies of the limitations of reason," entails the engagement of a source that transcends what human intelligence can know, but which is nevertheless not opposed to it.
>
> *Jones, "Classical Realism in a Democratic Context" [p.258].*

---

6. Conclusion: The Need for a True Political Realism Today

When discussing the intersection between political science and realism, what we are inevitably led to is a problem of first principles. Modern thought shifted its underlying first principles such that no discussion would be possible in political theory without taking into account its "meta" principles. The same has happened with ethics, and so we now argue about "metaethics" before discussing a particular case, as differing first principles will lead to dramatically different analysis and conclusions. On this topic of first principles, Strauss noted what he famously called the theologico-political problem (that is, the relationship between faith and reason with respect to political authority and philosophy) as one key underlying issue. Strauss found this to be particularly relevant in modernity due in particular to the modern rejection of God in the political sphere, regardless of whether God is discussed within the context of metaphysics or theology. Yet, in the modern effort to avoid God, anything which may eventually lead to God has also come under fire. It is not simply that God has been removed from metaphysics, but metaphysics itself as a whole has been swept aside. As a result, modern philosophy as such (both practical and theoretical) has largely forfeited its own absolute grounding in truth. Without metaphysics acting as the foundation, modern thinkers have inevitably forgotten the place of political philosophy as the "queen of the social sciences," that is, as the true science of human affairs. Rather than being guided by "*what is*" (the object of metaphysics), modern thinkers wish to follow their "autonomous will" instead.

Scholastic thought, contrary to the moderns but similar to the Greeks and Romans, was centered on being itself, such that theology and philosophy each involved a knowledge of the true whole, of universals. Modern thought, having given up on universal being, tends to retreat instead to the particular. While the traditional outlook in Western civilization had been to believe in the absolute nature of scientific knowledge, moderns have reoriented science (in the classical sense) so as to focus on what is relative and empirical. Having preferred the universal to the particular, modern philosophy cannot claim scientific knowledge in the proper sense; it can only be a matter of opinion.

This is an untenable state of affairs. Man still desires real knowledge of some sort. If philosophy cannot do this, Gnosticism will impose itself instead, masquerading as the new science. Hegel was a good example of this, as he attempted to forge a philosophical system which could serve as the key to unlocking all the mysteries of being itself. Marx took this into the practical realm, stripping Hegelianism of any traces of spirituality, focusing instead on making the material world the highest form of being. Again, the modern problem rears in once more, as even with those systems which claim absolute knowledge of being in its entirety, the ultimate focus (at least implicitly) is a transformation of being, rather than a discovery of *what is*.

The relationship between an actual pursuit of metaphysics (that is, metaphysics pursued from the standpoint of classical realism) with political philosophy could then be summarized as the following: metaphysics, in its study of being as it really is, recognizes its proper hierarchy. In other words, a proper metaphysical study would demonstrate to us that the human good in particular is not in fact the greatest good; man's "autonomous will" does not surpass being itself. Metaphysics reveals the true nature of the good in terms of *what is*, thereby providing a concrete foundation for the questions of practical philosophy, which will explore in its own way particular questions regarding the good itself. For instance, seeking the best regime in political philosophy presupposes a true good that ought to be discovered. If political philosophy is to be a science, then it must involve a search for this true good on universal terms, and this can only be done on the basis of a true philosophy of being.

References Historically Layered

ARISTOTLE (384—322BC).

c.348—7aBC. *Posterior Analytics* (in the *Basic Works of Aristotle* prepared by Richard McKeon, in the English translation by Hugh Tredennick (New York: Basic Books, 1941): 110-187 (complete)).

c.348—7bBC. *Politics*, Book VII (in the *Basic Works of Aristotle* prepared by Richard McKeon, in the English translation by Benjamin Jowett (New York: Basic Books, 1941): 1127-1324 (complete)).

c.348—7cBC. *Metaphysics*, Book IV (in the *Basic Works of Aristotle* prepared by Richard McKeon, in the English translation by W. D. Ross (New York: Basic Books, 1941): 689-934 (complete)).

c.335/4aBC. *Politics*, Book I (in the *Basic Works of Aristotle* prepared by Richard McKeon, in the English translation by Benjamin Jowett (New York: Basic Books, 1941): 1127-1324 (complete)).

c.335/4bBC. *Nicomachean Ethics* (in the *Basic Works of Aristotle* prepared by Richard McKeon, in the English translation by W. D. Ross (New York: Basic Books, 1941): 935-1126 (complete)).

c.330BC. *On the Soul* (in the *Basic Works of Aristotle* prepared by Richard McKeon, in the English translation by J. A. Smith (New York: Basic Books, 1941): 535-606 (complete)).

BROADIE, Alexander.

1968. "The Practical Syllogism", *Analysis* 29.1.

GERSON, Lloyd P.

1994. "Why Ethics is Political Science for Aristotle", *Proceedings of the ACPA* vol.68: 93-107.

HOBBES, Thomas (5 April 1588—1679 December 4).

1651. *Leviathan* (Cambridge: Cambridge University, 1996).

MACHIAVELLI, Niccolò (3 May 1469—1527 June 21).

1532. *The Prince* (Oxford: Oxford University, 1998).

MARITAIN, Jacques (18 November 1882—1973 April 28).

1946. *The Twilight of Civilization* (New York: Sheed & Ward).

1968. *Integral Humanism* in *The Collected Works of Jacques Maritain*, vol. XI (Notre Dame, IN: University of Notre Dame), ed. by Otto Bird, trans. by Joseph W. Evans of *Humanisme intégral: problemes temporels et spirituals d'une nouvelle chrétienté* (1936).

STRAUSS, Leo (20 September 1899—1973 October 18).

1953. *Natural Right and History* (Chicago: University of Chicago).

VOEGELIN, Eric (3 January 1901—1985 January 19).

1952. *The New Science of Politics* (Chicago: University of Chicago).

1968. *Science, Politics and Gnosticism* (Washington D.C.: Regnery Gateway).

Classical Realism in a Democratic Context

A Response to Francisco Plaza[1]

Brian Jones
PhD Candidate
University of St. Thomas, Houston TX

In this response to Francisco Plaza's paper, I have two primary aims. First, to highlight and further explore Plaza's critique of what I will call the "content" that makes up modern thought, especially as it relates to certain broader cultural movements in the Western world. Second, to provide a more nuanced interpretation of the socio-historical component of political science, exploring what could be called the "context" of modern democratic life. In doing so, I hope to explore some of the possibilities and limitations of the field of political science and its ability to recover classical realism in our post-modern world.

I. Introduction

In this response to Francisco Plaza's paper, I have two primary aims. First, to highlight and further explore Plaza's critique of what I will call the "content" that makes up modern thought, especially as it relates to certain broader cultural movements in the Western world. Second, to provide a more nuanced interpretation of the socio-historical component of political science, exploring what could be called the "context" of modern democratic life. In doing so, I hope

---

[1] Correspondence to editors@realityjournal.org.

Table of Contents

to explore some of the possibilities and limitations of the field of political science and its ability to recover classical realism in our post-modern world.

2. The *Content* of Modernity

Plaza's critical emphasis upon the *content* of modern theory puts him in good company with the predominant post-war Aristotelian and Thomistic scholarship in the United States. This interpretative tradition is critical of the philosophic and political currents in the West, and America in particular, and can trace its proximate origins in the re-emergence of the theologico-political problem initiated by Leo Strauss. The critique offered by Plaza is also a welcome variant of recent critical works analyzing the contemporary American social and political fracturing that has become increasingly normative in academic and public discourse. Plaza's critique of modernity, wherein he intersects political theory and religion, positions Plaza most notably alongside the works of Patrick Deneen, Joshua Mitchell, Mark Mitchell, Mark Lila, and D.C. Schindler, to name just a few.

In continuity with this particular interpretative tradition, Plaza portrays modernity in a manner that recalls the all-too-common monistic methodology stifling the fields of political theory and political science in recent decades. Rogers M. Smith[2] has observed this trend to be the overwhelming focus of contemporary political science, and the particular sub-field of American political thought, known as historical institutionalism. According to Rogers, this broadly "scientific" approach primarily examines the interactions between and across institutions, outlining how these institutions become a leading catalyst for various social conflicts or movements. In addition to this, historical institutionalism tends to prioritize the role of political parties, group organizations, and the plethora of government agencies as the leading explanations characterizing modern political life.

While it is certainly the case that these two methodological approaches in political science are necessary components of its practice, they often neglect a primary locus of social and political life. The truncated form that is

[2] Rogers M. Smith 2014: "Ideas and the Spiral of Politics: The Place of American Political Thought in American Political Development," *American Political Thought: A Journal of Ideas, Institutions, and Culture* 3 (Spring): 126-36.

contemporary political science tends to either reject, or at least significantly downplay, the fundamental role *theory* and *ideas* play in human affairs. Too little serious attention is given to the fact that public policy, the deliberative process guiding legal jurisprudence, and the structures of governance and political rule are continually nourished by the ideas of all those involved. Political structures and institutions receive the form they have from the worldview of those who gave life to these institutions, as well as by those that continue to sustain, and work within, them over time.

As such, the predominant methodology of contemporary political science tends to neglect the *explanatory power of ideas* in shaping, and changing, the course of political life. Perhaps there is no more recent witness to the deficiencies of political science today than the 2016 American presidential election. Not only did it become evident that the predictive tools were incapable of accurately portraying *who* was most likely to win: more than this, there was an alarming inability to *give an account* for why Donald Trump was able to win the presidency. Embedded within the public commentariat was a deeply entrenched Rawlsian approach, attempting to analyze data politically, not metaphysically. This was bound to fail in its explanations. The "end of history" dialectic of the post-1989 democratic world, and the immutability of progress, became unhinged from its deterministic trajectory.[3] Yet, the present models used to interpret the prevailing data could not comprehend the election results.

In returning to Plaza's account, it becomes clear that modernity is not simply a particular historical time period that follows the late medieval and renaissance era. Rather, his ahistoricist explication underscores the fact that the modern age needs to be conceived as a set of first principles, whose inner logic "constrains" one to go in the only direction such principles allow. In this respect, Plaza's insight echoes Etienne Gilson's, specifically drawing attention to the relationship between first principles and conclusions:[4]

---

[3] See Michael Anton 2016: "The Flight 93 Election," https://www.claremont.org/crb/basicpage/the-flight-93-election/. See also Laure Mandeville and Joshua Mitchell 2018: "Democracy in Danger: Confusing the Symptoms of Disorder with its Cause," https://www.atlanticcouncil.org/blogs/new-atlanticist/democracy-in-danger-confusing-the-symptoms-of-disorder-with-its-cause.

[4] Etienne Gilson 1941: *Unity of Philosophical Experience,* revised ed., 243.

> In the first place, philosophers are free to lay down their own sets of principles, but once this is done, they no longer think as they wish—they think as they can...any attempt on the part of a philosopher to shun the consequences of his own position is doomed to failure. What he himself declines to say will be said by his disciple.

The logic of modern philosophic thought can also be readily witnessed in the present politicization of human sexuality and gender, especially prevalent in Western nations. In a 2018 op-ed essay for the *New York Times,* author Andrea Long Chu details the personal experience of transitioning from a biological male to a female. What we read in this curious and shocking account is that the narrative framework for the author hinges upon the modern reversal of a central axiom in classical political realism, namely, that "art imitates nature." As the author contends, the purpose of seeking the transition from male to female is not in order to attain some level of happiness. Rather, the goal is to display the individual will's ability to transcend the limits (maybe even disorder) of nature itself. The author concludes the story with the following declaration:[5]

> ...I still want this, all of it. I want the tears; I want the pain. Transition doesn't have to make me happy for me to want it. Left to their own devices, people will rarely pursue what makes them feel good in the long term. *Desire and happiness are independent agents.*

What is worth observing in the above judgment is the *new conceptual framework* the author places before the reader. In short, a plea is being made for medical practice to be more firmly grounded in the patient's desire as the standard for health. To increase the patient's health would seem to entail increasing one's autonomy regarding the very purpose and function of the human body. Such an understanding with respect to medical practice is indicative of more than just a shift in patient care. Indeed, patient care is being pulled by a grand philosophic shift. Being healthy becomes centered around a manipulation grounded in one's personal preferences or desires, thereby undermining the doctor's capacity *qua* doctor to realign the patient with the healing source that is nature itself. Interestingly enough, Pope Francis has

---

[5] Andrea Long Chu 2018: "Why My Fake Vagina Won't Make Me Happy", *New York Times*.

described this phenomenon as the *technocratic paradigm.* This self-enclosed paradigm,[6]

> exalts the concept of a subject who, using logical and rational procedures, progressively approaches and gains control over an external object. This subject makes every effort to establish the scientific and experimental method, which in itself is already a technique of possession, mastery and transformation. It is as if the subject were to find itself in the presence of something formless, completely open to manipulation. Men and women have constantly intervened in nature, but for a long time this meant being in tune with and respecting the possibilities offered by the things themselves. It was a matter of receiving what nature itself allowed, as if from its own hand. Now, by contrast, we are the ones to lay our hands on things, attempting to extract everything possible from them while frequently ignoring or forgetting the reality in front of us.

In theory, much of modern science has rejected the Aristotelian doctrine that the aim of science is to discover the form or nature of what things are.[7] Modern science has exchanged knowledge of nature with the ability to manipulate it for the sake of greater power and dominance. This is precisely the stated goal of Francis Bacon's *New Organon,* whereby knowledge is reduced to engineering and coercion. In the same way, this is how Pope Francis portrays modern science, conceived in the Cartesian vision of "a technique of possession, mastery and transformation." For Pope Francis, without seeing nature as "form," it eventually succumbs to domination and procedural control. In this light, the relationship between human beings and nature is more vividly portrayed as one of antagonism, where "human beings and material objects no longer extend a friendly hand to one another; the relationship has become confrontational." Much of the extreme environmentalism today is grounded in precisely this vision of human beings and nature as enemies.

---

[6] Pope Francis 2015: *Laudato Si*, §106.

[7] It is worth mentioning, however, that trends of contemporary scientific practice can certainly be placed within the categories formal and final causality, which are the hallmarks of Aristotelian and Thomistic definitions of science. See Michael Tkacz 2013: "Thomistic Reflections on Teleology and Contemporary Biological Research," *New Blackfriars* 94: 654-75.

3. The *Context* of Modernity

Plaza's critique of modernity is offered with respect to a unique shift in the history of thought, one which is ultimately concerned with the intellectual *content* characteristic of the modern age. As mentioned above, numerous cases have been made that such an approach is almost entirely neglected in contemporary political science.[8] And while this is certainly the case, recovering a kind of realism in political science, or in politics more generally, necessitates something of a more nuanced *account* of modern democracy. While more could be said with respect to this judgment, let me give two brief preliminary remarks.

First, it is easy to consider modernity or liberalism as an *entity* that has some kind of actual existence in an abstract realm. In principle, I do not see anything wrong with this understanding of modernity. However, I am in agreement with Adrian Vermeule's claim that critics of the modern age can tend to neglect the personal desires and intentions of modern individuals themselves.[9] A second preliminary observation stems primarily from Alasdair MacIntyre's fundamental insight about all forms of tradition-constituted inquiry. The aim of recovering a classical realist vision which gives credence to the proper order of being (metaphysics as *first philosophy*) will always be interpreted through the particular lens and categories of thought that constitute a given condition. This can be understood by observing Alexis de Tocqueville's remark that Americans are the most "Cartesian" of all democratic nations. That Americans can be seen as the descendants of Descartes is not simply a judgment of philosophical doctrines. The interpretive key is Tocqueville's qualifier, which is that Americans have never actually read Descartes. Somehow, the generic intellectual framework of Americans with respect to authority, reason, and truth cannot be entirely explained as the effect of the "modern intellectual turn."

In this respect, it becomes clearer why we must attend to the *context* that is modern life, and more specifically, democratic life. This is not to be portrayed as a fundamental disagreement with respect to Plaza. Rather, as mentioned above, my approach is to highlight what might aptly be considered the other side

---

[8] See Paul DeHart 2014: "Political Philosophy after the Collapse of Classical, Epistemic Foundationalism," in *Reason, Revelation, and the Civic Order: Political Philosophy and the Claims of Faith,* 33-63.

[9] Adrian Vermeule 2018: "Integration from Within," *American Affairs Journal,* 2.1 (Spring).

of the same coin. In this vein, I will briefly turn to Tocqueville, and his insight concerning the socio-historical nature of modern democratic life.[10]

There is no better description of Tocqueville's perceptive vision of democratic life than his primary distinction between the social conditions of aristocratic and democratic man:[11]

> Aristocracy links everybody, from peasant to king, in one long chain. Democracy breaks the chain... Each man is thereby thrown back on himself alone, and there is a danger that he may be shut up in the solitude of his own heart.

According to Tocqueville, what is unique about modern democratic citizens is that they are brought into this new world *cut off.* No longer is their identity encompassed by one's name, family, or geographic place. Democratic citizens will come to have the normative experience of being uprooted and unsettled. Seeing the world generationally, wherein we could look forward, envisioning our great-grandchildren and also remain connected to the past by living near our families, has reached its end. While it is certainly the case that every age and civilization must address the perennial human task of how to live together in this world, we cannot neglect Tocqueville's judgment with respect to the modern world: "a new political science is needed for a world entirely new."[12]

There is a profound and unsettling feature of this new reality. Tocqueville illuminates this existential angst by portraying the democratic citizen as one looking over the ruins of a bygone world and celebrating its end. However, filled with an almost crippling fear of what lies ahead, democratic man cannot muster the courage to look forward at the new world not-yet made. What is it that makes this turn to an unmade world so terrifying? In short, it is the stripping away of those various identities that were the fundamental component of life in society. As the associations of civil society continually wither away, citizens live in a condition whereby the gap between them and the state is void. Churches,

---

[10] Defining democracy in the following way is not to claim that this is the *only definition* of democracy given by Tocqueville. For an exploration of Tocqueville's multi-layered understanding of democracy, see James T. Schleifer 2000: *The Making of Tocqueville's Democracy in America*, 2nd ed., 325-39.

[11] Alexis de Tocqueville 1835: *Democracy in America*, eds. Harvey Mansfield and Delba Winthrop, 483-84. All references to *Democracy in America* are from this edition.

[12] Ibid, 7.

families, and neighborhoods become undermined by an administrative state apparatus that, slowly and softly, fills the void once bolstered by the various forms of associational life. The good that arises from the variety of freedoms we experience in this new age can leave us with a renewed type of civic vigor. Civil society will become the locus of creating new identities. In this vein, being stripped of long-held identities, we might come to see ourselves as "more than kings."[13]

The administering of this Tocquevillian lens is not novel. Among other reasons, the account that I have laid out here hopefully focuses attention upon the challenges related to the common criticisms of modernity. Perhaps more than any other, the most proximate challenge to the call for a recovery of classical realism is the rise of identity politics. The scourge of identity politics is not easily rebutted by a rhetorical endeavor that looks to recover the classical realism of Platonic or Aristotelian political thought.

My brief attempt to implore Tocqueville hopefully answers the reasons for this. At one level, the increasing rates of social isolation and loneliness in Western nations provide conditions for types of conformity and civic breakdown that do find a real origin in this new social condition that is modern liberal democracy. I hesitate in calling this an "epidemic," but it is certainly the case that Tocqueville's over-arching worry for democratic citizens is a proclivity towards isolation.

In conjunction with this is the emergence of the "holy" in contemporary politics,[14] exemplified by identity politics more broadly. It is certainly the case that traditional religion has been on the decline over the last several decades. This, however, does not mean that religion has disappeared. It is has simply moved to a different domain, namely, the realm of politics. In this respect, liberal or democratic politics can morph into a kind of religion. As Adrian Vermeule contends,[15]

> ...liberalism has a soteriology, an eschatology, a clergy, and sacraments, centered on the confession and surrender of privilege, the redemption of declaring oneself an "ally," the overcoming of the dark past of prejudice and

---

[13] Ibid, 665.

[14] James V. Schall 1984: *The Politics of Heaven and Hell: Christian Themes from Classical, Medieval, and Modern Political Philosophy*, 289-303.

[15] Vermeule 2018: "Integration from Within."

> unreason—a past that is itself always in motion, so that the night of unreason may well suddenly come to mean what everyone believed last year.

Echoing Vermeule, we could add that a movement such as identity politics is not merely a new form of religion. This contention would usurp its own self-understanding. As a religion, identity politics is not only a set of doctrines, but is patently *liturgical.* The pseudo-liturgical activity of identity politics reveals its connection to the new condition of modern man. Its worship is made visible in public denunciations of illiberalism, racism, xenophobia, hatred, privilege, nourished by its nominal *telos* where humanity become witness to the final overcoming of all forms of discrimination and oppression.[16] The vitality and tenacity of identity politics becomes intelligible by seeing it within this deracinated liturgical context. In this way, liturgy truly is the "source and summit"[17] of identity politics.

This intellectual swindle on the part of the Gnostic could be restated as an act of self-deception, one that is animated by an underlying will to power that disguises itself as an intellectual move. Such an impetus within man beckons him toward absolute mastery. It results in a complete rebellion against the transcendent itself, as the subject feels imprisoned within the order of being. Even though man is nowhere near the top of this hierarchy, he wishes to be. In examining the depths of the will to power, Nietzsche states:

---

[16] I say "nominal" here because a significant part of the ideology concerning identity politics is that injustice in this world, ultimately, appears to have no end. Thus, the actualization of equality is not simply the goal of the movement, but the goal that can never be realized.

[17] 1963: *Sacrosanctum Concilium* argues that "...the liturgy is the summit toward which the activity of the Church is directed; at the same time it is the font from which all her power flows. For the aim and object of apostolic works is that all who are made sons of God by faith and baptism should come together to praise God in the midst of His Church, to take part in the sacrifice, and to eat the Lord's supper." (§10) If we can envision identity politics as a pseudo-religion, with a public liturgy that is the true source of its apostolic works, then the employment of this quote becomes clearer. In this light, Schall's argument that one of the best ways to understand modern political movements is through the study of ancient Christian heresies proves illuminating. See n.14 above.

"To rule, and to be no longer a servant of a god: this means was left behind to ennoble man." Through this will to power, then, the Gnostic man attempts to make himself God ruling over all of existence. This profound self-deception becomes the dogma of a political mass movement which hails the Gnostic thinkers as "prophets." These mass movements in turn take on the character of a religion, but it is only a kind of ersatz religion with man at the head, rather than God. To identify oneself as a Marxist, then, becomes akin to identifying oneself as a Christian or Jew.

Plaza, "Political Science and Realism" [p.239-40].

The deeply religious character of modern politics allows us to affirm Plaza's reliance upon Voegelin and Maritain as rather illuminating. To overcome the disorientating forces stemming from an excessive emphasis upon particulars, or an abstract utopian lens, something more than reason will be needed. To put it differently, the battle against Enlightenment rationalism, what Benedict XVI called the "pathologies of the limitations of reason," entails the engagement of a source that transcends what human intelligence can know, but which is nevertheless not opposed to it. I would contend that, contra Strauss, without the medieval tradition and a more robust account of the relationship between reason, revelation, and political life, the attempt to recover the principles of classical political realism will be deeply insufficient.[18]

---

[18] Robert C. Bartlett claims that liberal democratic citizens are sorely in need of recovering Aristotle's defense of the primacy of contemplation. However, in doing so, Bartlett's Aristotle is transformed into a materialist, because the object of contemplation is nature self-enclosed on itself, since there is nothing that transcends nature. Bartlett's concern with rise of religious fanaticism makes him turn away from a much richer account of the relationship between faith, reason, and political life. See Robert C. Bartlett 1995: "Aristotle's Science of the Best Regime," *American Political Science Review* 89.1: 152-60. While providing a more nuanced defense of the practice of political theology, Mark Lila falls into a similar problem that Bartlett does, namely, by neglecting to consider the thought of Augustine and Thomas Aquinas. See Mark Lilla 2007: *The Stillborn God: Religion, Politics, and the Modern West*.

The Christian understanding of revelation, in a real way, can help to save philosophy and political life from its own distortions and misunderstandings. Political life is necessary for human beings, since we are naturally political. Human beings are also religious animals, but politics is not the locus of salvation. Perhaps this is the most disturbing component of modern political movements, namely, the attempt to conceive of politics as salvific. Plaza is right that we need to recover a metaphysics that is true, one which gives us access to *Being.* This ability to access the ground of existence will continually need the strength to be unhinged from the short-sighted lens of a philosophical and political rationalism. In this respect, we will need *both* classical realism and religious faith, rightly understood.

References Historically Layered

ANTON, Michael.

2016. "The Flight 93 Election" in *The Claremont Review of Books* Digital Exclusive <https://www.claremont.org/crb/basicpage/the-flight-93-election/>. Retrieved 2019 October 17.

BARTLETT, Robert C.

1995. "Aristotle's Science of the Best Regime", *American Political Science Review*, 89.1 (March): 152-60.

BERGOGLIO, Jorge Mario [Pope Francis] (17 December 1936—).

2015. *Laudato Si.*

CHUA, Andrea Long.

2018. "Why My Fake Vagina Won't Make Me Happy", 18 November, *New York Times.*

DEHART, Paul.

2014. "Political Philosophy after the Collapse of Classical, Epistemic Foundationalism", in *Reason, Revelation, and the Civic Order: Political Philosophy and the Claims of Faith,* eds. Paul DeHart and Carson Holloway (DeKalb, IL: Northern Illinois University Press): 33-63.

GILSON, Étienne (13 June 1884—1978 September 19).

1941. *Unity of Philosophical Experience*, revised ed. (San Francisco, CA: Ignatius Press).

LILLA, Mark.

2007. *The Stillborn God: Religion, Politics, and the Modern West* (New York: Random House).

MANDEVILLE, Laure and MITCHELL, Joshua.

2018. "Democracy in Danger: Confusing the Symptoms of Disorder with Its Cause" in *New Atlanticist* <https://www.atlanticcouncil.org/blogs/new-atlanticist/democracy-in-danger-confusing-the-symptoms-of-disorder-with-its-cause/>.

MONTINI, Giovanni [Pope St. Paul VI] (26 September 1897—1978 August 6).

1963. *Sacrosanctum Concilium.*

SCHALL, James (20 January 1928—2019 April 17).

1984. *The Politics of Heaven and Hell: Christian Themes from Classical, Medieval, and Modern Political Philosophy* (Lanham, MD: University Press of America).

SCHLEIFER, James T.

2000. *The Making of Tocqueville's Democracy in America*, 2nd ed. (Indianapolis: Liberty Fund), 325-39.

SMITH, Rogers M

2014. "Ideas and the Spiral of Politics: The Place of American Political Thought in American Political Development", *American Political Thought: A Journal of Ideas, Institutions, and Culture* 3 (Spring): 126-136.

TKACZ, Michael

2013. "Thomistic Reflections on Teleology and Contemporary Biological Research", *New Blackfriars* 94: 654-75.

TOCQUEVILLE, Alexis de (29 July 1805—1859 April 16).

1835. *Democracy in America*, eds. Harvey Mansfield and Delba Winthrop (Chicago: University of Chicago Press, 2002).

VERMEULE, Adrian (2 May 1968—).

2018. "Integration from Within", *American Affairs Journal* 2.1.

For more about REALITY, please visit https://realityjournal.org.

The editors of REALITY would like to thank all our contributors as well as our advisory board. We would also like to thank all those who helped proofread or brought errata to our attention.

Compiling this first issue was a long labor of love—though we hope to produce many more in the coming years.

Though this issue is published and thus completed, if you find a problem in scholarship or philosophical argumentation, feel free to submit a review (comment or response) to be considered for publication online to editors@realityjournal.org.

Made in United States
Troutdale, OR
12/27/2023

16480350R00149